£15.99

D1436254

JUDGE'S DIARY

1967-1973

JUDGE'S DIARY
1967-1973

GORDON STOTT

THE MERCAT PRESS
EDINBURGH

First published in 1995 by Mercat Press
at James Thin, 53 South Bridge
Edinburgh EH1 1YS

ISBN 1873644 434

Printed and bound by
The Cromwell Press Limited,
Broughton Gifford, Melksham,
Wiltshire

For Nancy,
who made it all possible.

CONTENTS

I have altered a few names in order to meet the requirements of the Rehabilitation of Offenders Act; and in the introduction to each year (which was actually written at the end of the year) have changed the present tense into the past. Otherwise the extracts remain as written at the time.

1967

At the end of September 1967 the resignation of Lord Strachan caused a vacancy on the bench, and I was entitled to put forward my own name for the vacancy. I had enjoyed my three years as Lord Advocate, and if I could have been certain about another vacancy arising should have been content to wait. But there was no certainty about that; and on 27 October I was installed as a senator of the College of Justice. I had no doubt that during my three years I had won the goodwill and respect of my colleagues; but it was a sobering thought to look back and realise that I had accomplished practically nothing. I could at least claim that I was leaving the cause of law reform in a healthy state. The Scottish Office team was a good one, but the Secretary of State's indecisiveness and readiness to be influenced by press criticism meant that much of the work he had done had gone for nothing. One factor which while not affecting my decision helped to reconcile me to it was my growing dissatisfaction with current politics. The Americans continued their destruction of Vietnam, and the British Government continued to give them verbal support. At home, the Government's economic policy, such as it was, had been a failure. There was no satisfaction to be got out of defending a policy that was manifestly wrong— no one in either party willing to call the financiers' bluff, and the rate of interest higher than ever—and it was pleasanter to be a judge. I made it my practice, instead of waiting for the shorthand writer's note of the evidence, to decide the case on the notes I had taken myself. This meant that I was able to dispose of cases as they came along, and finished the term with nothing left to be done in the vacation—a situation which did not, I think, apply to many of my colleagues. To my surprise, I found that extempore dictation of an Opinion on a debate was by no means difficult. This was a great relief: it saved quite a lot of work at home, besides being an agreeable thing to do. In court there was always something of interest cropping up, and I always looked forward to the day's work with pleasurable anticipation, without the worry of preparation that bedevils the life of a busy counsel.

JUDGE'S DIARY

January 2nd
Dominion Cinema: *The Russians are Coming*. With a lot of little touches of wit and humour, it was something of a revelation. One could not have imagined Americans making a film like this a year or two ago—not only making fun of themselves but showing a Russian submarine crew as likeable human beings the same as anyone else.

January 8th
Braid Church: Rev. Professor F. Hildebrandt on Psalms 89:15. He had nothing specially notable to say, but his sermon could have served as a model for effective preaching of the Word, which was the subject of his discourse—interesting, powerful, well composed and well delivered, with scholarly precision of language and working up to a fine climax.

January 11th
Phoning Nancy from a call box in Aldwych, I made desperate efforts to push a sixpence, or alternatively a shilling, into the machine, before realising that it was working quite well without them. We had a long conversation without my paying anything.

To the Aldwych Theatre to see the Royal Shakespeare Company's 'documentary', *Us*—a peculiar affair, with no scenery except a heap of debris. The first part was a kind of illustrated commentary on the history of Vietnam and the war. It did not quite come off, and the man sitting next to me indulged in an expressive form of criticism by falling off to sleep and starting to snore. But the second half, an eloquent, thoughtful discussion of the pros and cons of the American action, and indeed of the whole philosophy of living, was much more worthwhile and worked up to a compelling climax which must have sent everyone home with something tough to think about.

January 12th
I never go to bed at the London flat without feeling a little glow of satisfaction at being so comfortable and peaceful, but last night it did not work out so well, because what sounded like an overflow of water from a flat below my window kept up an irregular gurgling sound throughout the night.

Finished reading *Robert Burns*, by David Daiches. I took this out of the library in order to get some information for proposing the

Immortal Memory at Cramond Association's Burns Supper, and finding it unexpectedly interesting decided to read it through. It puts Burns in a much more favourable light as a poet and as a man than I had imagined. Any theory that he ended life drunken and debauched, or that he ever became corrupted from his independence by the influence of Edinburgh patrons, is untenable; and I was persuaded that quite apart from his love songs, which I always admired, he had written satirical poetry, such as 'Holy Willie's Prayer', of superb artistry and power.

January 13th
Sinclair Shaw told me that when he was visiting Captain Brander Dunbar of Pitgavenny, Dunbar informed him that in the old days when he was a commissioner in Nyasaland he never took any important step without consulting a witch-doctor. His immediate superiors had disapproved of this, but it always had the strong support of Whitehall.

January 16th
Houghton has demitted office in a Government reshuffle, being replaced by Gordon-Walker. He had nothing like the same grip of the Committee, nor was his summing-up at the end of each discussion as clear or decisive. Mabon with his usual ebullience interrupted the Lord Chancellor in full flood and, prefacing his remarks by saying, 'I think this is the point that the Lord Chancellor is trying to make', proceeded to put his own view succinctly and vigorously. No one paid any attention to him, and when he came to an end Gardiner resumed his dissertation from the point where he had been interrupted.

Notting Hill Gate, the Classic Cinema: *Four in the Morning*, a film of the London riverside at dawn, genuine and well done, with lots of authentic little touches, but very slow. It is as inconclusive as life, and to that extent loses in dramatic effect what it gains in reality. Before this picture I saw the greater part of *The War Game*, the much-disputed film about the effect of nuclear war on Gravesend and Rochester which the BBC commissioned and then refused to put on. The panic aspect may be a little overdone, compared with the physical horrors—though these are as gruesome as one could imagine. The grimly sardonic commentary points the moral that civil defence in a nuclear war is the sheerest fantasy.

January 17th

Burlington House: an exhibition of Millais paintings. No give and take about Millais: his figures stand out starkly from their background, and there is never a smile on the face of anyone he paints—they all gaze at one another with the same blank, enigmatic stare. I found one exception: the drummer boy in 'Idyll of 1745' who leans against a tree with quite a charming smile while his small comrade, seated beside him, entertains some ragged country girls with a tune on the pipes.

To the Academy 2 Cinema to see *The Round-Up*, a Hungarian picture. It suddenly erupts into a scene of brutal violence, and from then on held my attention until the brilliant climax: the loud blare of the Austrian National Anthem as the patriots are seized for slaughter. Though not exactly entertainment, it was an unusual, finely conceived film. To my mind however it was surpassed by a film called, I think, *Johnny and Jessica*, which ran for less than half an hour but was a perfect little gem of a picture—about two very small children in the streets and waste ground of north London, one black and one white, who between them make nonsense of their elders' racial prejudices. Without a trace of sentimentality, it brings out, in the most moving, realistic fashion, the essential humanity and happiness of life. I should like everybody to see it.

January 18th

A Lighthouse meeting at George Street. At the end, I consulted the Commissioners about a letter I had from someone describing himself as 'a student of law at the University of Edinburgh' and enquiring whether Scots Law applied to the island of Rockall. Robertson was at least able to say categorically that Rockall was outwith the jurisdiction of the Commissioners of Northern Lights.

January 25th

To the Crematorium to attend Basil Paterson's funeral service: the usual nonsensical affair. But for him, I should probably be a school teacher in Dumfries.

A letter from Niall McDermott intimating that they were proposing in the next Budget to impose a charge to Income Tax on receipts coming in to professional men after cessation of business. This exception, based on the theory that barristers and advocates cannot sue for fees, has never been defensible, though it is of course a valuable concession—it has meant a considerable financial advantage to me since I gave up private practice.

January 29th
To church for Communion, at which I was serving bread. Mr Kelly preached a brief, pointless sermon on Exodus 12:11. I had to go back in the afternoon, and Mr Kelly preached the same sermon again. He had improved somewhat, and it seemed to make better sense. I had heard in advance about this practice of his, and did not find the repetition as boring as I had expected.

January 31st
I appeared in the High Court to deal with objections to the competency of the indictment in *H.M. Advocate v. Cairns*. The accused was originally charged with the murder of a man named Malcolmson, a fellow-prisoner in Barlinnie whom he was alleged to have stabbed. The Crown witnesses at the murder trial consisted of a succession of other prisoners, two of whom kept to their precognitions and said they saw Cairns stab Malcolmson, but most of whom said they knew nothing about it. One witness, Lindie, after at first refusing to say anything, was assured by Douglas Johnston, the presiding judge, acting on the instigation of Ewan Stewart who was prosecuting, that he could give evidence freely without any fear that action might be taken against him; and thereupon declared that it was he himself who had stabbed Malcolmson. Amid all this confusion it was not surprising that the jury, by a majority, found the charge Not Proven. Cairns thereupon went to the *Daily Express*, admitted that he had murdered Malcolmson, and persuaded them to pay him £100 for the right to publish a long, detailed story of the crime. I was satisfied that it was impossible to take proceedings against Lindie in view of Lord Johnston's assurance to him; and as there was no instance in the history of the law of Scotland of an accused person being prosecuted for perjury in giving evidence in his own case, the general view in the Crown Office was that nothing could be done about Cairns. It seemed to me however that it was important to discourage people like Cairns from going to newspapers and confessing to crimes of which they had just been acquitted, and I instructed that Cairns should be indicted for perjury: that he had given evidence that he had not stabbed Malcolmson, the truth being, as he knew, that he had stabbed him. The strength of the defence case was that I could succeed on the

present charge only by leading evidence to contradict the verdict of the previous jury; but anomalous as this might be it seemed no more so than the contention the defence had to make, that so far as the commission of a crime was concerned an accused giving evidence on his own behalf must have complete licence to commit perjury, provided at least that it was successful and that a jury had been persuaded by it to bring in a verdict in his favour. Strachan and Wheatley sat with the Lord Justice-Clerk; and Grant, after a short consultation with the others, intimated that they repelled the objection. The case against Cairns cannot succeed unless there is some corroboration of his admission; and as both the prisoners who gave evidence against him have disappeared it is not possible to proceed with the trial. Even if they are discovered, there is no certainty that their evidence this time will be the same. All this however does not seem to me to matter—I am not concerned so much with getting a conviction against Cairns as with letting the inmates of Barlinie know that they are not free to go to the press with confessions of crimes of which they have been acquitted. So far as that goes, today's ruling is very satisfactory. Edward Keith mentioned to me that he had been told by one of the *Express* people that in view of this prosecution their paper would not handle any story of that kind again.

February 7th
Dalgetty, Hume and two other officials came to see me about the Inner Ring Road—the main topic of controversy in Edinburgh at present, arising out of a proposal to amend the Development Plan so as to provide for a four-lane carriageway starting at Haymarket, tunnelling under Donaldson's Hospital and proceeding by Inverleith to Leith Walk. After more tunnelling under the Canongate the road will follow the line of the Pleasance and come along the Meadows to Tollcross, so back to Haymarket. The estimated cost, without any proper survey, is about £50 million, and it seems plain that the whole thing is a complete fantasy which will never be carried into effect. It has all been taken very seriously, and upholders of amenity and residents all along the lines of the road are voicing their opposition at a public enquiry before W. A. Elliott. The City Engineer in cross-examination maintained that the plan had the approval of an official of the Scottish Development Department, Ross, who had been a member of the joint working party which agreed to the proposal for an Inner Ring Road; and Elliott has acceded to the objectors' request

that Ross should be asked to come and give evidence. Hume was perturbed about this, and wondered whether counsel should not be instructed to appear with Ross and support him if he was asked questions which he was not prepared to answer. It had been made clear at the outset that Ross had been at the working party merely to give such advice as he could on general policy, and that his presence committed the Scottish Office to nothing; and I did not see why Ross when giving evidence should not say so, and go on to answer any question he was able to answer in aspects of the matter with which he was acquainted. I said that if Ross's personal view as an expert on such matters was that the Ring Road was a piece of fantastic nonsense I saw no reason why he should not say so, while making it clear that that was only his personal opinion. Ross, who was present at today's meeting, assured me that he had no intention of expressing any such opinion, or indeed any opinion at all about the merits of the proposal. He seemed to me a competent person, well able to look after himself. I felt that intervention by counsel would tend to lead to the controversy that Hume wanted to avoid; and in the end we all agreed that Ross should answer all questions that Elliott allowed, relevant or irrelevant, merely saying that he did not know, or had come to no conclusion, on any question when that was the true answer. Ross indicated that most of his answers would probably be to that effect.

February 11th

Motored with Nancy to the Castle for an official banquet to Mr Kosygin, the chairman of the Council of Ministers of the USSR. Government cars were in operation as usual to ferry guests up from the Esplanade to the Banqueting Hall, but as we got to the loading point a car arrived with the General Officer Commanding, who got out and proceeded to inspect the guard drawn up at the gate. While this pantomime was going on, we were left standing in the cold for about ten minutes. In the vestibule we talked to George Thomson and his wife, then joined a group which included Emrys Hughes and Moira Anderson, the singer—much nicer-looking than her television appearances suggested, with pretty auburn hair, and most pleasant and unassuming. Hughes was starting to tell me his experiences with that far from impartial judge, Mr Justice Swift, when we were called through to meet the official party. Mr Kosygin was a thickset man, with a rugged face and a deadpan, solemn expression even in his more humorous moments. I thought he was rather attractive, and his daughter was definitely so. She had been a student of English at the university, and spoke good English. The party was not long in going in to dinner, at which I was seated between Mrs Thomson and Mr Djhavakhishvili, Prime Minister of Georgia: a big, cumbrous-looking man, but despite his stolid appearance lively and agreeable. Mrs Thomson told me that George in his work at the Foreign Office had been struck by the extent to which everyone there was devoted to the memory of Ernest Bevin. They were people trained in the art of saying agreeable things, but George was sure that their admiration for Bevin went a long way beyond that. Bevin had expressed the view that if anyone was right four times out of six he was doing very well; he would have to be something of a paragon to be right five times out of six. Mabon was talking to the Russian ambassador, and we heard him telling him that if he got a letter which began 'Dear Comrade' and ended 'Yours fraternally' he could be sure that there would be something pretty hellish in between. Kosygin, like his host, appeared to be a teetotaller. Ross as usual made an excellent little speech, and Kosygin made an appropriate reply, apparently extempore. Mr Djhavakhishvili joined heartily in the tune of 'Auld Lang Syne', which on Ross's suggestion was sung with all joining hands in the approved manner. There could not have been a friendlier occasion.

February 14th

Looking through a file about the Russell Committee, I found two minutes written by Lord Craigton when the committee was being appointed. In the first he writes: 'Who says Miss Herbison would be a good choice? Not I for one. She has a closed mind'. In spite of this, Miss Herbison was approached but declined, and in the second minute Craigton writes: 'I would not have Mrs Hart at any price—her political purpose in life is to disrupt—if you gather what I mean'. He seems to have got his way this time, Mrs Cullen being appointed.

A meeting with the Attorney-General about experimental speed limits. Dingle Foot was brought in, being, as Elwyn put it, 'the expert in this kind of thing'—he had given the opinion that the Minister of Transport, after making an order containing a speed limit, could alter the limit to a higher or lower figure. I briefly expounded my own view, contrary to his, and Elwyn concluded that we should advise the Ministry that there was considerable doubt whether they had power to do what they wanted to do. Dingle Foot said nothing, but seemed to find this acceptable.

Legislation Committee: I corrected the Lord President's pronunciation of 'multures' in the course of a brief consideration of a Bill which Davidson is introducing for their redemption, but otherwise kept quiet until we got to the Royal Assent Bill, which the Lord Chancellor is sponsoring for the purpose of putting an end to the interruption of Commons business by incursions of Black Rod and enabling the royal assent to be given by sign-manual and thereafter merely notified to each House. I myself was sorry to see the passing of the old ceremony, with its Norman-French formula, *'La reine le veult'*, but was horrified to find from the Lord Chancellor's paper that instead of replacing it by a simple notification it was proposed that on each occasion the Speaker was to read out a lengthy rigmarole about the Queen not being able to be present in Parliament in person, and having been graciously pleased to signify by Sign Manual her consent to diverse measures—and so on for half a page. I had got Gibson to write the Lord Chancellor's people intimating my objection to this, and had a patronising reply stating that the formula had been agreed with everyone concerned and would have to stand, but the Lord Chancellor was grateful to me for taking an interest in the matter. Gardiner was not present today; Dingle Foot explained the object of the Bill. I at once raised my objection, saying I was quite in favour of a bit of verbiage if it was picturesque or traditional or historic, but if we had made up our minds to modernise the procedure it should be done by simple notification rather than by inflicting on the Speaker on each occasion a rigmarole that was far from elegant and certainly otiose. I put it to the Lord President, with his much greater knowledge of those matters than I had, that by the two hundredth occasion the House would have got a little tired of it. 'Well', said Crossman to Foot, 'what do you say to that?' Dingle replied that he always liked to have regard to what was said by the Lord Advocate, but there had been lengthy discussions with everyone concerned including the Palace, this was the formula that had been agreed, and it was important that they should get leave to introduce the Bill now. Crossman pointed out that they could go ahead with the Bill and think again about the formula. McDermott moved that the formula be simple notification that the Queen had given her consent, Gordon-Walker made sympathetic noises, and everyone seemed to be agreed. 'If people choose to go and consult the Palace before they consult us', said Crossman, 'then it's just too bad for them'. I was pleased about the success of this objection. Though no doubt a trivial matter, I felt that it would in time make rather a farce of Parliament—once approved, it would probably have gone on for a century or so, so that it seemed worth while to take up a little time in raising the objection now.

February 16th
Bowen showed me the printed agenda for a conference tomorrow under the auspices of the Law Society to enquire into the working of criminal legal aid. The Scottish Office had requested the Society to undertake an examination of this, but I doubt if they expected that the Society would do it by holding a kind of public meeting—certainly I did not. Anyhow I was horrified to see that the agenda comprised a list of 'criticisms' for discussion, and that one was that Legal Aid certificates were given too freely for employment of senior counsel for the defence and that prosecutions in the High Court were not being adequately presented. I phoned Laurie and pointed out that the second part of this alleged criticism was no concern of the Law Society and that it was shocking that such a statement should have appeared in their document. He read me out a long rigmarole of an 'answer' which had been prepared—how experienced the Advocates Depute were, no one had produced any examples of a case bungled by Advocates Depute, and anyhow the Crown had lots of other resources which the defence did not have. I got an admission from him that no one in the Crown Office had authorised this line of argument, and objected strenuously to any argument along these lines. Laurie rang back shortly afterwards to say they had agreed to delete this item from the agenda. That did not satisfy me; I told him I should require some expression of regret and an assurance that the Law Society regarded any such suggestion as appeared on the agenda as completely without foundation. He accepted this, and I told him to send me a proposed form of words.

Interviewed Macaulay in connection with a case in which Norman Buchan is interesting himself and in which Macaulay was prosecutor: two brothers, Eric and Hugh Webster, charged with assault and robbery on a man and his wife. The two assailants had got away with a bag of money, and were pursued by police who came on the scene. They lost sight of the leading escaper, but came up with the second one as he was trying to climb on to a roof, brought him down and took him to the police station. He turned out to be Hugh Webster. In the course of the chase one of the policemen, turning a corner, had come face to face with Eric Webster, walking towards him. Having satisfied himself that Eric was not the man he was chasing, he let him go; but at an identification parade later on the victims of the attack identified both Hugh and Eric as their assailants. They insisted however that Eric was not the first man in the chase but the second, and continued to identify as Eric the man seen on the roof and in the police station—who undoubtedly was Hugh. The identification was thus most unsatisfactory, and there was uncontradicted evidence from the police that when they met Eric he was not in the least exhausted or out of breath, though they themselves were very much out of puff by that stage. Thus, despite a feeble explanation by Eric of his presence there in the middle of the night—he said he was out looking for his father, who had gone fishing—it seemed hardly possible that Eric could have been one of the men who were being chased. Apart from his condition, it would have required remarkable presence of mind for him to turn round as soon as he was round the corner and walk quietly back towards his pursuers. James Walker's charge seemed to be intended to be in Eric's favour, but I do not suppose that anyone on the jury would realise that that was so, and by a majority they found Eric guilty. Hugh had changed his plea to Guilty in the course of the trial. Despite Eric's blameless record, Walker sentenced each of them to five years' imprisonment. Macaulay readily agreed that there might well have been a miscarriage of justice, and Penrose, the young counsel who had appeared for Eric, took the same view when I spoke to him.

In the afternoon Masson arrived, shaky and apologetic, and showed me the form of words they were proposing to circulate at the conference. I was not satisfied with it, and sat down at once and made a draft of my own, to the effect that the presentation of cases in the High Court was entirely a matter for the Crown Office, not the Law Society, and no discussion of this item would be permitted; the Law Society considered that any suggestion that cases were inadequately presented in the High Court was without foundation, and regretted that this suggestion had appeared on the agenda. After I got home I was not finished with the Law Society's conference: a long teleprint from London had to be read to me over the phone requesting advice about a complaint by the Glasgow Bar Association that they had not been asked to be represented. Mrs Ewing had been persistently on the phone, wanting to speak to the Secretary of State in person—which had not been permitted. The Association's members are intimately concerned with criminal legal aid in Glasgow, and despite a long-standing feud between them and the Law Society it seemed the height of folly to have a conference about criminal legal aid without inviting those who were particularly concerned in it. I gave this as my view, but Kerr Fraser, Ross's private secretary, phoned later from London to say they had got the Law Society to agree that local Bar Associations would all be asked to a follow-up conference in March. Though agreeing with the protest made by Mrs Ewing and her colleagues, I had not much sympathy with them—it seemed to me that if they had had any sense they would have contacted me and got me to take the matter up with the Law Society, but as usual they have preferred to pursue their quarrel with the Society rather than try to get an amicable solution. Even as regards our own grievance, the Crown Office was to some extent to blame, for Laurie had written to Lionel Gordon three weeks ago about representation at the conference, with an annexe containing the agenda of proposed 'criticisms'—including the one I objected to—and Gordon had neither taken exception to it nor shown the letter to me. I could not take him much to task today, when he was in bad shape as a result of falling in the lobby on Tuesday and dislocating his shoulder.

February 17th
I had written Kerr Fraser on Monday complaining about the Scottish Command's treatment of guests at the Castle on Saturday night, and was amused to see a headline on the front page of today's *Scotsman* that the Scottish Command was to be abolished. I remarked to Nancy that it was a very prompt reaction to our complaint.

I have been having an interchange with Norman Buchan about a Scottish Office submission on the report of the Russell Committee on rights of succession relating to illegitimate children. The submission throughout referred to the children as 'bastards', with the explanation that they were following English practice adopted in the Russell Report. Buchan had written a note saying it was regrettable that the word 'bastard' was being used; he hoped they would revert to 'illegitimate'. Below this I wrote: 'Nonsense! Bastard is a perfectly good word'; and this morning there is a note from Buchan: 'I agree that it is a good word, but only when used between friends'.

February 18th
Bowen reported on yesterday's conference, which as we expected had

been useless, though he did not think it had done any harm. There had been a printed slip on everyone's seat with the apology and withdrawal that I had requested.

February 20th
Papers that came in today included one by the Lord Chancellor, in which he states that he has had another look at the formula for the Speaker's announcing the royal assent, and considers that the appropriate formula would be for the Speaker to say that he has it in command from Her Majesty to intimate her assent to the Bill.

February 23rd
The English Law Commission's dinner in the Middle Temple Hall: a lovely old panelled room. I walked through to dinner with Lord Pearce, who said that what always astonished him was the speed at which Scottish counsel got through their cases—in this lot, they had literally got through them at the rate of one a day. At dinner I had Sir George Coldstream opposite, and having always regarded him as a bit of a stick was surprised to find how pleasant he was. Denning when he saw me made a point of coming over, and recalled with lively interest the time I had appeared before him in *Watson v. Winget*. I thought it remarkable that he remembered the argument so well after so many years; he is an extraordinarily attractive character. Coldstream spoke highly of Arthur Goodhart, saying he had probably done more good by stealth than anyone else he knew.

March 10th
An appointment with Ross to discuss the expenses of the Fado-Fione hydro-electricity enquiry. We had a short talk about the mistake in certifying the EIS as a charity. Ross was concerned to know who had allowed this certification to go through; he was not interested, he said, in what senior person had nominal responsibility but who had actually done it. He complained about some other mistake for which Hume had accepted responsibility—to which Kerr Fraser replied that he had told him five times already that Hume had dealt with that particular matter personally and was indeed responsible. Kerr Fraser had seen the file, and could assure him that that was so. Hume then arrived in person, with a bevy of Development Department officials, for discussion of problems arising from selective tendering: a weird process by which central and local government authorities, after eliminating from

the list of tenderers for any project those who for some reason are unsuitable, proceed by some arbitrary method to reduce the number of firms actually invited to something like four or five. Ross invited me to sit in at this discussion. Like most of his consultations, it did not reach any conclusion—Kerr Fraser came in to tell him it was time for his next appointment.

To Glasgow for the Juridicial Society dinner: an enormous affair, Allan Walker a first-rate chairman.

March 11th
Got to bed soon after one, with the comfortable reflection that so far as I know I had no more dinners to attend until next winter.

March 13th
A meeting with Sir John Hobson to discuss the Abortion Bill. He was concerned about the case of Dr Ross, who recently pled guilty to two charges of abortion of girl students, and was sentenced by Grant to four years' imprisonment. It appears that Dr Ross was well known to Edinburgh medical students. When a girl came to him asking for an abortion, he made no attempt to examine her or consult with her relatives or her own doctor, but having told her it would cost £100 arranged that she would attend, not at his surgery but at a room he had rented on the pretext of requiring it for practising on the bag-pipes. He would meet her there and carry out the operation, after which the girl would hand over £100. Sinclair Shaw remitted him to the High Court for sentence, after Ross's counsel had talked a lot of nonsense about the girls' being suicidal and this being something in the nature of a therapeutic abortion. The danger of having counsel who would try to mislead the court was demonstrated by Dr Ross's fate. Ross might have got something like eighteen months, which would I think have been an appropriate penalty, but in view of what had been said in the Sheriff Court Harry Wilson, no doubt rightly, thought it his duty to explain that this case was nowhere near the borderline between criminal and therapeutic abortion, and that if the Bill at present before Parliament had been law it would not have made any difference to Ross's position. Hobson, proceeding appar-ently on some garbled account in the newspapers, had taken on himself to say that this was wrong and that Dr Ross could not have been convicted if the Bill had been enacted in its present form. He sent me a copy of a letter he had written to Bruce Millan to that effect, and I

accordingly wrote him in fairly strong terms: that I was at a loss to understand why he suggested that the Solicitor-General had been in error. Obviously he must have some information about the case that was not known to me, and if so he had better come and tell me about it. It was plain that he had no information, and though he waffled away throughout our conversation he was quite unable to justify what he had written. I was not impressed, although his very muddle-headedness made him a difficult person to argue with.

Home Affairs Committee; a proposal put forward by an unfortunate Under-Secretary at the Ministry of Works happened to encounter the opposition of Jenkins and Crossman. There was something to be said for the proposal, but under Gordon-Walker's feeble chairmanship it seems clear that the mandarins on the committee will always be allowed to ride roughshod over anybody else's views.

March 16th
Windsor: bus to Maidenhead, along flat roads bounded by fields in one of which a notice advertised: 'Clairvaux: St Bernards kennels'.

March 17th
Home Affairs Committee: the Lord Chancellor's paper on how the Government should deal with proposals for legislation on social problems like divorce and Sunday observance. Gordon-Walker waffled away as usual, assuring us with obvious truth that he had a completely open mind.

March 19th
To church, where Mr Kelly preached on Matthew 21:10–11. Having given his sermons what I thought was a fair trial, and concluded that no edification was to be got from them, I reverted to reading the Old Testament during the sermon.. I got completely absorbed in the story of Jacob, that extraordinary man who went round swindling everyone right and left until he amassed a vast fortune, unctuously ascribing his success to the special favour of Providence.

March 21st
A letter from one of our correspondents, Lt-Col. Rose, whose affairs are managed by a solicitor named Martin as curator while Rose is in a mental hospital in England. Miss Howat had a visit last week at Deans Yard from a man describing himself as Martin, wanting an

interview with me about Rose's affairs; but after some time, when she had taken him to see Mitchell, they realised that the visitor was Rose himself. She refused to let him see me, and suggested he should write—which he has now done, complaining that the curatory is being run on the authority of two fraudulent documents purporting to be extracts of Court of Session interlocutors. I thought I could at least confirm that the interlocutors were genuine, and the Deputy Principal Clerk of Session came up a little later to assure me that this was correct. I had had letters from Rose before, and found him a curious correspondent. He would write two or three pages of extremely able argument on the legal position, which made me begin to think that his detention was perhaps without justification, and then would follow a page in which he maintained that the proper place to try train robbers was in a signal box on the line outside his mental hospital, and if the court could be established at that point the whole mystery would be cleared up.

March 22nd
Wakened at 11.30 pm by a ring on the phone: one McClure of the *Scotsman* wanting to ask me a question. I told him politely but firmly that I did not answer questions at that time of night, and that he should bear that in mind for the future. I did not allow him to tell me what the question was.

March 23rd
Parliament House: I listened for a short time to the evidence in a petition by Lady Monckton which if successful will establish her right to the Ruthven peerage. Lady Monckton, the first Lady Carlisle, was sitting in court. She looked rather grim, and if Lord Carlisle left her for my Esmé it seemed to me that it was perhaps not to be wondered at. I am the respondent in the petition, which was being heard by Lyon. Shiach appeared for me, and asked one question in cross-examination of the witness, Sir Ian Moncrieffe of that Ilk. I had no idea what the question meant, but Moncrieffe said it was a good question and one that he found it difficult to answer.

A Kirk Session meeting tonight: great discussion on a proposal by the Women's Work Party that the elders when taking Communion cards should also take round a leaflet to the effect that the members of the Work Party were getting old and unable to cope with a sale of work, so instead of a sale they would have a coffee morning which members of the church could attend and bring a money contribution. A man named Watt protested and said he would be most unwilling to deliver such a leaflet; and he was supported by people who thought that the Work Party should try to recruit enough new members to run a sale of work. Mr Kelly, who seemed to be much in favour of supporting the Work Party, wheedled away at them, stressing how disappointed the old ladies would be if the Session turned them down; he really did it very well. I said nothing until the very end, when I observed that a sale of work was a futile way of raising money, wasteful of time and effort, and though I for one would certainly put the Work Party's leaflet in the waste-paper basket I did not see why others should not have an opportunity of considering it; I should much rather deliver the leaflet than try to persuade my family to help with a sale of work. 'Well', said Mr Kelly, 'that sums the matter up'. The leaflet was approved by 16 votes to 9.

March 24th
The list of gifts in the yearbook of the National Trust included: 'Anonymous: 500 prints of painting of Dysart Harbour'; 'Miss M Brown, Glasgow: Pair of spectacles traditionally worn by Tam o' Shanter's Granny'; 'F W Gordon, Edinburgh: 31 volumes of Royal Horticultural Society Journal'; 'R McLean, Edinburgh: Garden Seat for Grey Mare's Tail'.

March 31st
For the first time to my recollection Miss Howat was at the office before me. I got her to make a booking for Nancy at the Stanhope Court Hotel before taking her to task for a note she had sent Miss Black demanding that all the Lord Advocate's department files should ultimately be kept in London, and Miss Black should file the papers under London file numbers so that they could later be incorporated in Miss Howat's filing system. Miss Black was upset by this silly note, and I instructed Miss Howat that she must consult with Miss Black about any change and be guided by her. I pointed out that when the law officers were no longer in Parliament the Edinburgh office was more important than the London one. She had not much to say in justification of her note—directed towards building up her empire and justifying the appointment of an additional clerical officer that she had persuaded the Treasury to allow.

Train to Wimbledon, and from Wimbledon to West Croydon. At

Merton Park another, abandoned, loop line had gone across to Tooting —a path across this line at the end of the platform with a notice: 'Passengers leaving the station must cross the line by this path'. I noticed that without exception the passengers leaving the station stepped down on to the line and crossed it at the opposite exit, beside a notice saying: 'Passengers not to cross at this point'.

April 2nd
A typically Londonish type of occurrence in the Underground when I got on at Kensington High Street. A pigeon came on with me, and after the train started continued to peck unconcernedly among the crevices of the floor boards. When we reached Gloucester Road, it stood at the door looking up until the doors opened, when it flew out.

April 7th
A complaint from a correspondent in Fife about some charges of assault which he maintains were maliciously laid against him. In one of the assaults the alleged weapon was a dead octopus.

April 10th
In the absence from Edinburgh of all the Scottish Office ministers, we had been asked to act as hosts to Professor Petrovsky, the Russian Minister of Health. No one could have been more friendly than the amiable Minister and his wife. He showed me his wristlet watch with an inscription which he said showed that he had got it from the King of Afghanistan in recognition of an operation he had carried out in Moscow on one of his children.

April 11th
10.30 flight to London. Lord Dalkeith was on the same flight, and I introduced myself to him and thanked him for a courteous letter he once wrote me about a constituent who claimed to have been as-saulted by a policeman. In his initial letter, Dalkeith had said he could not let the matter rest until I could satisfy him that the police had been free from blame, and I had pointed out in reply that a policeman like everyone else was entitled to the presumption of inno-cence, and I could not order a prosecution on insufficient evidence. To this Dalkeith had replied that he now understood the position, and was sorry he had been stupid.

April 12th

To Windsor for a Privy Council. It was apparent that apart from its historic interest the Castle was very much in use: as we were standing at the end of the hall two small children on tricycles suddenly emerged from a recess and whizzed along the polished floor. The equerry remarked that the Castle was an ideal place for children—the main corridor round the buildings on that floor was a quarter of a mile long. A car was to take me to the airport, and as there was plenty of time I suggested that we should keep clear of the motorway. So we had a pleasant run along minor roads, through Datchet and another pretty Thames-side village.

Walked with Nancy to Blackford Pond, telling her about Woodburn and his recollections of Jowitt, who he said was lucid and good at explaining things, just as Cooper was. Jowitt however seemed to have no particular principles or beliefs, and this detracted from the effectiveness of his arguments. Woodburn recalled however that on one occasion some forestry question came up, and it appeared that forestry was a subject in which Jowitt took a passionate interest, with the result that his contribution to the discussion, in which he could employ his forensic talents on something he believed in, was quite outstanding.

April 16th

Finished reading *Rescue in Denmark*, an account of how Danish Jews were saved from the Nazis. While paying tribute to the courage of the Danish populace, the author is strangely critical of the failure to resist the German invaders at the outset—comparing this attitude unfavourably with what happened in Norway. He has to record that the consequence of the futile resistance put up by the Norwegians was an immediate campaign of terror against Jews, which only eight hundred survived. In Denmark even after the Nazis started a terror campaign against the Jews the Danes were able by playing it quietly, and by acts of individual heroism in place of armed force, to get almost all of them out to safety.

April 20th

Finished *The Company I've Kept*, by Hugh MacDiarmid, a rambling, undisciplined book, though I personally find him most stimulating. One of the odd things about him is his professed loyalty to the Communist Party, when every chapter of the book includes an abundance of evidence that almost every aspect of a Communist Party regime would be anathema to him.

April 24th

10.30 flight to London—several MPs on the plane. I gave John Mackintosh a lift in to Westminster. In contrast to Norman Wylie, who was complaining not long ago about how boring parliamentary life was, Mackintosh thought it fascinating.

A meeting with Elwyn Jones in connection with a project for joining the Common Market. The main points put to us by the Cabinet related to the sovereignty of Parliament after accession to the Treaty of Rome. It seemed to me that if we adopted the provisions of the treaty into law the legislation would have the same effect as any other legislation, and if Parliament later passed another Act in conflict with the legislation adopting the treaty it would give effect to the later Act, in accordance with normal rules of construction. No doubt in doing so we should put ourselves in breach of our obligations under the treaty, but that seemed to be a matter of international relations, not of law. I was somewhat shaken by a case to which Gibson referred me where an Italian gentleman refused to pay an account of about 22 shillings to the Italian nationalised electricity undertaking on the ground that the Italian Act setting up the authority was in breach of an article of the Treaty of Rome. The Italian court, in a convincing, well-reasoned judgment, held that as Mr Costa had bought electricity from a body set up by Act of Parliament he was bound to pay for it, whether or not the Italian Parliament had breached the treaty by passing the Act. But the European Court of Justice held that once the Italian Parliament had adopted the treaty it was disabled from thereafter passing any legislation repugnant to the treaty provisions. No one could tell me what had been the attitude of the Italian courts to this pronouncement, or whether Mr Costa had to pay his 22 shillings; and despite the judgment of the European Court I could not conceive that a British court would give overriding effect to a vague provision in the treaty if it were faced with a subsequent Act of Parliament in explicit terms to a contrary effect. This seemed also to be the view of the English law officers, and in general we were prepared to affirm an excellent draft which Hetherington had done. But the two men from the Lord Chancellor's department caused a bit of trouble. They seemed principally anxious that no definite opinion should be expressed. I thought this was absurd, and said so with some force; and there was no difficulty in getting Elwyn to overrule the Chancellor's people and keep the draft as it was.

April 27th
Papers before me today relating to a question put down by Dempsey, whether the Secretary of State would 'take steps to prohibit the use of females wearing topless dresses in Clubs and other establishments in Scotland'. Gordon and Cowperthwaite had concocted a draft reply, that 'the Lord Advocate and I will watch for any developments of this kind'.

May 1st
A talk with Norman Buchan, who wanted to discuss the Webster case. He is not as clearly convinced of Webster's innocence as I am; he seems however anxious to try to have something done. His private secretary is a strong supporter of my view. We discussed a proposal by the Glasgow magistrates that the police should have power to arrest anyone found carrying an offensive weapon, if they have reasonable cause to believe that he is doing so without excuse or authority. At present they can do this only if they have cause to believe also that the weapon is likely to be used, and this makes it difficult for the police to deal with gangs of youths carrying knives, since no one can tell whether they are going to be used—probably even the youths do not know, depending as it does on how much they have to drink or whether they meet up with some rival gang. I thought it more important that police should have power to deal with these gangs on the spot, and so discourage them from carrying knives altogether, than that in such a matter we should be sticklers for the right of the individual to carry a knife if he wants. But the politicians are hesitant about it.

May 6th
Zurich. Having already travelled on the main line to Zug, I had arranged that on our way to Lucerne we should go by the old line, on which the slow trains travel. A steady flow of passengers from station to station: the type of wayside station that Dr Beeching would have had shut up long ago. During our tour so far I have not seen a single disused station. There is a good service of trains everywhere, and the public obviously make use of a good service when one is provided. At Lucerne we had made no arrangements for accommodation. Nancy thought we might get something on the north side of the lake, and

the Royal—a little off the road, up a steep hill—looked nice. We found a friendly proprietrix, with whom we bargained for a room with private bath, demi-pension, at forty francs each per night. We were taken up to a lovely big room looking out on the lake some distance below, with a balcony affording a magnificent view across the lake and wooded promontory opposite, the towering rocky ridge of Pilatus to its right, the black mass of the Burgenstock to its left, and a whole range of snow-covered mountains beyond. We saw a resident in overcoat and homburg hat arrive home at his flat in the street below. Although the streets were in no way muddy—in this country everything is kept beautifully clean—he carefully wiped his feet on a shoe-scraper at the door and having gone in emerged at once again with a broom, with which he swept away any dust he might have left when cleaning his shoes.

May 7th
The main road seemed very busy, and traffic continued into the early hours. But on our commanding heights we only had the muted roar of it in the distance, hardly disturbing at all—much better than Zurich, where on our last night the noise outside was too much for even me to sleep through: shouting and yelling at midnight as if a revolution had broken out. One wonders who takes part in this revelry, for during the daytime everyone looks most staid and respectable: no beatniks, or long-haired youths, or mini-skirts, or transistors.

May 8th
At 6.45 am a squad of men with a crane and a bull-dozer started work on the demolition of a house just below us. It was a pleasure to watch the efficient, methodical way they set about their work: everyone fully occupied, and even a man spraying the work continuously with a hose, to keep down the dust.

May 10th
Transport Museum. Although several exhibits had the usual notice asking visitors not to touch them, there seemed to be no attendants. Visitors were free to wander round, unaccompanied, on the assumption that they would behave themselves—as all of them apparently do.

May 11th
Basle had good milk, but it has nothing else. The airport bus took us

across the Rhine and through the frontier marked simply by a little notice saying 'France'. We landed at Turnhouse in a misty drizzle. Nancy remarked on how odd it was that we had had breakfast in Lucerne, coffee in Basle, lunch over Paris, tea over Manchester, and supper at home in Midmar Gardens.

May 12th

Nancy had ordered a corgi puppy and went for it this afternoon. The cat treats it warily, but does not seem to have any real objection to it. It is not at all concerned about the cat.

May 23rd

The Lord High Commissioner's banquet at Holyrood. Mrs Grimond was a lively, agreeable companion, who had plenty to say about any kind of topic—it was sometimes difficult to get a word in. I had Lady Reith on the other side, a pleasant old lady whose interests I did not succeed in discovering. The food was good, but I did not help myself to sufficiently large portions and was still quite hungry when the meal ended. In greeting Hughes, I had remarked that I had seen nothing of him for a long time. He replied that there was nothing so strange about that, but what was peculiar was that he had seen nothing of the Secretary of State, although they worked in the same office. Midnight before I got to bed. The puppy was lively, jumping and nipping at the cat all the way down to the scullery when the cat went down to be served with its fish. The cat tolerated the nuisance for some time, then lifted one paw and gave the puppy a push which sent it sprawling.

May 26th

Harry Wilson, who is in attendance on the Lord High Commissioner in his capacity of Solicitor-General, told me that they had been this morning to the Free Church Assembly. Reith had remarked to him that he felt rather frightened at the prospect, but in the result he had got on extremely well. He and the Free Church people seemed to be on the same wavelength. They had congratulated him on the high standards he had set for the BBC, and he had made an excellent speech in reply, seeming much more relaxed and at home with them than in his own Assembly. In the *Scotsman* today there was an article on the theme that there seemed little likelihood 'that either of Scotland's law officers will be found a seat in the House of Commons'.

The Liberals, it was said, claimed that there could be no law reform without a law officer to pilot the legislation through Parliament. 'But in Labour circles this criticism has been dismissed as nonsense because of the amount of legislation already handled by Mr Stott'. It is odd that Ross, who keeps rushing round doing everything under the sun, gets persistently criticised for doing nothing, while I, who do practically nothing, am paid tribute for doing so much.

May 29th
I had asked James Walker to have a talk with me about the Webster case. He was very affable, and seemed to remember the case well. He would have given Webster the benefit of the doubt, but it was a jury question, and the jury having taken a different view he did not seem to think there was any need to interfere. He thought it would be difficult from a constitutional point of view to overturn a jury's verdict by administrative action, but suggested that now that the evidence had been extended some question on it might be referred to the High Court.

A Devizes schoolmaster has written to know which portion of the Bible is considered to be most memorable from a literary point of view. I have referred him to the passage in which Abraham bargains with God about the number of righteous people in Sodom that would justify non-destruction of the city.

May 30th
Legislation Committee. The Foreign Office were promoting a Bill to provide for the relinquishment of sovereignty over Aden and the surrounding territories, including what seemed an extraordinary provision that 'the approval of Parliament is hereby given to the conclusion . . . of any agreement between Her Majesty and any other ruler or government as may appear to be expedient with respect to a transfer of sovereignty'. Crossman thought that, in view of the disturbances going on in Aden, and the controversy about giving it up, the Bill would be controversial. After some discussion, I suggested that the wording of Clause 2 might be reconsidered—at present it seemed to be designed to arouse the greatest degree of opposition. George Thomson, who was representing the Foreign Office, agreed to reconsider the clause. Gordon-Walker said that in such an important matter it seemed desirable for the Foreign Office to have some outside advice, adding the odd remark that it was well known that the Foreign

Office lawyers were a poor lot. Thomson replied that they recognised the importance of getting other advice, and had consulted lawyers in the Commonwealth Relations Office. 'They are just as bad', said Gordon-Walker. We went on to consider a proposal by Jenkins that Government time should if necessary be given to enable the remaining stages of the Abortion Bill to be completed. The proposal was supported by Crossman and the Chief Whip. Longford however objected, and embarked on a lengthy diatribe about some letters that had just appeared in *The Times* in which distinguished medical men expressed opposition to the Bill—a ridiculous argument, since letters from medical men taking one side or the other have been appearing in *The Times* since the start of the controversy. I butted in to say that as I understood it, while strong opinions could be expressed for or against the Bill, the question with which we were concerned was one of procedure, and I thought it would be disastrous if when so much time and public discussion had already been given to the Bill Parliament would not have the opportunity of coming to a decision on it. This argument did not penetrate to Longford; he continued to argue the merits of the Bill, on the basis that for the government to give time would lose a lot of votes in Catholic constituencies. Jenkins when asked to reply said he had nothing to add to what I had said. Despite Crossman's efforts to persuade Longford that the matter of principle was left open for the House to decide, he insisted that the matter be referred to the Cabinet. For my part, I was pleased at having been able to give some useful support to Crossman and Jenkins instead of being up against them.

June 1st

Nancy and I were invited to a reception at the Tunisian embassy. We did not stay long; and after supper went to listen to a band playing in the Embankment Gardens, then taking a ride on the top of a bus to Surrey Docks.

June 2nd

A reception which the Lord Chancellor and the law officers were giving to members of Law Societies from Common Market countries, at Lancaster House. We stood in line with Gardiner, Elwyn Jones and his wife, and the Foots, and shook hands with a great lot of people. There was a man at the door calling out names, but we were too far inside to hear what he said. I had some conversation with gentlemen from Luxemburg, Denmark, Holland and Germany; and we had a few words with Peter Rawlinson and his strikingly handsome young wife. Lady Wilberforce, speaking with a markedly foreign accent, told us that her husband when playing chess with her gave up the queen as a handicap, and they had some excellent games. A large number of those present, including Jones and Foot, were going on to a dinner which the Bar Council, I think, were giving in the Temple. They expressed some indignation that the Scottish law officers had not been invited, an omission that had not occurred to me, though I suppose it was rather an obvious piece of discourtesy—a welcome one so far as we were concerned. Jones and Foot seemed to take it seriously, and were still discussing it when I followed them into the cloakroom. They did not see me come in, and Jones appeared to be saying how shocking it was that I had not been invited—'and of course he's such a modest man'. Actually I was not at all in the mood for an extensive dinner, having partaken of the excellent refreshment provided at the reception. We made our way to a seat by the lake in St James's Park, afterwards walking along the lake side and up the Duke of York's Steps to Piccadilly. By the time we got to Coventry Street we were ready for something more to eat, and had a nice meal in Lyons' Corner House.

June 6th

To the House of Lords to hear a debate on the Criminal Justice Bill: the clause intended to give an English jury the right to return a majority verdict. It seems to be a complete myth that debates in the Lords are superior to those in the Commons. I do not think I have ever heard a debate so inconsequent and downright stupid. It was started off by Dilhorne, who propounded the theory that a majority verdict should be allowed only when the majority wanted to convict; acquittal should have to be unanimous—on the ground that acquittal by a majority would leave a slur on the reputation of anyone so acquitted. It would follow that a man who got ten votes against him would be convicted, but a man who got ten votes in his favour would have to go on being re-tried until he either got a unanimous verdict in his favour or ten people on the jury the other way. Apart from Gardiner, who spoke with his usual lucidity and good sense, none of the following speakers seemed to see the absurdity of Dilhorne's proposal, and they all treated one another's speeches with a deferential courtesy which none of them deserved. A meeting of Scottish ministers in Ross's room was equally tiresome. Ross and the others rambled at length round each point, coming to no conclusion. I was content to sit quiet and let them talk, but it seems an incredibly silly way of doing business. In the train to Earls Court, there was a long-haired, mini-skirted girl with a big button on her coat bearing the inscription 'Exciting new offer'.

June 8th

A meeting with Edward Taylor, the young Conservative MP for Cathcart, about a complaint by a constituent. Taylor in his political activities had given the impression of being rather a brash, pushing young man, but I found him extremely reasonable.

June 9th

To Parliament House to look for James Mackay and get his views on interpretation of the Land Commission Act. I was diffident about approaching him for an unpaid oral opinion, but as always he was enthusiastic and helpful, saying that he found these questions about the Land Commission Act most interesting—as indeed they are when one has to go properly into them.

June 13th

Kilbrandon came to see me about divorce. The English Commission, following on a meeting with Church of England representatives, seem to be going back to the old idea of proof of fault, instead of deciding whether marriage has in fact broken down. The Scottish Commission do not agree that the Court should have an overriding discretion to refuse divorce when grounds of divorce have been established, and they do not think that the Court should be entitled to refuse divorce on the ground that the parties have deceived or misled the Court—taking the view that to keep the parties tied together in matrimony is not an appropriate penalty for telling lies.

June 16th

Home Affairs Committee. Two Scottish Office law-reform papers were approved. Crossman said he supposed the bills would be introduced in the Lords. I said that they would, and added that the idea was that there would be a Scottish law-reform bill to start the business in the Lords at the beginning of each session. 'For all time coming?' asked

Gordon-Walker in some surprise, and I replied that that was more or less the idea. 'Well, it may be quite a good idea', said Gordon-Walker. This piece of kite-flying, if it succeeds, will get over the problem of parliamentary time which has always been the main obstacle to law reform. A talk with Gardiner about divorce. Like me, he thinks we should go ahead with legislation right away, and I told him that despite the unenthusiastic attitude of the Scottish Office we might be able to get Ross to put forward a joint paper with him. We agreed that the two countries should keep together, and that the differences between the two Commissions were of no importance. He said he thought our talk had been most useful, as I think it may have been. He was probably surprised to find support for his ideas from a Scottish minister—he obviously regards the Scottish Office as a bulwark of reaction on social questions. On my way back to the House through Westminster Abbey, I was intrigued by finding one of the floor slabs among the poets with the inscription, 'Robert Hawke, Knight, Murdered in the choir August 11 1378'.

June 19th
An appointment with Peterson, Sheriff-Substitute at Oban, and another of three nominees for transfer to Glasgow. He has been actively canvassing for the appointment, and I was thus surprised when he appeared to be undecided and wanted time to consider it. I made it clear that I thought it foolish of him to have sought the appointment without having decided that he wanted it, and suggested that if that were his attitude we had better just forget about it. This however did not suit him at all—but could he not just have an opportunity to telephone his wife. I agreed to give him till tomorrow morning; and as I expected he rang up later in the day and said he wanted to go.

June 20th
Dalgetty to see me about a Bill to give effect to the recommendations of the Russell Committee about giving illegitimate children rights of succession. We got bogged down in an impromptu discussion of Kilbrandon's recommendations regarding legitimation by subsequent marriage. I was impressed by the grasp of the problems involved shown by a young lawyer named Whitty who was one of the people Dalgetty had brought with him, and who seemed to have thought it out very fully—much more so than I was able to do while he was putting the problems to me.

June 22nd

A Faculty reception in Parliament Hall. I had a few words with E. M. Grieve, and introduced D. B. Smith to him as one of my Advocates Depute. Smith pointed out that he was not one of the Advocates Depute, adding that he hoped that when I came to appoint any I would not leave him out in the mistaken belief that he was an Advocate Depute already. Swann, the Principal of the University, was introduced to me by Kilbrandon. He was just asking me what I was doing to keep Tam Dalyell in order when Nancy Wheatley appeared. I introduced Swann to her, explaining that Lady Wheatley was Tam's mother-in-law and would probably be better able to control him than anyone else. She disclaimed any ability in that direction, and got involved in a vehement argument with Swann about the Dalyell family. Swann, though he obviously did not think highly of them, said a word in favour of Tam's mother which Nancy Wheatley repudiated with some heat. She stood up for 'Kathleen's side' of the Castle of Binns when Swann condemned the house as the coldest place he had ever been in. He agreed that he had not been in 'Kathleen's side'. His complaint against Tam was that he always asked if he could sit beside Swann if he encountered him in the aeroplane to London; if it was not Tam Dalyell, it was some other MP. Nancy Wheatley said that when someone asked to sit beside him he should say 'No'. He explained that he had not the strength of mind to do that, but usually tried to say he had work to do. 'Well, that's just a lie', said Nancy Wheatley. 'Oh, well, I have a University to run between times', said Swann, not at all put out. 'It may be a poor, second-rate kind of place, but it does mean a certain amount of work'.

June 27th

Half an hour to wait at Earls Court before a train for Kensington High Street appeared. I got into conversation with a lady who had just been to hear Billy Graham at Earls Court. She had been converted fifteen years ago, by the power of the Holy Spirit, and told me about the joy of belief, which had brought her to salvation. While appreciating the benefit this had obviously done her, and no doubt through her to those with whom she came in contact, I asked her whether there might not be some other road to salvation. What happened if one had really given a lot of thought to it, and decided that one could not honestly say one believed, and then it turned out to be true? Would salvation be open in those circumstances? She agreed that some special allowance would have to be made for those who had never heard the Gospel, but that of course was not quite the same point. She was a cheerful, friendly person, and said she knew two people who had been converted through Dr Graham—one of them her fishmonger, who since then had been a new man, completely changed.

June 29th
To Turnhouse to meet Hon. Aldo Moro, the Prime Minister of Italy. I was told that lunch would be laid on for me. Though I noticed a 'Reserved' ticket on one of the tables, I sat down at one of the other tables and ordered from the menu. Halfway through, the airport manager appeared, apologising profusely for not knowing about my arrival. He said the chef had laid on something special for me, so it was lucky for me that I had not been recognised. I told him to give my apologies to the chef, and tell him that I had had a very nice lunch. After lunch I was joined by Dr Trinchieri, the Italian Consul-General, a friendly, talkative old gentleman. On his way from London the Prime Minister had stopped at York to see the Minster, a change in his plans which had necessitated a complete revision in the Scottish Office's plans for the day. After he came down from the plane, he made quite a speech, while cameras whirred and the wind blew. I had not thought about saying anything, but said it was a pleasure to see him in Scotland and the Government hoped he would enjoy his visit. We all piled into limousines to drive to the Caledonian Hotel. I travelled in the first car, with Mr Moro and the Italian ambassador, an elegant, rather quizzical man with hair carefully brushed back over his head. Mr Moro himself was tall, slightly stooping, and rather languid. His expression seldom varied—he hardly smiled at all, but looked interested all the time, and I think his interest was genuine. He spoke in low, even tones, without any emphasis; it was difficult to imagine him flurried or excited, or indeed displaying any emotion. Harry Wilson had agreed to look after him throughout the afternoon. Dinner at the Castle. On my right I had Diana Younger, the wife of the Conservative MP for Ayr, who despite being mother of four children looked young and attractive—a very agreeable table companion. On her other side she had Trinchieri, who flirted with her throughout the dinner.

June 30th
Today's programme was scheduled to start at 8.50 with a visit to the

Forth Bridge. The Prime Minister however had gone to church, and had still to have breakfast when he got back—much to the annoyance of the British Government hospitality man, who complained that they were 'a lousy undisciplined crew'. Some Italian hangers-on were wandering about the lounge, among whom was the Ambassador, looking rather the worse for wear, and remarking that it had been cynically observed of the profession of diplomatist that it was carried on more with the feet than with the head. We were driven to the Forth Bridge, then to Sighthill, where a visit was scheduled to the premises of a company called Nuclear Enterprises, run by an enthusiastic family named Pringle. A press conference followed. Moro was asked mostly about Britain's entry to the Common Market, of which he is a strong supporter; no doubt this is why the Foreign Office are cultivating him so assiduously. We had a lunch engagement at the City Chambers, but at the Prime Minister's request a visit to the National Gallery had been inserted into the programme. The Ambassador remarked on the number of Canaletto paintings in this country, and told me that when some of the old Italian buildings were being reconstructed after the war they were able to make use of paintings by Canaletto's nephew, so perfect was the detail. We all piled into the cars again and were driven to the City Chambers. I had expected that the Lord Provost would meet us at the door, but he was not there. When the City Officer had led us up the stair, we were all left standing at the top while the Officer went away to the Lord Provost's room. When he came back he asked if everyone else would stay where he was, and the Prime Minister and His Excellency would come with him. The interpreter went with the Prime Minister, and so did I. To my amazement we were shown into a small room off the corridor, with four hard-backed chairs and a table, and left there by ourselves. We waited a few minutes before I went out and, finding the City Officer in the lobby, asked him where the Lord Provost was, adding that it was outrageous that the Prime Minister of Italy should be treated in this way. The only reply I got was that it was not his fault, and that the Lord Provost was in his room and knew his guest had arrived. I instructed him to tell the Lord Provost to come and receive his guest immediately, and was considering following him into the Lord Provost's room when he emerged and took the three of us in. The Lord Provost received us without a word of apology. Moro, as appears to be characteristic of him, gave no indication of having taken offence, but sat down at the Provost's table and conversed

politely with him until lunch was served. Brechin made little attempt
to converse with his guest, preferring the easier task of talking to me.
His excuse for his boorish conduct was that he had just come in from
viewing the film 'Ulysses' along with the magistrates, who—as the
film has been refused a certificate by the Film Censors—had to
decide whether it should be licensed for showing in Edinburgh. It
was, said Brechin, a most disgusting film, which should never have
been made. We did not have much of a lunch, and afterwards had to
return to the reception room, where a procession of people were
waiting to be introduced. Moro, as is his way, talked to each in turn
with exemplary patience. A brief call at the hotel, where we picked
up the Ambassador. In the car, making for Turnhouse, I asked him
to give Moro my apologies for the seeming discourtesy of the Lord
Provost, who had been engaged on the judicial duty of licensing a
film. Moro waved this apology aside, saying that he knew well in his
own country that circumstances sometimes made that kind of thing
unavoidable. I then asked the Ambassador to tell him that apart from
any official appreciation of his visit I had had the greatest personal
enjoyment in having the opportunity of meeting him and going round
with him over the past few days. This was true. Behind his quiet,
unassuming manner he gives the impression of a warm, interesting
character, and I should imagine in his undemonstrative way a very
determined one. I liked and respected him, and thought it unfortunate that what seemed to have been otherwise a successful visit should
have been marred by Brechin's disgraceful behaviour—particularly
as his appointment at the City Chambers had necessitated his being
hurried away from the National Gallery, where he had obviously
been enjoying himself.

July 1st
Drafted a Minute to the Secretary of State, narrating what had happened at the City Chambers and suggesting that they should be omitted
from the programme of any distinguished visitor until Edinburgh
Corporation learned how to behave in a civilised manner.

July 3rd
A telegram had come from Rome:

> *Reintrando in Italia desidero rinnoverli il mio vivissimo ringraziamento*
> *par le corisia usatami nel carso della mia visite in Scozia conformambole*

in mici sentimenti di deferenza a diestime Aldo Moro.

I asked Miss Black to find out from the Scottish Office whether it was usual to reply to such messages, but their answer was that they did not know—they had not had such a message on this occasion or on any other. I thought it would be courteous to reply, and drafted a form of words.

July 14th
A phone call from one Dr Harper, who in a feeble voice told me that Colonel Rose had died. He rang off abruptly when the pips sounded. I should certainly not accept any message about Colonel Rose unless I had official confirmation—quite likely it was Colonel Rose himself speaking.

July 15th
George Emslie came up in a state of some perturbation at the news that the Bill dealing with corroboration was to be published in September. The Faculty had a strong committee examining Kilbrandon's report on this, but it could not possibly report to the Faculty before October. Emslie thought it would destroy all chance of cooperation between the Government and the Faculty if the Bill were published before then. I explained my difficulties about parliamentary time, and the importance of having the Bill ready for the start of the session. Emslie was most cooperative and understanding, as he always is, and undertook to explain this to the Faculty and to give them my assurance that their views would be welcomed and taken into account as the Bill proceeded through Lords and Commons.

July 18th
A Minute from Miss Macdonald of the Scottish Home and Health Department recording that after consultation with Gibson they had decided that it was not possible to have two Law Reform Bills ready for the start of the session, and so they had decided to concentrate on the Legitimation Bill and leave the Miscellaneous Provisions Bill— the one that will deal with corroboration—over. It was suggested that in view of what had been said by Ministers at the Home Affairs Committee the Whips should be warned not to expect two Scottish Bills at the beginning of the session. When I had successfully overcome what I had always thought was the bottleneck of parliamentary

time, it was maddening to find that the bottleneck was going to be in my own department, and that this first-class opportunity for law reform was to be frittered away on legitimation. I interviewed Gibson about it as soon as he came in, and he undertook to hold up any further moves until we decided which Bill was to come first. The excuse for postponing the Miscellaneous Provisions Bill is that the Scottish Office want to include a provision to set up machinery of collecting officers for alimentary payments, and this will not be ready. Though I did not think much of this point—if the collecting-officers provisions are not ready, the collecting officers will just have to be left out—postponement of the Bill would have the advantage of meeting the point that Emslie put to me. I felt there might be something to be said for it provided it did not jeopardise the Bill's chances for this session, or our position with the Whips in relation to the tentative understanding about a Law Reform Bill at the start of each session. I asked Gibson to consult with the Scottish Office and see how matters stood in those regards, while making no secret of my annoyance that they should have purported to take this decision without consulting me or even advising me that what I had undertaken to the Home Affairs Committee was supposed to be impracticable.

To Kings Cross to meet Elizabeth off the train from York. Elizabeth had been included in an invitation to the Royal Garden Party at Buckingham Palace, and I had written asking her if she would like to go and whether Miss Blake would let her away a day early—the Mount does not finish until tomorrow. She replied that she would like to go, and would ask Miss Blake, but later phoned Nancy to say Miss Blake had refused. Quakers did not approve of dressing up, and this was not the kind of occasion for which leave of absence would be given. Elizabeth asked Nancy to get me to write, and I did so—saying nothing about Miss Blake's refusal but pointing out that Buckingham Palace gardens were one of the sights of London, and I hoped that Miss Blake would give me the opportunity—which might not occur again—of showing them to Elizabeth. This brought the right reply; and Elizabeth appeared in a nice outfit of pink skirt with matching blouse and jacket. We strolled round the lake, and back along the edge of a herbaceous border, for tea at one of the little tables set out on the grass. After tea Elizabeth went off 'exploring', as she put it. She seemed to be enjoying herself. Ross had rung up yesterday to say that he had been invited to tonight's performance of the Georgian State Dance Company, and to ask us to go with him.

Shortly after we had taken our seats, the Russian ambassador appeared with his wife and two other men; they also had their wives with them. The ambassador and his wife are friendly and unassuming. The dancing was fast and furious, and carried out with perfect precision.

July 19th
Gibson had left me a file of correspondence, which I read through with growing dismay. It was apparent that it was he who had raised the objection to having the two Bills, and written to St Andrews House to say that Ministers could not commit the draftsman to a timetable without previous consultation. He was not prepared to take draftsmen from their existing commitments in order to meet the convenience of the Scottish Office—apparently not realising that our office ought to be at least as keen on getting on with law reform as the Scottish Home Department, nor appreciating the importance of what had been offered in regard to parliamentary time.

A long letter from Colonel Rose, which confirmed me in the doubts I had had about his demise. 'What proof is there', he asks, 'that I am still alive?'

A meeting with Dalgetty and two men from the Scottish Education Department, who raised an interesting question about certificated teachers who decline to go on the Register of Teachers which is to be compiled under the new Act. I expressed a doubt as to whether mere failure to register was justifiable cause for dismissing an otherwise unexceptionable teacher; but it is difficult to see how the proposed scheme can be worked out if some teachers register and others refuse. We agreed that there was no satisfactory solution, and that the more time that elapsed before the Act was brought into operation the better.

July 20th
Nancy had stayed on in London for a tea-party yesterday at 10 Downing Street. Jay Wilson had been with her, and Nancy had introduced George Brown to her, whereupon Brown observed that it was interesting to see someone connected with the Solicitor-General for Scotland and to know that these people actually existed.

July 21st
A visit from R. S. Johnston, who wanted to know what were his prospects of being appointed a Court of Session judge. I said I thought he had the same chance as anyone else of comparable ability. R. F.

Johnson, Dalgetty and three others from St Andrews House came to talk about divorce. A letter I wrote to Ross has borne fruit—I stressed the importance of Ross's being in on the paper, and Ross added a short note saying he agreed generally with what I had said. The officials apparently took this as indication to go ahead, and scrapped a terrible draft submission which had been sent to Gibson for his comments—that Gardiner should be allowed to go ahead with reform in England, and nothing done in Scotland until public opinion had 'crystallised'. Gibson had had no comment of any consequence, but it seems that Johnson himself must have taken a hand in it, for the draft that came to me was very different, reaching the conclusion—to his own surprise, as Johnson put it—that we should reject the Scottish Commission's proposals, accept the broad principles of what the English Commission recommended, with breakdown of marriage as the general ground of divorce, and go ahead with them in the same Bill. I did not regard this submission as a genuine rejection of Kilbrandon, thinking that the difference between Kilbrandon and Scarman is more verbal than real, but I agreed very much with Johnson's conclusion. Johnson accepted that since we were all agreed on the best line of action there was no need to put the conclusion in such a provocative way; and he is to discuss with Kilbrandon and Gardiner's people how far we can have common ground. They all smiled when I remarked that we should take advantage of a favouring breeze from the Secretary of State while it lasted. I took the opportunity of mentioning the Law Reform Bills. Johnson did not seem to think there was any reason to suppose that a short postponement of Miscellaneous Provisions would interfere with its passage this session; and on that indication I agreed that the Legitimation Bill would come first, and later told Emslie that we should probably be able to wait for the Faculty's observations. Clyde appeared with a message that Strachan had decided to resign and a new judge would be required in October to replace him. I feel I shall have to take this vacancy myself. It is a pity that Strachan's resignation has come so soon, and I should be sorry to exchange the interesting life of the Crown Office for the much less interesting job of a judge of the Court of Session; but there may not be another vacancy under the present administration, and I should not want to risk having to go back to the toil of an ordinary practice at the Bar. I said nothing to Clyde about this, merely remarking that it was rather awkward, since I had no one in mind at the moment who was altogether suitable as a judge.

July 24th

To the Hume Tower, the big new University building in George Square, to deputise for Ross in opening the International Congress of Celtic Studies. I had begun by explaining that I did not know a single word of Gaelic, and ended by saying I had been asked to finish with a few words of welcome in that language and had been told that if I gave them a note of what I wanted to say they would have it translated and send me a tape recording so that I should know how to pronounce the words. But I thought that was rather artificial, and with their permission should simply welcome them in my native tongue. Swann, who made a few short remarks, had an amusing follow-up to this, saying he was one up on the Lord Advocate—indeed two up, for he knew two words of Gaelic. He might not be able to pronounce them properly, nor even to spell them properly, but he thought that was probably the better bet—and he turned round and picked up a piece of chalk, pulled down the blackboard behind us, and wrote two Gaelic words of welcome. The whole affair took less than half an hour. The *Daily Express* phoned to query part of my speech where, recounting the encounter that Ross McLean and I had had with the two little girls on the island of Barra, and commending the grace and charm with which these two small Gaelic speakers had conversed with us in English, I had added that mainland children would probably not have been allowed to speak to us at all, though it passed my comprehension how any child could learn the art of civilised conversation, let alone civilised living, if they were to be frightened off from conversing with any but females. I declined to make any comment; but I daresay I may have got myself into trouble with the newspaper headlines.

July 25th

Bought copies of the Scottish morning papers—relieved to find that the *Express* had nothing at all about the Congress of Celtic Studies, or my speech.

July 26th

Sat on the steps of the throne in the House of Lords and listened to their Lordships dealing with the Abortion Bill. They were obviously much interested in the Bill, but were as hopeless as ever. They seem to have no idea of relevance; anyone could get up and talk on some remotely connected topic without any regard to whether it was relevant to the amendment under discussion. They were supposed to be debating whether abortion should be permitted on the ground of risk of injury to the health of existing children, and one man got up and read out a mass of statistics about mortality rates which had no bearing whatever on the question before the House. From time to time a peer who was obviously a lunatic stumped through the House waggling his hand and with an insane grin on his face. The best speakers were the women—best of all Lady Stocks. I was agreeably surprised by Lord Ferrier, who made a remarkably liberal and fairminded contribution to the debate. Lord Platt, a physician, seemed to take a delight in contradicting his colleague Lord Brock, who is a surgeon—the man who had given the maternity statistics.

July 27th
A dinner to the Crown Agent on his retiral. We had invited the whole staff of the Crown Office. So far as anyone knew, it was the first time that the whole staff had met together round a table, and all appeared to think it had been a good idea. Harry and his wife were hostesses on Monday night at a reception to the Celtic Congress delegates, and he told me that two separate people, addressing him as the Lord Advocate, had told him how much they had enjoyed his speech opening the Congress.

July 28th
A visit from a Glasgow psychiatrist, Dr Sclare, complaining about Peter McNeill, who he said had thrown aside the unanimous views of five doctors and sent a man to prison when the doctors were agreed that he was mentally ill and should be in Carstairs maximum-security hospital. In fact he has now been sent there, since when he got to Barlinnie it turned out that for all practical purposes he was a raving lunatic. On studying the papers, I discovered that Peter had not had five reports before him, but only three, and that the three psychiatrists were by no means in agreement. Two for the Crown thought he was unfit to plead; the defending solicitor brought Dr Sclare, who reported that in his opinion the accused was not unfit to plead. He added that he should be dealt with under section 63 of the Act—which in fact only applies when an accused is found unfit to plead—and be sent to Carstairs. Peter after pondering it for a fortnight found the man was fit to plead, and sent him to prison. Under another section he could have sent him to Carstairs even after finding him fit to

plead, but it seemed to me that the confusion had been caused mostly by the psychiatrists themselves. I had no difficulty in persuading Dr Sclare that that was so. I assured him that Peter McNeill was the last sheriff who would be likely to dismiss the views of medical experts without giving them consideration. Dr Sclare said he would inform his colleagues that they had all taken it up wrong.

August 6th
Lyme Regis: the parish church, where Rev. P. N. Howard preached on the transfiguration. Though not much of a preacher, he was a nice old gentleman. He thought that the number of occasions when we experienced anything like the transfiguration were rare—at any rate, it was with him. It was not more than once or twice a year that he felt himself to be really among the company of angels and archangels.

August 16th
I had phoned Ian last week and arranged a meeting at Hamdon Hill. We all picnicked in a sheltered spot on the grass. On the way back in the car, Richard remarked in a friendly way on the difference between the two brothers: 'He does everything for his wife, and you don't do anything at all'.

August 17th
Lyme Regis Conservative fête. Mr Ernest Partridge, formerly MP for a Battersea division, told us how unfortunate it was we had parted from Sir Alec Douglas-Home, but we had to do the best we could with our present leader, and he had plenty of able assistants.

August 20th
We all walked to church, where Rev. A. R. Wallace, formerly headmaster of Sherborne, preached on Mark 10:15. He denounced in no uncertain terms the modern theologians who—no doubt unwittingly—were doing Satan's work by expressing doubts about the virgin birth and whether God might have made a mistake at Aberfan.

August 24th
We all left shortly before eleven for Taunton, where I parked the car at the station before taking the train to Minehead—a line I had not been on before. Richard had a pleasant surprise, having expected to find some small place at the end of the line, with colliery bings. It

was indeed a pleasant surprise to all of us: a good stretch of sand, and all the requisites of a pleasant seaside resort.

August 31st
Motored to Parliament House. After a month's disuse, the Hillman battery was flat, but it started the engine with its last dying gasp. A lot of work to attend to; and after being, like the battery, out of use for a month I found it quite exhausting. I signed an authority to Collins' to print a new edition of the Bible—no edition of the Bible can be printed in Scotland without my permission.

September 6th
With Elizabeth and Richard to Musselburgh for a round of golf on the Monktonhall course—the charge for children only one shilling each. I gave them a stroke a hole, and played their better ball; and the game ended on the fifteenth green with a win for them. Richard had driven his tee shot into the river, so it was a critical hole for Elizabeth. She proceeded to play it perfectly, making the green in three long shots straight down the fairway. Richard was delighted. 'You must count', he said; 'it's very important'—Elizabeth often does not bother to count the number of strokes she takes for a hole. She carries only three clubs, driving with a brassie and continuing to use it for subsequent shots, whether on the fairway or in the rough, until she comes within measurable distance of the green, when she takes a putter.

September 12th
Picked up two Canadian girls who wanted to go to Grangemouth, where, they had heard, they would probably be able to find a ship going to Norway. They asked if there was a Youth Hostel in Grangemouth, which I thought unlikely. A police van came along as we got into the main street, and I went across and consulted the sergeant who was driving. He said that if the girls would go to the police station, a few yards along the street, they would all be back shortly and would probably be able to fix them up. I returned to my passengers and instructed them to go to the police station, where the police would no doubt do what was required. 'What did you ask them for?' they asked; and were amused when I replied, 'A ship to Norway and accommodation for the night'.

September 16th

A Minute from St Andrews House to say that they had got Treasury consent to the filling of the vacancy on the Bench, and that I could now go ahead with a nomination; no doubt I would consult the Lord President!

September 19th

Wrote Ross, intimating that I thought I should take the vacant judgeship and asking him to let me know that he agreed. I have not mentioned it to anyone else except Miss Black.

September 20th

Interviewed Clyde about a request from St Andrews House that he allow Cameron to serve as chairman of a committee on inshore fishing. Told him that the arrangements for appointing a new judge were going ahead, and he should have one by some time in October. I took the opportunity of consulting him about an Auditor of the Court of Session. He promised to think the matter over and let me have a suggestion.

September 22nd

Went across to the House through Westminster Abbey, and stopped to look at some of the monuments, including an odd one where 'the Loyall Duke of Newcastle & his Dutches' are laid out flat on top of a big pedestal, above eye level, so that only one side of the Duke can be seen and the Duchess is practically invisible, though the inscription relates almost entirely to her. 'Her name was Margarett Lucas youngest sister to the Lord Lucas of Colchester a noble familie for all the Brothers were Valiant and all the Sisters virtuous. This Dutches was a wise witty & learned Lady which her many Bookes do well testifie she was a most virtuous & a loving & carefull wife & was with her Lord all the time of his banishment & miseries & when he came home never parted from him in his solitary retirement'. The monument to Pitt is peculiar—he is set up on high above a miscellaneous collection of deities, cupids and others, holding up one hand in an admonitory gesture above their heads. I noticed that one finger was missing.

September 26th

Home Affairs Committee. Gardiner had several papers, including his proposals for a Divorce Bill. A lot of tedious waffling from Cledwyn Hughes and Shackleton, who were all in favour of reform but had to warn us at great length how very dangerous it was and what tremendous opposition there would be. In the end, permission was given for drafting a Bill for presentation by a private Member. Gordon-Walker having become Minister of Education, his place as chairman of the Committee has been taken by Michael Stewart. As I had expected, he proved a sensible chairman who guided the Committee to a proper conclusion. A lengthy discussion about the site for the new British Museum library. A site in Bloomsbury was chosen in the early 1950s, but after sixteen years of wrangling the conclusion has been reached that this site is out of the question and should never have been considered. Gordon-Walker is thus faced with the task of telling Lord Radclyffe, the chairman of the Museum trustees, that after waiting sixteen years for their library they would have to start looking for another site. He was anxious to offer some positive alternative and had some vague idea about a site at Covent Garden. Crossman did not approve, and it was amusing to watch Gordon-Walker's face— more like a melancholy bloodhound than ever—as it slowly dawned on him under the force of Crossman's argument that his alternative would not do and he would have nothing to offer Lord Radclyffe.

September 27th
A few words with Emslie about the vacancy on the Bench. We agreed that the only possibilities were one or other of us or Allan Walker.

September 28th
Emslie came up to say he was afraid he might not have made his real views clear to me yesterday. The ideal solution, he was sure, was that I should take the judgeship. From his own standpoint all he wanted to say was that he would not like to soldier on indefinitely as Dean of Faculty.

September 29th
A most interesting murder case: the case of a teacher's wife who had murdered her invalid father-in-law. The invalid was a cantankerous old man who was incapable of looking after himself and gave endless trouble in his son's household, where as there was nowhere else for him to go he had been dumped for the purpose of being looked after. The daughter-in-law was a diabetic, with a plentiful supply of insulin

to inject herself; and one night when she got the old man to herself she injected sufficient of it into him to kill him. As he had been suffering from every conceivable malady except diabetes, and was equally liable to die any moment or live for ten years, the doctor had no difficulty in certifying that death was due to natural causes; and as the presence of insulin is apparently not discoverable even by post-mortem examination it seemed as effective a method of murdering the old man as could be devised. Suspicion was however aroused through the intervention of a daily help, and prolonged scientific tests on the deceased's tissues by experts from Burroughs Wellcome have now revealed that he must indeed have had an injection of insulin. It seemed obvious that the young woman had acted only when driven to distraction by the old man's tantrums; and I soon made up my mind to mark the papers 'No Pro'—after which Bowen and I set out finding sufficiently good grounds in law for this deci-sion, which we had little difficulty in doing. Lord Strachan's resignation was in this morning's papers, and the car-park attendant in Parlia-ment Square told me he had been reliably informed that the vacancy was to be filled by the appointment of Allan Walker, whose position as Sheriff of Lanarkshire was to be taken by the Solicitor-General.

September 30th

A visit from Lyon. He has just issued his 33-page judgment in favour of Lady Monckton, holding that she is entitled to the Scottish barony of Ruthven. It appears that the judgment of the Lyon Court granting someone the right to matriculate the arms of a peerage is generally accepted by the Lord Chancellor as sufficient proof to enable him to summon the peer to the House of Lords, unless he has some infor-mation to the contrary; and we have had Coldstream on the phone asking if I would satisfy myself that Lyon had considered certain House of Lords authorities, in which Lord Mansfield and others had spoken of a settled presumption in Scots Law that where the terms of a peerage destination were unknown it must be regarded as having been to heirs male. Before Lyon arrived, I read through his judg-ment, from which it was obvious that he did not think much of Lord Mansfield and his noble colleagues. He made a number of sneering references to the opinions expressed, and from a lengthy examination of the history of the Scottish peerage concluded that the destination in the Ruthven peerage must be presumed to be to 'heirs of tailzie and provision'—by which it seemed to me that he meant anyone whom the ancestor cared to name. This morning he was full of glee about this pronouncement, which he thought if it had been made in earlier times would have saved many of the old Scottish peerages from extinction at the hands of the English barbarians in the House of Lords. Anyhow there is no doubt that he considered Lord Mansfield's presumption, and demolished it, at least to his own satisfaction, and I shall have no difficulty in assuring Coldstream that we have no information to set against the judgment of the Lyon Court.

October 1st
To church, where Mr Kelly preached on Matthew 22:2. I continued reading Exodus, and was interested to find, sandwiched in among directions about the furnishings of the temple and robes to be worn by priests, a delightful little story about an occasion when the children of Israel, despondent at Moses' failure to come down from the mountain, got Aaron to make them a golden calf. God, annoyed about this, decided that they were hopeless and told Moses he was going to destroy them; but Moses retorted that that would not do at all—everyone knew that God had brought them out of Egypt, and would not think much of a god who did that only to destroy them in the wilderness. God was impressed by this argument, and changed his mind; but just to keep things in order Moses had 3,000 of the people killed, apparently on his own initiative.

October 3rd
Sir Douglas Haddow came, at my request, and I told him my intentions about filling the vacancy. He said he was not altogether surprised, and told me that the first step was for the Secretary of State to have a word with the Prime Minister. I said I had written him a fortnight ago; I did not know what he had done about it. 'Nothing', said Haddow with a smile. 'You can be quite sure he'll have done nothing. He would put the letter in his pocket'. He undertook to take it up with Ross when he comes back from the Labour Party conference.

On television tonight there was a documentary on Vietnam—odd that the Americans persist in this crazy war when they all seem to realise that nobody wants them there and that they are doing no good at all.

October 4th
Clyde had intimated yesterday through the Justiciary Office that he could not provide a judge for a circuit at Oban on October 26th.

There is only one fairly short case, and the suggestion was that it should be transferred to Glasgow, where a circuit was going on anyhow. This was not practicable, as the indictment had been served, and defence solicitors were no doubt already preparing for a trial at Oban on the 26th. The only way of getting the case to Glasgow would be to drop the indictment, and serve a new one. Having had no explanation as to why a judge could not be available, and accepting that Glasgow juries should not be burdened with cases from all over the country, I had agreed that the Justiciary Office's proposal be rejected. This afternoon Clyde told me that in addition to a Valuation Appeal Court he had eleven proofs out for the Court of Session on the 26th, and had no judge to send to Oban. I pointed out that the circuit dates had been fixed with his approval a long time ago, and that the Justiciary Court in any event took precedence of the Court of Session and the Valuation Appeal Court. 'Oh, well', he said, 'if you say that on your authority there is to be no Valuation Appeal Court then of course I'll cancel it'. I replied that I had nothing whatever to do with the Valuation Appeal Court. It was entirely for him what arrangements he made, but there would have to be a circuit at Oban. 'Well', he said, 'you can have your circuit but there won't be a judge for it'. When I pointed out that what he was saying was that he was not prepared to rearrange Court of Session business so as to provide a judge, he proceeded to storm up and down the room, saying I had no business to put words into his mouth. I calmed him down, saying there was no point in that kind of thing when the two of us were there by ourselves, we had got on together quite well, and it would be silly to quarrel over a matter of this kind. In any case, as I pointed out, he would not have enough judges for eleven proofs even if the Oban circuit was abandoned, and would be dependent on some of the proofs settling. He agreed that this was the fact—an indication that the problem was a trumped-up affair, for every week Macdonald fixes far more proofs than he has judges for, expecting that sufficient will settle before the date of the proof. So I did not give much encouragement to either of Clyde's compromise suggestions: that we should reduce the Oban charge and take the case in the Sheriff Court, or drop the sitting at Glasgow arranged for the 24th, in which event he would be able to give us a judge for Oban. We parted reasonably amicably, on a suggestion by me that the Lord Justice-Clerk ought to go, and Clyde should use his powers of persuasion on him instead of the Crown Office. I undertook to put his two suggestions to the Crown Agent, indicating however that it was most unlikely that either would be practicable. Bowen confirmed this, and showed me the indictment in the Glasgow case, from which it appeared that it would finish in one day or two and so allow the Glasgow judge to go on to Oban anyhow. I did not think it was our business to point this out—it must be equally obvious to the Justiciary Office, and if we suggested this and for any reason it chanced to fall through we should get the blame. We agreed that I should say nothing more to Clyde, and leave him guessing for the time being—time to cool down, as Bowen put it. Bowen remarked that in the old days this problem would not have arisen; Clyde would have made his way to the Crown Agent's room and had a quiet word with him, and Mr Gordon would have lifted the phone and told the Procurator-Fiscal at Oban to drop the indictment. My comment was that if that method of communication had stopped—as it appears to have done, Clyde not having been seen upstairs since Gordon left—it was all to the good. It seems obvious that Clyde is out to make trouble, but he does not seem to me to have chosen his ground very well—once circuit dates have been fixed by Clyde and the Justiciary Office, all the Crown Office is concerned with is having our cases ready to be tried on those dates. It is not for me to ask for a judge, it is simply for Clyde to supply one, and what he does or does not do about it is officially no concern of mine.

October 7th

An exceptionally pleasant flight north, in company with a Falkirk business man and a charming American girl whom I encouraged to take the seat between us. An appointment to meet Ross; he said he had spoken to the Prime Minister about my position.

October 9th

A pleasant surprise, when Sharyn Seaton arrived in my room—the girl I had met on the aeroplane. This morning, with a blustery wind and showers, was good enough for city sightseeing. I motored Sharyn to the Castle, where we climbed up to the top; then down the Royal Mile and round the park. I asked Harry Wilson to arrange lunch for us. Sharyn came fully up to expectation. Besides being very pretty, she was bright, intelligent and friendly, and took a lively interest in everything. We pointed out the way for her to reach Greyfriars Bobby while we returned to work.

1967

October 10th

Motored to Balmoral for Privy Council. Elwyn Jones, Shackleton and
I walked across to the garden, and out through a gate to the hill. Here
a young policeman emerged from the trees and asked who we were.
Elwyn explained, and asked about him. He was one of a dozen members of the Metropolitan Police who are drafted to Balmoral to be on
duty in the grounds for ten weeks while the Court is in residence.
They volunteer for this, and he seemed to find it agreeable; negotiations were proceeding to see if they could have their wives and children
with them. The Council was held in a small room lined with reference books; and we then went through with the Queen to the
drawing-room. She had had to get her horse back in good order to
the Castle when the animal went lame as she was out riding this
morning. She said that for years she had always carried in her pocket
one of those things for taking stones out of horses' hoofs. This morning she had gone without it, and for the first time in her life had
needed one. She said her sister had had an unfortunate experience
there with her Russian horse, which had crossed four bridges quite
happily and when it came to the fifth bridge had refused to cross it,
though there was absolutely no difference between that bridge and
the other four. She gave a graphic imitation of the expression on the
horse's face when she found it standing there with Margaret, completely failing to respond to Margaret's efforts to persuade it to cross
the bridge. She seemed in a vivacious mood, but was rather damped
down during lunch, with Crossman carrying on a rapid-fire conversation on the one side with Sir Martin Charteris, and Shackleton booming
away on the other in his slow, tedious way. The Queen had perforce
to lapse into silence, looking glumly ahead of her while the noise
went on on either side. Crossman was talking about Jerusalem—a
tawdry city, he thought. The Queen remarked that it was curious
that the cause of these divided cities was always religious. 'Or political', added Crossman—'Berlin'. 'Yes', said the Queen, 'as soon as I
had said it I was saying to myself, "That's silly, for what about
Berlin?"' Talking about the Montreal Exposition, she told us that the
only thing to be seen in the American pavilion was an enormous
picture of Elizabeth Taylor. 'But she's not an American', someone
said. 'No', said the Queen, not to be outdone in knowledge of film
stars, 'she came from Liverpool, didn't she?' She told us they had
had the Shah of Persia at Balmoral, and thought they had behaved
rather cruelly to him. Apparently he is a keen shot, shooting any kind

47

of living creature in Persia, and they took him round showing him all the stags and game birds he could have shot on the Balmoral estate, but as it was Sunday it was not possible to let him shoot anything. In that part of Scotland shooting and fishing were tabu on Sundays. You might perhaps be allowed to fish for trout, but not salmon. She was indignant at the Wee Frees for sending a petition protesting against her having a priest in Buckingham Palace and attending mass. It was explained to them that there had of course been a priest at Buckingham Palace when the King of the Belgians was staying there, but the Queen had never been near any mass. The next thing that arrived was another petition, which she explained—rather oddly, I thought—that she had happened to open herself, and she found it was exactly the same except that the bit about attending mass had been left out. There must be few people so completely frank and outspoken as the Queen, and there is never the slightest doubt that her expressed opinions are absolutely genuine—which is no doubt what makes her such a stimulating host. We were given a nice lunch, and when we got back to the drawing-room Elwyn asked her about the police. She gave a completely incredible explanation that there were only fourteen policemen in Aberdeenshire, and so they had to bring them up from London. I should suppose that the more likely explanation was the one I suggested: that the average Aberdonian policeman would not appreciate a ten-weeks tour of duty wandering round the Balmoral estate, though a Londoner might find it a pleasant change. She said that at Balmoral they were not much troubled with intruders, though last week two French girls had been found peering in at the windows. There had been some mystification as to how they had got there, in view of the police guard on all the gates and approaches, but it turned out that they had waded across the river. The Queen did not stay long with us after lunch; and some argument arose between Shackleton, who wanted to go to Loch Muick, and Crossman, who had been there last year and wanted to accept Charteris' proposal to take us up into the forest. This was settled by what Crossman described as a compromise, giving him his own way. Shackleton, who like the rest of us was in a lounge suit, proceeded to change from head to foot, putting on corduroy trousers, long boots, and a reefer jacket, as if he were going on an expedition to the Antarctic, and all six of us piled into one of the Queen's cars. Charteris took us up a rough track into the pine woods. We walked up a path to the Falls of Garrault, in a lovely wooded glen. Returning to the car, we came down a track that was really just a watercourse, and to Charteris' delight saw a capercailzie, which flew up into a tree. Up on the moor, Charteris let us out to walk down the road, beside a sparkling peaty burn. We started some blackcock, in addition to grouse, and over the hills in the distance could hear the occasional roar of a stag, like a cow's moo. Tea was laid out for us in the visitors' lounge— conversation starting off from Macmillan's memoirs. Crossman said he had liked the second volume much more than the first. 'He says some very nice things in it about you', said Elwyn Jones, and Crossman agreed, adding that that was not why he liked it. Crossman obviously thought highly of Macmillan, with whom he had been in Algiers during the war. As Minister of State Resident in North Africa, he said, Macmillan had been the epitome of a British pro-consul. He and Eisenhower had been in complete charge of everything; and since it took 24 hours to get a telegram through from London Macmillan was able on the plea of urgency to do pretty much what he pleased. He recalled how often Macmillan had been delighted at some thunderous rebuke from Churchill when it was too late to do anything about it. There was a gaiety about Macmillan that Crossman had found irresistable. He admired him too for the long years he had spent on the back benches when, having quarrelled with his party leaders, he seemed to have no prospect of anything different. Crossman observed that he had had the same experience himself. While the lamented Hugh Gaitskell was in charge, Crossman had no hope of ever getting anything. He would no doubt have been offered some junior office, which he would have refused, and that would have been the end of him. But on Hugh's death the whole position changed; he knew he would be in the Cabinet. There were a lot of people in the Government who would never have been there if Gaitskell were alive. 'You're one of them, Elwyn.' Elwyn agreed, but added that he might perhaps have been Solicitor-General. Someone asked if there were other people who got nothing under Wilson but who would have been in office under Gaitskell. Crossman did not think there were many. Wilson had selected his Government with extraordinary care, making sure that everyone was included who could possibly have made trouble from any point of view. Woodrow Wyatt would probably have got a Department from Gaitskell, and Desmond Donnelly would have been in. 'Surely not', said Elwyn in horror. 'Yes', said Crossman, 'Desmond would have got an under-secretaryship'. Elwyn wondered how much Macmillan would have got out of his memoirs. 'I know how much he got', Crossman said. He had sold them outright—all the rights in them—and got £100,000. Eden had got £250,000. The general run of authors, they thought, were poorly rewarded. Crossman said he had never made anything worthwhile from any of his books. The exception was in school textbooks; a man who compiled sets of sentences for translation into French could make thousands. Crossman told us that when he and his family went on a journey by car his wife drove the car and he read aloud to the children. He read to them a great deal: *King Solomon's Mines* and *The White Company*. 'They like being read to', he said, 'and I like reading aloud'. 'I should say you did', remarked Elwyn.

October 11th

I got Gordon Brown to come up to the Crown Office, and asked him about judges' robes. He promised to take this in hand. My decision was news to him—it is extraordinary how widespread the rumour is about Allan Walker. Brown, who had been in Glasgow, said people were approaching him there to say they had heard they were about to lose their Sheriff. R. E. C. Johnson came by appointment, and said the Warrant had now been signed by the Secretary of State. He thanked me for the help I had given them at St Andrews House during my period of office. 'You've been a tower of strength', he said.

October 12th

Walked across from Deans Yard to Downing Street for Cabinet: the Lord Chancellor's divorce proposals. The general discussion was interesting and impressive. Like most things, the Prime Minister's conduct of Cabinet meetings had improved with experience. He was completely in control. He gave everyone a fair chance, and if any backchat developed might allow it to continue for a moment or two before stopping it by simply calling on someone else—possibly someone who had given no indication of wanting to speak. By good luck, Cledwyn Hughes was not there, and Lord Longford had only Gunter to support his negative view. Actually Gunter made a very attractive little defence of the old-fashioned point of view—much more effective than Longford's irrelevancies. Crossman and Michael Stewart were effective on the other side, and Barbara Castle made a surprisingly neat contribution, summing up the Lord Chancellor's case in a few succinct sentences. The Prime Minister was obviously content at the way things were going, and advanced no argument himself until he came to sum up at the end—the decision as he expressed it being that a Bill should be drafted for handing to a private Member, that it should start in the Commons and that there should be a free vote for all Members, including Ministers, on all clauses. I demurred to the extent of suggesting that if we had a separate Scottish Bill we might be allowed, if we thought fit, to start in the Lords, and the Prime Minister accordingly added that Scotland should have the option of coming in or not when the English draft Bill was available for us to see. Crossman, no doubt thinking I was pulling a fast one on them, intervened to say they must have an option too to say whether the inclusion of Scotland would make their Bill too complicated. I accepted this, saying it would be an option either way. 'Option either way', said the Prime Minister, and the meeting ended.

Back through Westminster Abbey. One of the delightful things about the Abbey is that the size of monuments bears no relation to the eminence of those they commemorate. In the midst of ordinary-sized statues of statesmen and Prime Ministers one will find an enormous memorial to some obscure naval captain—one big one erected by the East India Company to the memory of Sir Eyre Coote peculiar in as much as the face of the main figure—presumably Sir Eyre Coote—was almost completely covered by a representation in stone of the visor of a helmet. The memorial to one naval gentleman ended with a somewhat obscure couplet: 'Dying, he led Britannia's thunder roar, and Spain still felt him when he breath'd no more'. A fulsome epitaph to Dr Hugh Boulter concluded that he had been 'consecrated Bishop of Bristol 1718. He was translated to the Archbishopric of Armagh 1723, and from thence to Heaven Sep^{br} the 27th 1742'. Another man with a distinguished naval career was 'Philip de Sausmorez Esqr': 'When the Enemy after a long & obstinate Resistance was again routed, in pursuing two Ships that were making their Escape, he gloriously but unfortunately fell'.

October 13th

Brown has got Strachan's robes—an excellent fit—and assured me that everything would be ready for installation on 24th October. That would provide an amicable solution to my dispute with Clyde about the Oban circuit on the 26th: I should be able to take one of the Court of Session proofs myself, and thus free another judge to go to Oban. I have not yet said anything to Clyde about the appointment, explaining to Johnson that in view of the trouble that arose in the earlier case I had established this precedent when nominating Alex Thomson and Robertson—though of course no objection would have been taken to either. 'When did you actually tell him?' he asked; and when I explained that I had not told him said, 'You mean to say he didn't know until he saw it in the papers?' I assured him that there had been no complaint, and that there could hardly have been in view of Clyde's vulnerable position after his behaviour in relation to the Leechman appointment. Lionel Gordon rang up, and indicated that he had just heard about my decision. Now that he knows the secret, it will be a secret no longer; but it is remarkable how long the news has been kept from Parliament House by reason of the fact that neither Clyde nor Gordon knew about it.

October 16th
A note from the Clerk of Justiciary, intimating that on the instructions of the Lord Justice-General the sitting at Oban had been cancelled.

October 17th
Told Clyde that he could expect to have his new judge announced by the end of the week, but that as I was the nominee the judge would not be available to take the Oban circuit—it is not permissable for me to try cases the indictment in which is in my name. He could not have been nicer—saying he thought it was a good thing, that it was right that these things should keep in a proper pattern and not have some junior person promoted before his time, and that if there was anything he could do for me I had only to ask. I remarked that now I should have to do what I was told, to which he replied, 'Oh, no, not at all. We work on a very light rein here'. I told him that Harry Wilson was likely to succeed me, and said I thought he would be generally acceptable—he seemed to get a good hearing in court. 'We never give anyone a good hearing', said Clyde, taking the words out of my mouth. He agreed when I said that perhaps I could put it that he was treated with less disrespect than some people. He was always prepared to take advice—'perhaps unlike his predecessor'. 'I've said nothing about that', said Clyde. Oban was not referred to; and when Bowen asked me what had been decided I advised him to wait until this afternoon and if he heard nothing to assume that the circuit was off. Another day can be fixed for Oban later on.

1967

October 18th

This morning's *Scotsman* carried a complimentary article headed 'Lord Advocate may forsake politics for the Bench'. Referring to me as the likeliest candidate, it narrated that although there had been opportunities in recent years I had so far always declined to elevate myself. It had been felt that there was always too much important Scottish legislation requiring my attention to permit my departure to the Bench. 'The Liberals have criticised Labour for failing to find seats for their law officers and claimed there could be no question of law reform without a Scottish law officer to pilot it through the Commons. But in Labour circles this criticism has been dismissed as nonsense because of the amount of legislation already handled by Mr Stott. It is unlikely, in view of his fine work in the administration, that the Government would stand in his way if Mr Stott chose to nominate himself. Should he do so, the Government would be faced with the problem of finding a successor for such an eminent law officer, so experienced in handling legislation'. The *Glasgow Herald* had a similar prophecy on its front page—a remarkable coincidence that both papers should publish this forecast on the day after I had told Clyde who the new judge was to be. Amusing to think that I, who have made no concessions to the newspapers, should get such a good press, whereas Ross, with his Information Office and perpetual worry about what the newspapers will say, is constantly, and quite unfairly, slated.

October 19th

10.30 flight to London. I chose a seat beside a nice-looking girl who turned out to be Dianna Page, a Mormon on her way back to Salt Lake City after eighteen months in Scotland as a voluntary missionary. I cross-questioned her on the history and doctrines of Mormonism, and we had a most interesting and entertaining discussion. Dianna had a delightful sense of humour, and took all my comments in good part. They accept the literal truth of all that appears in the Bible, and thus believe that all mankind is descended from the sons of Noah; and they have a delightful explanation for the presence of a seemingly indigenous population in America—Red Indians, Incas and the like—that there were two migrations across the Pacific from Arabia, the first about the time of building the Tower of Babel, the second about 600 BC. It seems that the risen Lord appeared to the faithful in America shortly after the Resurrection, but the record of this was lost until recovered by the prophet Joseph Smith. The Mormons believe in a second coming, which may happen at any time; but Dianna assured me that, contrary to the tenets of Jehovah's Witnesses, there would be salvation not only for Mormons but for all the righteous, justification being by works, not by faith. She gave me her copy of the Book of Mormon, a kind of American supplement to the Bible.

Leaving the office for lunch, I noticed a class of schoolchildren, aged about eleven or twelve, going into the Abbey, more than half of them black. It was a pleasing sight to look at them in their green school blazers, all chatting and laughing with one another quite irrespective of colour; I thought it would be a good thing to show to all the silly racialists who stir up trouble in Notting Hill or Smethwick.

October 24th

Motored with Nancy and the dog to Auchtermuchty. We found Aunt Jeannie at home, and she recalled that when Uncle David was torpedoed and got stuck in a hatchway after going below, with his lifejacket on, to bring the cat—when everyone else but the captain had gone off the ship—the captain was shouting impatiently for David to come up because he himself could not swim and was expecting David to help him in the water.

October 28th

Saw in the *Daily Express* a paragraph recording that 'bangs and thuds' had been heard during the installation of the former Lord Advocate, caused apparently by workmen 'dismantling wooden cabinets beneath the crowded courtroom'. James Leechman had remarked on this after the ceremony, saying he had thought it must be some of my supporters trying to get in.

October 31st

A defended divorce, *Williams v. Williams*. The defender is a professional criminal, recently released from Dartmoor after serving a sentence of seven years: a hefty, good-looking man, with a pleasant smile and proud of his reputation as a housebreaker. It had all started, he said, when he began going down Garscube Road and met in with criminals there. Up to 1953 he had not got the hang of it, but in 1954 he was in with the team, and money started to come in. He got put away for a safeblowing in 1955, when there was only £109 in the safe, and the haul included some bags of farthings. Flo—his wife—was supposed to dump the farthings, but she didn't dump them, and he got 18 months. His wife did not think much of his career as a criminal. He would do something, she said, and the next she knew was that the police were on to him; he always got caught. On one occasion he sheltered a well-known housebreaker, who was caught hiding under floorboards in the Williams house. In December 1960, when released after a 21-months sentence, he did not come home direct, as he admitted in evidence that he ought to have done, but—as he put it—unfortunately bumped into two of his old pals, and of course the whisky bottle came out. When he got home, his wife was annoyed, and went off with the children to her parents. Early in 1961 he was sent back to prison, on what he claims was a frame-up—the only one in his career. There was a reconciliation in August 1962, but at the end of the year he went off to Blackpool and took part in the robbery which got him the 7-years sentence. He has produced a bundle of letters from his wife showing that up to January 1964 she was writing at least once a week in affectionate terms—a delightful series of letters such as few prisoners could have had the good fortune to receive, displaying in a remarkable way her lively, generous personality and her apparent affection for her husband:

'I have stopped counting birthdays a long time ago, so I'll be quite young when you come home, anyway you're only as old as you feel and I feel just 21 years. I know I don't look it but there you are I'm still a kid at heart.'

She tells him all about her doings and the children's and what is happening to their friends and acquaintances.

'Wait till I tell you about Sandra, she came in from school on Monday and she asked me could she learn the Violin so that she could get into the school Band. I said by all means hen you do so, well on Tues, she comes in with the Violin and I'm not kidding you, she makes some awful noise with it, she goes into the wee room to practise and the door is closed. I am in the livingroom, door closed, T.V. on, and I still hear her trying to knock a tune out of it, but I will let her carry on and encourage her all I can so that she will be able to play it, so we may have a fiddler by the time you come home, anyway she is a tryer and is determined to play the instrument. The Clyde tunnel is a wonderful piece of workmanship, and brightly lit and done with pale green tiles. I was through it when it opened, and now the buses have started to go through it now, the No.19 goes from Drumchapel to Govan Cross.'

In the autumn of 1963 she took up with another man, John Ferguson, who also has since served a prison sentence, and Ferguson and she have been living as man and wife since December of that year. 'John Ferguson', she said in her evidence, 'is a different kind of person. He showed me love, affection, kindness, consideration, which Sonny never showed me. He has been good to me and kind. He made me a different person'. The defender maintains, no doubt rightly, that this is the real reason for her wanting a divorce, and that until she met Ferguson she had no thought in her mind except to look forward to living happily with her husband when he came out of Dartmoor. Her explanation that her letters were written out of pity was barely credible, though it is odd that even after she fell in love with Ferguson she was still writing her husband in affectionate terms until the letters suddenly stopped in January 1964. He continued to write but got no answer. Two of his later letters have been produced: remarkable too, in a different style—verbose, bombastic, and full of possessive but seemingly genuine affection.

'Don't be angry, my dearest. Its hardly worth while in this life, because it is so short in any case, besides us mortals are in enough anguish without wishing more on each other.'

On the pursuer's own evidence I thought her case was hopeless. She seemed a nice person, as frank and open as her letters suggested, and it seemed absurd that she should be tied to a gaol-bird when she was in love with another man; but I did not see how it was going to be possible to do anything for her. There was no medical evidence, and her letters did not suggest that she was afraid of him or worried about his conduct—or indeed anything but delighted at the thought of having him back with her.

November 3rd
Nine undefended divorces. The cruelty founded on was of the most trivial character: the husband had shouted at his wife, or had kept changing his job. Not thinking it right to keep the parties together

when they were agreed on wanting a divorce, I granted decree in all the cases without comment; but it seemed to me that the divorce law had become a complete farce since the days when I was at the junior bar.

November 6th

Spent the morning in drafting my judgment in *Williams v. Williams.* In the light of the averments which seemed to pass muster in cruelty divorces, I had not much difficulty in finding grounds on which to grant the pursuer her divorce.

November 10th

A petition to presume the death of Miss Margaret Stanley. She emigrated after the war, and the last heard of her was a Christmas card in 1950 with an Australian postmark. Actually I did not think there was any reason to suppose that Margaret Stanley was dead—she is still comparatively young, and just does not seem to be the kind of person who keeps in touch with anyone; nor indeed does she have anyone much to keep in touch with. But apparently where all possible enquiry has been made it is thought to be reasonable to find that the person is presumed to have died; and there is provision in the Act whereby the 'deceased' can turn up at any time within thirteen years of the decree and claim what is due to her.

November 11th

In one of my divorces the adultery alleged was with the defender's former husband, who had divorced her in 1963 shortly before she married the pursuer. Within a year she was back with her former husband, and when an enquiry agent visited the house she said, 'We realise we were meant for each other'.

November 18th

Undefended divorces. In one of the proofs, when I had just given decree on the evidence of an enquiry agent that the defender was living in England with another woman—whose photograph was produced—a woman stood up in the court who appeared to be the woman in the photograph and asked if she might say something. 'No', I said, 'I'm afraid not', adding that she ought to have put in a Minute. She left the court saying something to the effect that it was not she, or that she had not been there. I was somewhat disconcerted, but as no one officially connected with the case made any move I did not think it was my business to investigate the matter—particularly as decree of divorce had been pronounced.

November 21st

Cross actions of divorce on the ground of cruelty—out in the Roll for today and the next two days. It was apparent that each party wanted a divorce but was not prepared to be divorced by the other. No question of custody arose, and it seemed ludicrous that three days should be occupied in deciding which was to blame. Both were on legal aid. Coutts appeared for the husband, O'Brien for the wife; and eventually both agreed to a short adjournment so that they could have a talk with their respective clients. They were not very hopeful, saying that they had had discussions already. I pointed out that the averments of cruelty were thin, and it would be unfortunate for everyone if the cases proceeded as defended actions and led to no useful result. It had occurred to me when I first saw the papers that it might be a salutary lesson to parties who insisted on cross actions if the Court made a practice of refusing divorce to both—though of course I did not put it in quite that way to Coutts and O'Brien. I sat reading in the Cedar Room for twenty minutes until they reached agreement: that the wife's action would proceed undefended. I was pleased with my morning's work, which must have saved the tax-payer £500 at the very least. Incidentally I had given myself a holiday for the rest of the day.

November 23rd

A divorce action: the pursuer complains that her husband came home late at night with lipstick on his shirt. The defender admits that he came home late, but says he had been playing cards with his wife's uncle.

November 28th

A divorce proof, *Carnegie v. Carnegie*. Gow moved for expenses against the co-defender, but had forgotten to prove that the co-defender knew that Mrs Carnegie was a married woman. As the co-defender, with whom Mrs Carnegie is living, has been maintaining her three boys and herself, as well as another baby, and seems likely to have to continue to do so, I was glad of the excuse not to award any expenses against him.

November 30th

My Employers' Liability Bill has found a taker among Members successful in the ballot: Mr Cronin, the Labour MP for Loughborough. I had thought it would have appealed more to some Trade Union member, but Mr Cronin is a surgeon.

December 1st

Divorces, one insanity and six cruelty. The defender in the insanity case, who had been married in a Baptist church, had in a fit of depression cut off both his hands with a circular saw. The pursuer in one of the cases said that her husband had kicked her and knocked her about because the bus was late coming back from the bingo. He had accused her of 'standing blathering on the way home'. In another case I had occasion to speak severely to a girl who came to give evidence in support of her mother, and who came into the witness-box chewing gum. My macer is a stickler for etiquette, and keeps telling people in the witness-box to stand up when they innocently take a seat—whereupon I always invite them to sit down if they prefer—and he was apologetic for not having noticed the girl's aberration. It was the first time that people in my court had heard me speaking sternly to anyone; and there was an uneasy hush in court while the girl was giving her evidence. Before she left the box I asked her one or two friendly questions, so that we parted on good terms.

December 12th

Wheatley recalled a trial in which Sherry, a well-known housebreaker, had given evidence on behalf of his friend Dandy Mackay, when the latter was up on a safe-blowing charge. Sherry had already been dealt with in respect of the safe-blowing, so that he was free to say, as he did, that he had done the job on his own, without any accomplice. The safe in question had been removed from Turnhouse golf club; and Jack Hunter, cross-examining as Advocate Depute, had taken Sherry through all the procedure he was supposed to have carried out: that he had lowered the safe out of a window, loaded it on to a trolley, wheeled the trolley to a van and driven the van to Craigmillar, where he had taken the safe up two flights of stairs to the house where it was blown open. Having got Sherry to agree that he had done all this entirely by himself, he invited him to step down from the witness-box and show how he had lifted the safe. Sherry after much puffing and blowing had to admit that he was unable to move it, then turning to Hunter said innocently, 'It's being in Saughton must have made me weak'. Wheatley recalled also an occasion when the police had been tipped off that Mannion and some of his accomplices had got away with a safe and were working on it in a house at Craigmillar. They piled into a police car, and drove hell-for-leather to Craigmillar where they climbed up to a house on the second floor and burst in, only to find a different gang altogether working on a safe. They hastily withdraw, explaining that they must have come to the wrong floor.

December 15th

A divorce case where the defender was a ship's captain. The pursuer, a part-time science teacher, was a gentle, innocent young woman whose evidence was refreshingly naive and convincing: a masterpiece of understatement. Asked whether the marriage had been happy, she said that it had been happy at first, but later on her husband had not been very kind to her. She hastened to assure us that he had not been violent or assaulted her physically, but he had been rather unkind. She had gone with him in his ship to Basra, where he had sent her off at night in a small boat 'with a person who was not very sober'. Later he could not agree with the cab-driver about the charge for a taxi to take her five miles back to the ship, and she was left walking about in Basra at one o'clock in the morning. She was led by her counsel to tell us, very diffidently, about occasions when he came home at three in the morning and insisted on arguing with her, saying she need not think she was going to get to sleep yet. She agreed reluctantly that before this he had stripped off her night clothes, so that she was rather cold.

1968

A judge, it seemed, was not required nor invited to take part in public or social activities, and I spent a peaceful, uneventful year. I continued to enjoy my work. I had no difficulty in making up my mind, and for the most part, I thought, managed to achieve a substantial measure of justice in the cases coming before me. I was of course very much at home with the criminal work, and continued also to enjoy charging civil juries. I put our relevancy procedure to more use than was commonly done, disposing of seven actions on a debate on the pleadings without any enquiry. There was unquestionably a great deal of rubbish, particularly in undefended divorces—I dealt with no less than 484. With British politics in the doldrums, political interest shifted to the United States. The Vietcong launched a major offensive against all the cities in Vietnam under American control, and all the delusions about victory and pacification were blown skyhigh. The resulting disillusionment might have had no very concrete result but for the dogged persistence of Senator Fulbright, the leading critic of the Vietnam adventure, and the emergence of a new figure on the American presidential scene—Senator Eugene McCarthy. Senator McCarthy was something that American or even British politics had not seen for a long time. He had no use for sham or shibboleths; he made no concessions to party bosses or even to his own supporters. He said what he thought, and spoke as he manifestly was: wise, civilised, magnanimous, kind. In the few months before he was overwhelmed by the Democratic Party juggernaut he brought to the surface all the latent opposition to the war, particularly among younger people, and brought about the conditions under which a start could be made, however shakily and insecurely, on negotiation for peace. His defeat at the Convention by the poor, pedestrian Hubert Humphrey was hardly a surprise. It seemed poetic justice when the Democrats saw their candidate lose to Richard Nixon—a non-choice if ever there was one.

January 9th

Bruce appeared for a Minuter who wanted a reduction in the weekly payments that Milligan had ordered him to make to his wife on divorce: a motion to allow the Minute and Answers to be adjusted. The motion was not opposed, but I demurred to it, observing that this was meant to be summary procedure and I saw no reason why time and money should be wasted on adjustment. I asked if there was any Rule of Court which laid down the procedure, and was told not; but, said Bruce, it was common practice to allow a Minute and Answers to be adjusted. Sibbald confirmed this; but I refused the motion, thinking that if this was common practice the sooner it was changed the better. A proof can proceed perfectly well on Minute and Answers unadjusted. In a desertion case, in which the wife had given evidence in the usual form—that her husband had left her and she had been willing to have him back—I asked the pursuer, as I sometimes do, what had been the cause of the trouble. Why had he left her? She replied that it was because he disliked her.

January 16th

A ministerial broadcast by Roy Jenkins, on cuts announced today as answer to the economic crisis. Jenkins did not convince me that there was any economic crisis, or if there were that what the Government proposes to do could possibly provide a remedy.

January 21st

Braid Church. I was impressed by a girl in the choir who I thought was the kind of girl I did not like the look of—on account not so much of her very short skirt as of her built-up fuzzy hair and long dangling ear-rings. But when she sang her whole appearance was transformed; she seemed to be giving herself with such wholehearted sincerity to the music of the anthem.

January 30th

Stephen v. Stephen. In 1951 the pursuer bought a small farm out of the proceeds of a legacy. She gave her husband a half share, in the hope that he would settle in and get rid of his drinking habits. She said however that he regularly went away drinking, leaving her with all the farm work to do, and coming home late at night with drunken companions who, according to a son-in-law, 'shouted Mrs Stephen up if she was bedded'. The married daughter, a convincing, unpartisan witness who insisted that the defender had been a good father to her, gave a graphic account of one occasion when she and her husband had to barricade their room door against the defender and a gentleman named Smith. They 'chappit and chappit', then came round to the window where she heard Smith say, 'Will you gat a barra and row this heap of muck to the midden?'—a reference to her father. He regularly came rolling home from the bus, on one side of the road one minute and the other side the next, often landing in the ditch. In matter-of-fact language she told of his unwillingness to be helped, and how one night they said 'Oh, leave him', and they just left him. The defender said he had never had to be carried home—'nae as far as I ken'. I found the pursuer entitled to divorce—the first time I had attempted an extempore judgment in a proof.

February 1st
Barton v. William Low & Co.: the pursuer an Aberdeen housewife who bought a pound of corned beef in the defenders' store at the price of tenpence halfpenny. She and her daughter ate it and contracted typhoid fever. She avers that the number of people who contract typhoid fever in the United Kingdom in a year seldom exceeds 200; between May and July 1964, 400 people in Aberdeen contracted it, the great majority of whom had eaten corned beef purchased in the defenders' shop or food which had been in contact with it. The pursuer ascribes the start of her illness to the defenders' corned beef and is suing them under the Sale of Goods Act. The beef had been corned at Rosario in Argentina, where water from the River Parana was used for washing cans, and the suggestion is that a bacillus from sewage in the river may have got into the can. The question today was whether averments to be sent to proof should include a report of the Milne Committee set up to enquire into the cause and manner of dealing with the epidemic. R. S. Johnston for the defenders argued that it was impracticable to incorporate into the Record 74 pages of argument and discussion on a variety of matters ranging from the slaughtering of cattle in the Argentine to food hygiene education and the public relations activities of the Aberdeen Medical Officer of Health. For the pursuer, Robert Taylor appreciated that he could not support this, and what he was seeking to incorporate was now restricted to specified paragraphs. These still numbered 41, plus an appendix, and I wasted a good deal of time teasing him about some of the 'averments': opinions of the Medical Officer of Health

later found to be erroneous, and such observations as that 'the later victims of the outbreak—as we shall explain in Chapter XXX—probably arose from cross-contamination of meats on the counter'. This one gave scope for a good deal of badinage—Chapter XXX was not one of the parts which Taylor sought to incorporate, and anyhow did not contain anything about cross-contamination.

Looked in this afternoon on Harry Wilson, and found Clyde with him—they seemed to be on very good terms. I also am on unusually good terms with Clyde at the moment, and we are allied against most of the other judges in resisting a proposal from the Law Society that the Court should sit on Mondays instead of Saturdays. I gave Clyde some information I had from Layden about extra expense and inconvenience for divorce witnesses; and he promised to let me see his reply to the Law Society before he sends it.

February 3rd
Nicholas and Gillian Croan sledging in the road. Nicholas remarked that God had put frost under the snow, which he found very convenient. He is a solemn, serious little boy. A few months ago when I gave him a lift home on his way from school he had been worried, having been told not to accept lifts from people he did not know. They pointed out to him that he knew the Lord Advocate quite well, to which he replied, 'But it might have been somebody else who disguised himself as the Lord Advocate'.

February 4th
Drafting an opinion in the typhoid case. I am refusing to remit to probation the pursuer's averments about the report.

February 5th
In Harry Wilson's room last week I had been surprised to hear talk about a meeting he had been attending of the Parliamentary Labour Party—what I had always supposed to be simply a meeting of the Labour MPs. Today a curious sequel: a letter from the secretary of the Parliamentary Labour Party, to the effect that he had been asked by the Party's Liaison Committee to write me following reports they had received of my attendance at a Party meeting on Wednesday. The Committee had taken the view that not being Members of the House the Solicitor-General and I should not be present at Party meetings. They understood that the practice of attending meetings of

the Scottish Labour Group had gone on for some time, and saw no objection to that. I replied: 'Never having attended a meeting of the Parliamentary Labour Party, I am at a loss to know why your Committee should have asked you to write me in the terms of your letter. You may say to your Committee that their understanding that it was my practice to attend meetings of the Scottish Labour Group is equally devoid of any foundation in fact'.

February 18th

A cruelty action in which the pursuer at the age of twenty had married a man of fifty-one who could not read or write and who was deaf and unable to speak properly. When her child Carol Ann was born the following year, she began to suffer from glandular trouble, which caused her to put on weight—she now weighs over fifteen stone. The marriage was a disaster from the start. She never forgave her husband because of a beating he gave Carol when she was five months old, and he never forgave her because a girl she had had living with her in the house went off with £76 of his savings that he kept hidden in the back lobby. He swore at her and assaulted her, on one occasion with the fireguard, and on another with a poker. She seemed a frank enough witness, and volunteered the information that one night when he was in a temper and tried to get her by the throat—she was then weighing 14 stone—she got him down and sat on top of him. I understood her to say that no one else was present on the occasions of the fireguard and poker incidents, and it was odd to have evidence from two witnesses who claim to have come in as the incident began and gave diametrically opposite accounts of what happened. Each insisted that the other was not there. The pursuer had a quaint way of putting things: 'Every time we had a row my hair started to fall out'.

February 21st

The only witness today was the defender, and his evidence did not take long since it was almost impossible for anyone to understand what he was saying. Sometimes he just stood and looked blankly at the questioner, at other times he wandered off into a rambling monologue. It was possible to conclude that he admitted giving his wife a punch on the nose but maintained that it was only a little one. It was a curious feature of his way of speaking that he always referred to his wife as 'he' and 'him'. He gave an extraordinary imitation of her laughing at him, which sounded most sinister.

February 22nd
Seven undefended divorces. In one of them the pursuer said that her husband started fighting with his brother just after the wedding and had spent the first night of the marriage in prison. Shortly afterwards she had to go along to a bookmaker's office where he had tried to hang himself in a back room, none of his horses having come in. The pursuer described an incident when he said his dinner was cold and hit her with the dinner. 'I just lifted the poker up and hit him'. 'What did he say to that?' I asked, and she replied with a smile, 'He had to go to hospital'. She seemed rather a pleasant woman.

March 11th
'World in Action' on television tonight was following Richard Nixon's campaign as a presidential candidate. I have never shared the general revulsion from Nixon; he is a pragmatist and a practical man, far less dangerous as president than any right-wing ideologist and perhaps than some left-wing ones.

March 12th
Television extracts from the Senate Foreign Affairs Committee's hearing on Vietnam, with Mr Dean Rusk making a wholly ineffective attempt to stand up to the questioning. I was impressed by a young senator from Idaho, Senator Church; and Senator Fulbright is always magnificent; his suave courtesy and slow Southern drawl, combined with keen intelligence and mastery of dry sarcasm, make him a formidable inquisitor, a role which he combined with that of chairman of the Committee with a delightful disregard for any idea that a chairman should be impartial.

March 13th
Television tonight produced Senator Eugene McCarthy. It is a pity that this really great man—intelligent, courageous and eminently sensible—should be such a bad speaker.

March 18th
BBC pre-Budget profile of Roy Jenkins. From what I had seen of him, I had hoped that he might bring some new thinking to the Exchequer, but he seems to be as much thirled as the rest of them to

the Treasury nonsense about adverse trade balances and stimulating exports by taking away people's money by taxation so that they will not be able to buy too much. In this latest 'crisis' of a rush on the world's gold supplies he had nothing to offer, and for the first time in my life I felt I should like to be someone like a Chancellor of the Exchequer so as to be able to put forward a sensible solution. We have the old guff about the necessity for stern measures in tomorrow's Budget, with a massive increase in indirect taxation and a consequent increase in the price of everything and demand for wages to match—intensifying the inflation it is supposed to remedy.

March 19th

A defended action in which the pursuer accuses his wife of cohabiting with a man named Drury. When Drury was on night work, the defender stayed in his house with the children. There could, she said, be no harm in her staying overnight there because she took the dog with her. The relevance of this was not clear; but the pursuer on being asked whether his wife had taken the dog replied tersely, 'No dog'. He never accused the defender of any improper association with Drury—his complaints against her were quite different: thriftlessness, excessive drinking, never giving him a proper meal. He had lost interest in her, and in early 1965 wrote a message for her on a mirror, telling her in rather obscure language to clear out. He was not very frank about this. At first he denied that anything had been written on the mirror. Then he agreed that maybe he had written on the mirror, but it was not a message. Then, if he had written a message, it had not necessarily been meant for his wife; and finally if he had written a message for his wife on the mirror it had nothing to do with the case. The defender seemed intelligent, and gave her evidence convincingly.

March 20th

The proof was concluded—Drury the only witness. He seemed a sensible man, and except for harking back unnecessarily to the dog gave a good account of himself. Brand hardly attempted to cross-examine, having apparently lost any faith he may have had in the case. I gave judgment, assoilzieing the defender.

March 22nd

A slight contretemps in one of today's cases when a photograph was put to the pursuer for identification purposes and on being asked whether that was a photograph of his wife he firmly replied 'No'. His counsel had another attempt with the photograph. 'Look at it carefully. She may have a different hair style, or it may have been taken at some earlier date. Are you sure it's not your wife?' The pursuer considered it, and replied, 'It looks like her leg'.

March 23rd

Ten undefended divorces—one where the pursuer was a delightful old fellow from a tenement in Upper Grey Street whose wife had deserted him thirty-four years ago. While he was giving evidence, I remarked that that had happened a long time ago. Why had he decided to apply for a divorce now? He said he felt he should get everything straightened out before he died; and his counsel brought out in evidence that he had been living for ten years with a woman who had been a very good wife to him and he wanted to put everything right before it was too late. Sibbald mentioned to me afterwards that the doctors had given the pursuer notice that he had only a month or two to live; but he seemed perfectly cheerful, and content that he was doing the right thing.

March 30th

Granted decree in a proof continued from last week to enable the pursuer to identify his wife's signature in the Register of Births. He said he had to pay two shillings to do it, but I told him it was cheap at the price since it got him his divorce. A nullity case was rather unusual: the pursuer had married an American seaman from the Polaris base, who later went home to the United States without her. Assuming without much reason that he had divorced her there, she married another American seaman from the Polaris base. He also went off to the United States without her. Shortly afterwards her first husband came back to this country. The two settled down together; and today she was seeking to annul the second marriage on the ground that it was bigamous. Her husband is intending to take her home with him this time to the United States, along with their child, a child of the second marriage, and another child the pursuer had before marrying either of the Americans. He is arranging to adopt the two latter children.

April 1st

A surprise development in America: President Johnson has suddenly announced not only a stop to the bombing of Hanoi but a decision not to stand for reelection. So Senator McCarthy's campaign has had an undreamed-off success, but whether it will lead to peace or to Johnson's replacement by some more irresponsible political figure on the right is impossible to say.

April 14th
To church. Mr Kelly preached on Mark 16:6; and I occupied myself as usual in reading Leviticus. Among all the quaint regulations and prohibitions—forbidding, for instance, any blind or lame man to approach the altar, 'or he that hath a flat nose, or any thing superfluous'— it is interesting to come on some humane provisions very much applicable to present-day problems:

'If a stranger sojourn with thee in your land, ye shall not vex him. But the stranger that dwelleth with you shall be unto you as one born among you, and thou shalt love him as thyself; for ye were strangers in the land of Egypt: I am the Lord your God.'

April 21st
To church, where Rev. R. A. K. Martin, of Beath, preached on II Thessalonians 1:3. His illustrations and way of expressing himself were odd—he told us that when we were following Christ we must not stand still, for that would be going backwards. But he seemed a well-meaning, genuine man.

May 6th
'World in Action' tonight had a film taken by a cameraman accompanying an American platoon in the fighting line in Vietnam. Several soldiers were briefly interviewed, but their insipid, mass-produced opinions were far from edifying. Most of them seemed to be just cannon fodder for the Pentagon.

May 13th
'Panorama' had a bunch of Labour MPs discussing the party debacle. We switched off the sound, and were able to watch Mr Shinwell, Mr Woodrow Wyatt and the rest of them mouthing away with that egregious ass Robin Day, to the accompaniment of a Brandenburg Concerto on the wireless.

May 14th

To the city education offices to get a form for a University grant for Elizabeth. A handsome young negress who was in charge of the reception counter told me it was too late; applications had to be in by the end of last month, and she had no form left. I did not take this obstacle too seriously, and on going in to the next counter succeeded in getting a form there.

May 28th

I had to move to the Second Division court for my proof, *Caird (Dundee) v. North of Scotland Hydro Electric Board*, an action for repayment of £17,773 which the pursuers say they were overcharged for electricity for their jute-spinning mill between 1956 and 1964. In view of the large number of productions, it was thought convenient to have the proof in a larger court than mine. R. S. Johnston, when I rose at four, had not completed his examination-in-chief of the first witness, a consulting engineer. He left no pebble unturned. Indeed it could be said that he took each one up and considered it from every angle two or three times. It looks as if the case will take a long time.

May 29th

Several divorce cases in the Motion Roll, including one with rather a delightful plea in law: 'The pursuer's averment that the defender treated the pursuer like a dog being irrelevant and lacking in specification should be excluded from probation'. The proof in the Dundee case continued, with still the same witness throughout the day. Though slow, it is quite interesting.

May 30th

The proof continued throughout the morning. Emslie got some useful admissions from the witness with the help of an enormous graph that the defenders had produced. It seemed to me that there was not much left of the pursuers' case when Emslie had finished with their expert witness; and when we resumed in the afternoon Emslie announced that the parties had agreed on a settlement. He said to me afterwards that they had got an offer of settlement that it was impossible from a commercial point of view to refuse. He said there were some weaknesses in their graph, apart from anything that the witness had got hold of, adding that he thought I had come pretty near it in some questions I had asked.

June 6th

Neil v. Neil, the case of a young couple who took in a girl named Wedlock as a lodger. The pursuer found that her husband stopped taking her out and took Miss Wedlock out instead. She gave Miss Wedlock notice to leave, but, some time after she had left, the pursuer came home one day and found her husband in the house and Miss Wedlock hiding in an upstairs room. She then left him, and put an enquiry agent on to the job. The enquiry agent visited the house where the defender lived, and the defender took him into the livingroom, where a girl was sleeping on a couch by the fire. The reason for the visit having been explained, the defender denied having associated with any woman. This conversation took place without any reference to the fact that a girl was sleeping on the couch. The enquiry agent explained in evidence that he and the defender just ignored her. The girl however woke up and admitted that she was Miss Wedlock. The Prime Minister's tribute on television to Senator Robert Kennedy, who died today from gunshot wounds received at the hand of an assassin. The Prime Minister always does these things well. Then we had Harold Macmillan—tears trickling down his cheeks as he wallowed in sentimental recollections of 'Bobby'. It seemed a bit overdone, even for this wonderful old ham actor, but no doubt it was genuine enough.

June 8th

Ten undefended divorces. In one, evidence was given by an old Glasgow woman who had gone with her son to the tenement where the wife was living with another man, and had found her and the man sitting on a couch. Asked by counsel, 'Was there a bed in the room?' she replied indignantly, 'There was nothing in the room—just the couch and a carry-out'.

June 14th

To the Lyceum: *Who's Afraid of Virginia Woolf?* A magnificent performance by a cast of four: Stephen Murray, Antonia Pemberton, Elizabeth Hughes and Del Henney. But two acts of wrangling and abuse, however brilliant, found us at 10.30 limp and exhausted, with another act still to come. I was not averse to Nancy's suggestion that we should come away. A remarkable play, but just too much of a good thing.

June 17th

To the Lyceum to see the end of *Who's Afraid of Virginia Woolf?* Got there after ten, and slipped into vacant seats near the back of the Dress Circle. There was still about twenty minutes of the second act to go. Coming to it fresh, and seeing it from a different angle, we found this very enjoyable. The third act, which we had not seen before, turned out to be rather phoney. However, it was satisfactory to have seen the whole play, and we had no doubt that the proper way to do it was by instalments.

June 18th

Finished reading *Memoirs, 1925–1950*, by George Kennan. At first I found the book dull, but when he gets launched into his diplomatic career it becomes fascinating and indeed terrifying. In plain factual narrative, without any indication of illwill, he exposes the ignorance and imbecility of those in the seats of military and political power in the United States, and their inability to comprehend what was happening in any part of the world.

July 12th

There has been a good deal of publicity for an arrangement which Frankie Vaughan the singer has been trying to make with young Glasgow gangsters to receive their weapons from them at a public confrontation at some open space at Easterhouse. It was pointed out that the only person who could give an amnesty to people with illegal weapons was the Lord Advocate; and I was amused last night to get a phone call from a man who said he was Ron Flockhart of the *Daily Mail* and wanted to know whether I had come to any decision about this. I said it was entirely a matter for Mr Wilson, and he would have to get in touch with him. 'Do I have to go through him?' he asked; and I assured him he had. I said he could get Mr Wilson at the Crown Office—a safe observation, as it was after office hours. He rang again half an hour later to say he had been unable to find Mr Wilson, and would I not tell him what my decision was to be? I assured him that only Mr Wilson could make a decision, and when he asked who Mr Wilson was told him he was the Lord Advocate. 'The trouble with you', I added, 'is that you're a little out of date'.

Today I had twelve undefended divorces. The pursuer in one of them had an averment that her husband had thrown a kitten at her; but although she was a talkative woman, anxious to go into everything at length, her counsel did not examine her on that averment.

July 19th
Among the divorces in my Motion Roll was one in which it was averred that the defender while under the influence of drink had climbed an electric pylon and would not come down until the pursuer told him she loved him. One stormy night he told the pursuer he was going to take a boat out on the loch, and when he came back showed her a note he had left for her to the effect that if he did not return he would be drowned.

August 6th
Dug one or two shaws of potatoes. We have not planted any this year—there are just a few potatoes that have re-seeded themselves from previous years. Ironically enough, they are very good: a big crop on each of the shaws, not a blemish on any of the potatoes.

August 8th
The Republican Convention on television: a clear win for Nixon, and a press conference at which he appeared—relaxed, and to all appearances reasonable. If I were an American, and if as seems to be thought inevitable Hubert Humphrey is to be the Democratic candidate, I should be inclined to vote Republican.

August 9th
Extracts from Nixon's acceptance speech were not very edifying, and his choice of running mate even less so: Governor Agnew of Maryland, who looked like a seedy version of Lyndon Johnson.

August 11th
To church. Rev. E. B. McCallum preached on Luke 18:8. He looked rather like an Egyptian, but said he came from 'a village on the west coast, called Campbeltown'.

August 13th
Finished reading *The Heir of Redclyffe*, by Charlotte M. Yonge, a most extraordinary book. On the face of it, it is the corniest stuff imaginable—old-fashioned sentiment and piety, and situations that could have been cleared up in a moment, given a little commonsense. But so far as I was concerned it had a compulsive effect. I found

myself reading on with mounting anxiety, turning over the pages to see what was going to happen, in the despairing hope that all might yet be well. While reading, I was utterly wrapped up in the fortunes of little Amy and her beloved Sir George, writhing all the while at the obstacles put in their way by their egregious cousin. I do not know what the secret is: perhaps just that it is a good book, that the people in it are good people, and that their emotions are genuine emotions so as to arouse a similar response in the reader. There is really no villain in the book. Everyone has his point of view which the author understands and makes allowance for; and her power of conviction never falters. She seems to me to have been a great writer.

August 14th

To the University library, where I took out a volume of Pepys' *Diary*. The set that I had been reading in Morningside public library has disappeared from the shelves—I suppose it must have been removed to make way for more popular books. Certainly no one but me had had the diary volumes out for a long time, to judge by the date stamps.

August 15th

Finished reading *The Constant Nymph*, by Margaret Kennedy. At first I thought I had read it too often and knew it too well, but before long I found it as fascinating as ever, and was regretful that seven or eight pages were missing towards the end of my old sixpenny edition—even though I had a good knowledge of what was in them.

August 18th

Overstrand. We went to the parish church for the 11 o'clock service. The rector, Rev. R. B. Budgitt, preached on Luke 19:42: an elderly, worried-looking man who preached a naive sermon. Instead of the Prayer Book service, they used a revised version from a little booklet which has been apparently authorised as an experiment for three years. Except for one prose psalm, there was no chanting, but apart from that it seemed that the new service was just as dull as the old, without any of its dignity. It seemed strange even to the local congregation, and the ritual was spoiled by the Rector's interrupting himself to say 'Stand up' or 'Sit down'. At least, as Richard said afterwards, it was amusing. In the afternoon Richard and I went in to bathe. I had brought the surfboards from home, and the surf today was not at all bad. I was quite bruised and battered by the force of the waves. On one occasion my bathing trunks were swept right off me. I found it exhilarating; and with the constant struggle to keep one's footing one did not notice the coldness of the water.

August 19th
To Cromer for the holiday show at the Pier Pavilion. It boasted two quite presentable comedians. Alan Wells, a cheerful extrovert, was surpassed by Billy Riley. This gentleman, by no means in his first youth, showed himself a master of the throwaway, gloomy type of humour. I thought he was extremely funny, though it appeared that my view was not shared by many in the audience: an explanation no doubt of why Mr Riley was appearing on Cromer pier and not in some televised show in London.

August 22nd
To Clacton, to meet Elizabeth at Butlins. It was surrounded by a high wire fence, like a prison camp, and it appeared that no one could get out or in without producing the appropriate pass. Inside, it was much the same: long concrete avenues between drab buildings. I had thought it would all be terribly jolly, but it was not even that—the inmates were mostly mooning about in a gloomy kind of way as if they had nothing better to do. There was a gate leading out to the beach, but it did not seem that the campers were free to get out and in even there. Elizabeth, as a member of the staff, was able to nego-tiate with the gate-keeper to let us out, where we found a nice stretch of beach. On coming in again, Elizabeth went to change into her working uniform so that I could take her photograph outside her coffee-bar. Her working shift this week is from 4.15 pm to 1 am. She seemed to be contented, and getting on all right.

August 23rd
Nancy was dismayed on opening my parcel of herring to find that they had not been cleaned. I undertook the job, cutting the heads off and gutting the herring. They were beautifully fresh, and one of them had two big roes in it—something we should not have got in Scotland.

August 26th
We motored to Wroxham to have a look at the Broads. Stopped in

North Walsham and went to look at the church: a spacious, handsome building which must at one time have been bigger, as there is a ruined bit attached to one end. Wroxham is a trippery place: cafes and motor coaches and postcard shops. My idea was that we might join one of the advertised boat trips. Richard however was all for hiring a motor boat, and with some misgivings I contracted to hire a small motor launch for three hours. This proved an excellent idea, much superior to the crowded, stuffy cabin cruisers which carried on the public excursions. I took the wheel and brought the boat through the crowded waterway opposite the Wroxham moorings. The Bure was a surprisingly wide waterway, between banks of tangled trees and shrubs which cut off all view of the country behind them. The boat went slowly, and its controls were simplicity itself. Richard took over after we got into the open river, and I sat in the open at the stern enjoying the sail. Twice we attempted a landing, but found that behind the bank there was a wilderness of reeds, head-high. Paths which appeared to lead through the reeds ended a short way in from the river. The landing, and tying-up of the boat, made a pleasant diversion; and the dog, which did not seem to be enjoying the cruise, was glad of the chance to get ashore. When we were putting off after the second stop, it leaped ashore again, and we had to heave to while Richard went ashore and brought it back on board. We got as far as Horning Ferry before turning round. On the way back we turned into Salhouse Broad: very pretty, with woods all round except where a grassy slope rose from the shore. At Wroxham I took the boat under a narrow bridge into the upper stretch of the Bure; and as our three hours were nearly up we turned across the river and made our way back—thus ending a very enjoyable little trip.

August 28th

A television programme of the Democratic Party convention in Chicago: a brief but decisive intervention by Mayor Daly, who seems to be the recognised Democratic Party boss. It appears to be thought that Senator McCarthy threw away such small chance as he had of the presidential nomination by being unable to find time to meet Mayor Daly; but from what we saw of him on television McCarthy's reluctance was understandable.

This morning the car refused to start. We walked up the road to the village garage, where they undertook to send someone shortly. The proprietor himself arrived half an hour later. Like me, he took off the distributor cover, but dried it more thoroughly than I had done. The engine then started at once. His charge of seven shillings and sixpence seemed a good deal for what he had done, but the work was cheap at the price in as much as it got the car going.

August 29th
The Democratic convention: Hubert Humphrey duly—and disastrously—adopted.

August 30th
Convention television this morning. I was quite taken with Senator Muskie, who has been selected for Vice-Presidential candidate: a sensible, plainspoken man. Even Humphrey was not too bad, but it was sad to think, when listening to his elegant, well-meaning platitudes, what might have been if McCarthy had had the nomination. We had a brief glimpse of McCarthy at his press conference after the convention: witty, imperturbable, friendly as ever, the very antithesis of Humphrey and all the other pompous, noisy, party-machine politicians. Mayor Daly's police apparently repressed all dissension outside the hall with the utmost brutality, and even carried the same tactics into the convention—having, according to the accepted jargon, 'lost their cool'. McCarthy, after thanking the journalists for taking the trouble to come along and meet 'the Government in exile', responded to their enthusiastic laughter and applause by saying that if they received him like that he might be led to give some visible display of emotion—might even lose his cool. Just to see and hear him for those few moments made one feel what poor creatures Humphrey and Nixon are by comparison, and what folly the American politicians have shown in giving the electors such a choice of candidates.

September 14th
Yarrow Show at Oakwood. The only Borderer known to me that I met was Lord Dalkeith—who seemed to know who I was, for he took off his cap to me.

September 23rd
Vice-President Humphrey talking to a panel of correspondents assembled by the BBC. As always in 'Panorama', the questioners were so silly that anyone else by comparison would have seemed a paragon of wisdom; but there was no gainsaying the fact that Mr Humphrey

answered the questions sensibly and vigorously, and within the limitations of American Government policy made a good show. Against all my inclinations, I could not resist the conclusion that he would be a better President than Nixon.

September 30th
Motored to Perth for the Perth circuit.

October 3rd
H.M. Advocate v. Duffy: two young women charged with assault on a girl of twenty in Victoria Road, Dundee, as a consequence of which the girl had suffered the loss of an eye. The girl was a civil servant who had been working as a part-time waitress in the Oddfellows Bar one night in May when Mrs Duffy was there with some friends. Mrs Duffy took umbrage because she thought the waitress was slow in serving her, and had not given her enough lemonade for her whisky; and when Sylvia came out of the bar at closing time, with a young man who also was employed there, Mrs Duffy was waiting for her, with her friend Mrs Kelly—who had not been in the bar. They ran across the street and Mrs Duffy butted and struck the girl; then, while she was engaged in a struggle with the young man, Mrs Rourke weighed in, knocked Sylvia down, and kicked her. Sylvia was helped back into the bar by the young man, Healy, and it was found that she had received a serious injury to her eye, which later had to be taken out. The doctors were certain that the injury had been caused by stabbing, and a knife was found lying on the street where the fight had taken place. Healy had meanwhile gone in search of Mrs Duffy, and brought her back to the pub, where she complained that if anyone was girning he would get the same as the girl had got—this arose when a member of the band had said that if it had been his girl that she had done that to he would have broken every bone in her body. On being taken to the police station, Mrs Duffy admitted the assault but said she knew nothing about a knife. Eventually she was persuaded to make a further statement, in which she told of finding a knife on the stair as she was coming down from her house and carrying it in her pocket to the scene of the crime. She had thought she might use it as a potato peeler. No one had actually seen her use the knife, but Healy and another witness—a woman who had been out exercising her dog—spoke of blood on Sylvia's face and her holding her eye, immediately after the initial assault by Mrs Duffy,

so that seemed to let Mrs Kelly out so far as the knife and the injury to the eye were concerned. In charging the jury I advised them to find Mrs Kelly guilty only of simple assault. I was pleased with my charge, which I was able to produce effortlessly and without being able to think of anything afterwards that I had omitted or should have preferred to put differently. I do not suppose that I left the jury in much doubt about what they were expected to do as regards Mrs Duffy, and they were out for little more than ten minutes before returning an unanimous verdict of guilty as libelled. Mrs Duffy at one point interrupted the proceedings by a tearful protest against her counsel's handling of her case. She chose a bad point: Penrose's failure to cross-examine the witnesses on the possibility that blood found on her clothing could have come from a cut on her finger, not from Sylvia. Penrose was right, since grouping tests had shown that the blood could not be Mrs Duffy's. I had no hesitation in sentencing Mrs Duffy to three years imprisonment. Mrs Kelly's part in the affair was no more than a typical street brawl, but I was not disposed to take a lenient view when she had joined in a vicious assault on a girl she had never seen before. I sentenced her to six months imprisonment, remarking that even though it was a first offence this silly violence must be discouraged. I had asked the jurors who had not been empanelled to come back at two, so we were able to go straight on to the last case, *H.M. Advocate v. Baikie*. With a short adjournment for tea, we went on till 5.30.

I got the car to take me back to the hotel, and changed quickly so as to have a run in my own car before darkness fell. I made for Dunkeld, and turned up the hill on the road to Blairgowrie. I had not remembered what a delightful road this was; even on a dismal damp evening, with darkness coming on, it was a lovely road winding among woods and lochs. I felt sorry that Nancy was not there to share it with me. In Blairgowrie I found a fish-and-chip shop, where I had supper for three shillings and threepence: a perfectly good supper, nice fresh fish.

October 4th

The conclusion of the Baikie trial. I did not think I charged the jury as effectively. I had no doubt that Baikie was guilty, but the jury were out for a long time, so that I began to think that I had put the case too weakly. However, they came back with a verdict of guilty, by a majority. Taking the week as a whole, I was pleased with how I had got on; it was satisfactory, and to me rather surprising, to find that I was able to deal with a succession of cases without any sense of tiredness or exhaustion. After each charge to a jury, I felt as fresh as at the start of the case.

It was getting on for 12.30, and I had it in mind to stop for a sandwich at the milk bar south of Kinross. But as I was coming out of Kinross I was hailed for a lift by two girls—students making their way back to Edinburgh—so I carried on without stopping for lunch.

October 8th

Procedure Roll debate in *Farrans v. Roxburgh County Council*. The pursuers, a firm of contractors, took on a contract for road improvements between Jedburgh and Carter Bar. They detail a lot of additional work they had to do, and are claiming a sum of £36,800. The contract included an arbitration clause, and the claim was referred to an engineer, Mr Alexander Fraser. A Record was drawn up; and Mr Fraser heard argument upon it, dismissed the claim, and found that no sums were due. It was submitted to me by Cullen for the pursuers, and later by Peter Maxwell his senior, that the contractors were free to raise the matter again on different pleadings. It is well settled that an arbiter's award is final. The pursuers however say that they are not challenging the award, but merely asking that the arbiter should consider the matter again—on what, as James Mackay for the defenders pointed out, seems much the same point. The pursuers say that by using the words *hinc inde* the arbiter meant his finding to be limited to a decision on the Record as it stood. It is not clear what *hinc inde* means, but it is difficult to suppose that it could mean what the pursuers suggest. I had given Cullen and Maxwell rather a rough passage, and felt I must try tomorrow to interrupt less during the remainder of Maxwell's speech.

October 9th

Peter Maxwell resumed his speech. I heard him for a time in silence, but then forgot my good resolutions and pressed him vigorously on a particular point, until at last he said that if I did not want to hear him there was no point in going on. I apologised, and persuaded him to proceed; and meeting him afterwards in the hall with James Mackay, after I had taken the case to avizandum, apologised again for any discourtesy. We parted on friendly terms.

With Nancy to the Zoo for lunch; and home, where I switched on

ITV for the Conservative party conference. Within minutes of switching it on, I fell sound asleep, and when I awoke the picture was of horses passing the Chase Hotel at York races.

October 11th
Eleven divorces. In one of them there had been difficulty in inducing the pursuer to specify the cruelty she alleged. Her marriage, she said, had not really been very happy. The defender had not behaved very well. His conduct had not really been good at all. He had not treated her properly. Pressed to say in what way his conduct had been bad, she at last replied, 'He was not consistent'. Her counsel was able to get from her that he had been drinking to excess, and came home drunk very regularly. 'He was consistent in that, at least', I remarked.

Finished drafting my judgment in *Farrans v. Roxburgh County Council*; I have found that the arbiter's decision is final, and dismissed the action.

October 15th
On television we had a documentary about four Texan millionaires. They seemed to be typical examples of the arrested development which affects so many adult Americans, and no doubt explains why the USA is landed with presidential candidates like Hubert Humphrey and Richard Nixon.

October 17th
An undefended proof in which Craik appeared and moved for the diet to be discharged, as the pursuer had failed to put his solicitors in funds and his Legal Aid certificate had been suspended. I did not see how Craik could move for discharge of the diet if he and those instructing him were no longer acting for the pursuer. It seemed to me that if solicitors were refusing to carry on without payment their proper course would have been to intimate that to the pursuer so that he could conduct the proof himself; and I expressed my displeasure at what they had done. There was nothing I could really do about it, and I agreed to discharge the diet.

To the City Hospital at 7.30 to see Mrs Shearlaw. She had been wheeled into the main ward, where a concert party were about to begin their show: eight men in white shirts, black trousers and black bow ties, who took it in turn to tender their pieces—'Edelweiss', 'Until', 'The Laird of Cockpen', 'The Hippopotamus Song', and the like. Most of them were pretty awful, and after one had given us 'Love's Last Word is Spoken Cherie' an old crone who had been lying motionless in the bed next to me suddenly exclaimed in a loud voice, 'That's terrible'. But I suppose it was good of an amateur concert party—who had all been engaged in their own work of bus driving or whatever it might be, during the day—to come at all, and for the most part the old ladies seemed to be enjoying it. The concert party were between me and the door, but luckily it was ascertained that a patient at the far end had her birthday today, and when the party all moved up to her bed to sing 'Happy Birthday to You' I was able to get out.

October 31st
Jury trial: *McCallum v. Paterson*. The pursuer was a housewife of 50 who had been a passenger in a car on the Ayr-Stranraer road. The car broke down. Her husband went to get help while she remained seated in the car, which during his absence was run into by the defender's car. The pursuer received a serious injury to her spine, resulting in complete permanent paralysis of all her limbs and organs below that level. She is confined to a wheelchair, dependent on her husband and daughter for assistance in everything she does. The defender admitted liability, and the case came up for trial on quantum of damages before Milligan and a jury, two years ago. The jury awarded her £23,000—just what any reasonable person might expect as an award for such catastrophic injury. The defender however enrolled a motion for a new trial, which came up before Grant, Walker and Cameron, and they overturned the verdict and ordered a new trial on the ground that the damages were excessive. This was a ridiculous decision, and just how ridiculous it was became more apparent every moment as the pursuer's evidence was deployed in the re-trial today. She had to be carried in, and Wylie brought out from her, with tact and skill, the measure of her sufferings and the awful life she had to lead when every normal function was paralysed. The evidence of the pursuer and her medical witnesses went unchallenged, there being no possible answer to it. We decided to leave the speeches over till tomorrow. I made a few additions to the notes I had made last night for my charge to the jury—designed as far as possible to ensure that they gave a similar award to what the pursuer was awarded before.

November 1st

The jury, though out for an hour, came back with an award of £22,000—a very satisfactory result.

November 6th

George Macdonald told me that the defenders' agents in *McCallum v. Paterson* had enrolled a motion for another new trial. I remarked that that was ridiculous—no jury would give less than £22,000, and it would be crazy if they did. Macdonald agreed; and Sibbald and Almond had also agreed, before the verdict, that the jury were bound to award pretty much what the first jury had given, if not more. There is a tender of £12,500.

November 10th

An article in yesterday's *Scotsman* recalls the rules laid down before 1914 for the conduct of hostilities between belligerents, and the War Office's warning: 'Should it be found impossible to count on the loyalty of the adversary, there is grave danger of war degenerating into excess'.

November 28th

Twelve undefended cruelty cases. The pursuer in one of them, a farmer's wife from Dumfriesshire, was one of the most attractive persons I have encountered: a tall, handsome woman with nice features, a pleasant smile, and a friendly, convincing manner of speaking, and yet her silly ass of a husband after marrying her completely neglected her in order to go off on motor-cycle rallies and throughout their married life would have as little to do with her as possible. There was no question of ill-treatment, so that the case on cruelty was pretty thin; but I had no hesitation in granting a divorce, in the hope that some more sensible man would have the good luck to get her as his wife.

November 29th

Eleven cruelty divorces. In one of them, the pursuer's father gave evidence about staying with the parties in Callander; and on being 'shouted through' by his daughter found her husband trying to strangle her. 'What did you do?' counsel asked. 'I said, "I've come here for a holiday, and if this is going to be the carry-on I'm going away home".'

December 3rd

A proof in *Semple v. British Railways Board.* The pursuer had abandoned a case against fellow-workmen of removing planks between two waggons from which he was working in a tunnel—which removal, he averred, had caused him to fall into the space between the waggons when the tunnel was blacked out by smoke from a train. The reason for this amendment was obvious when the pursuer came to give evidence. He was a transparently honest witness, and made it clear from the outset that he knew the planks had been removed, and had indeed taken part in their removal in order to put them on some trestles to enable the workers to reach a point on the tunnel roof. His case was now confined to blaming his employers for not providing enough spare planks and not giving a special warning when a steam train was due. The pursuer in his own evidence destroyed both these cases. He said that they always used the planks for trestles when they were not required for access, and would never have thought of looking for any extra planks, though he did not doubt that spare planks were available if he had wanted them. He said too that he had a warning by detonator that a train was approaching, and he would have been perfectly safe if he had not, for some reason which he could not explain, put his foot over the edge of the waggon where the planks had been. Other witnesses were to the same effect; and I gave judgment assoilzieing the defenders. The pursuer did not suffer any very serious injury: a temporary dislocation of some fingers of his right hand.

On television tonight a BBC documentary on Pakistani teenagers in Britain was an interesting commentary on last night's programme from Enoch Powell, and made nonsense of his idea that because someone is black he can have no contribution to make to the texture of English life. It is a pity that he is so wickedly wrong in this when he is almost alone in taking a sensible view on other things—a sentence quoted last night from one of his speeches could hardly have been bettered as a summation of what utter nonsense all this fuss about balance of payments really is.

December 4th

Guthrie lamenting to Milligan the state of the Court of Session. In the past week they had had motions in the First Division withdrawing five cases down for appeal from the Outer House and Sheriff Court, all because the House of Lords disregarded the law and restored judgments for pursuers after the First Division had found for defenders. Insurance companies knew that when they had come to the First Division and got them to find in their favour pursuers would just take the case to the House of Lords and the decision would be reversed. So, although the Division might have been quite prepared to do what the insurance companies wanted, the companies realised it would be a waste of money. It did not seem to occur to him that pursuers might conceivably be in the right.

December 5th

A proof: *Murdoch v. Colvilles*. A catwalk ran at a level of six inches above the floor. The pursuer was walking along it and slipped. He says that the defenders should have put studs on the surface of the catwalk. A photograph of the catwalk did not suggest the slightest danger to anyone, but the pursuer led the evidence of a consulting engineer, who supported his case for studs. My efforts to encourage Elliott to get a move on did not meet with much success; and just before lunch time the pursuer's panel doctor interrupted the lengthy re-examination to protest. 'It's my practice I'm thinking of'. 'Well', I said, 'I'm doing my best to stop him, as you can see'; but I assured him that we should let him away before lunch, and Elliott at length sat down.

I told Kissen about Guthrie's remarks concerning appeals to the First Division. Kissen observed that it was a good illustration of how hopelessly people could become corrupted in bad company.

December 6th

In the robing-room I found Guthrie and Migdale, who were engaged today along with Clyde in hearing the defender's motion for another new trial in *McCallum v. Paterson*. Wylie had told me that the court was very much against him, with Clyde shouting at him and saying that after the Second Division had held that the award of £23,000 was excessive he should have reduced the sum sued for. Guthrie gave me an opening by remarking 'Here's the man that's caused all the trouble'. I was able to say that the Second Division's judgment had been ridiculous and no jury would ever award less than £20,000. Guthrie asked what I should have awarded. I said I should have awarded £15,000 out of deference to the authorities, but my own valuation of the case would have have been £20,000. I thought I had made some impression on them, but whether they have been able to stand up to Clyde remains to be seen.

JUDGE'S DIARY

December 7th

My Bill to reverse *Davie v. New Merton Board Mills* got an unopposed Second Reading in the House of Commons yesterday. Hugh Brown had drawn first place in the ballot for private members' Bills, and Ewan Stewart had persuaded him to take this one, so it has every chance of being passed into law this session. The section of the Law Reform (Miscellaneous Provisions) Act dealing with corroboration came into force last week, and corroboration is no longer required in actions of damages for personal injury. Other sections, including that which makes criminal convictions competent evidence in civil cases, can be brought into force as soon as the Secretary of State makes an order. It looks as if most of the little law reforms which I listed when I came into office have been achieved after all, despite the slow progress I seemed to be making in getting them put through.

December 9th

Drafting my Opinion in *Murdoch v. Colvilles*. With some hesitation, I have found for the pursuer and awarded him £700.

A television documentary about the troubles in Northern Ireland, with Captain Terence O'Neill appearing on the following news programme to say how bad things were. He was a pathetic figure, like a drunk man who had reached the melancholy stage, and compared unfavourably with the Orange extremist Ian Paisley. If there is to be a rabble-rouser, he might as well be a good one, and Mr Paisley's loud voice, truculent manner, and clerical attire, certainly fill the bill.

December 10th

A cruelty divorce in which the defender conducted his own defence. The wife complained that when drunk he sometimes beat her up. The only corroboration came from marks seen on her on one occasion when she hit her husband four times on the head with a poker, and all he had done was to wrest the poker from her and hit her back. But though I thought that the evidence given by her and her witnesses was exaggerated it was obvious that he was a drunken nuisance and that the marriage was beyond repair; and I had no doubt that I could grant decree of divorce. After everybody else had gone, the defender and his daughter came back looking as if they wanted to say something, and when I called them up asked if he could appeal against my award of £5 per week as periodical allowance for the wife. I told them that he was entitled to appeal if he liked but that I did not think he would have much hope of success on that point. I stressed that he must not take that just from me, and advised them to see a lawyer about it. He was quite a nice little man, and I thought I should perhaps not have awarded so much; but he is working in Birmingham and earning good wages.

On television after supper we had *My Little Chickadee*, with Mae West and W.C. Fields: not much of a film, but they are a quaint pair and speak in an extraordinary clipped accent and stylised phraseology. Mae West was very funny in a completely deadpan style, not at all what I had expected. Went up to bed soon after ten, but came down again at 10.50 to see a film of the Thames from source to sea, against a background of Handel's *Water Music*. It was attractively photographed and had the great merit that not a word was spoken from start to finish.

December 11th

The divorce proof had been put out for three days, but as I had finished it in one I was appointed to take two Procedure Rolls. In *Allan v. Pochin (Joinery)* a motion had been enrolled to bring in the main contractors on the building site at which the pursuer was injured; they had erected the scaffolding which collapsed when the pursuer was standing on it. Sibbald assumed that I would allow the amendment, and if this was done there was not much point in having a Procedure Roll debate until all parties were in the case. Both pursuer and defenders however had pleas to relevancy; and on reading the Record last night it seemed to me that the pursuer was right and no relevant defence had been stated. If this was so, the case could be disposed of right away, and there was no use complicating it by allowing another party to be brought in. The defenders aver that the scaffold was stable until a tie securing it was removed by some unknown person on the day of the accident. If that were so, a failure to inspect at the start of the work would not have mattered—there was then no defect to be discovered. But the relevant Regulation requires that every scaffold shall be properly maintained: an absolute obligation. The removal of the tie meant that the scaffold had not been maintained, and the employers were responsible in law, whoever it was that had done the actual damage. Osborne argued that the regulation did not apply to a scaffold that was being erected or dismantled, but as no one suggested that this was such a scaffold the argument did not take him very far. His other argument, that it was not reasonably practicable to prevent a breach of the regulation, was equally futile, since the duty under the regulation is not subject to any condition of practicability. The debate had gone into the afternoon; and after one of the other clerks of court turned up and apologising on Sibbald's behalf explained that he had committed himself to another appointment, on the view that he would certainly be free before lunch-time. This no doubt was the explanation of why Sibbald had been so keen that I continue the case for debate at some later date when the Third Party had been brought in.

December 19th
The First Division were giving judgment in *McCallum v. Paterson*; they upset the jury's verdict and ordered a third trial.

December 20th
Debate on the Employers Liability (Defective Plant) Bill was prolonged by Members who wanted to hinder the progress of a Divorce Bill for England which had second place on the Order Paper, but in the end my Bill was given a second reading without a division.

December 27th
This morning's *Scotsman* had a good leader on *McCallum v. Paterson*, saying not that the Division are wrong but that since they must have a criterion of excess they should be able to state it.

December 29th
Pleased to see in the *Sunday Express* an excellent leader on the McCallum case, pointing out that Clyde's observations about civil juries' being an 'importation from England' were irrelevant and that many people would rather trust to a jury than to judges who deprived a terribly injured woman of compensation twice awarded. 'It would be much better for people who go to the courts if juries were permitted their proper function and Lord Clyde was no longer asked to administer laws with which he obviously disagrees'.

December 31st
At the cost of two pounds I took a ticket for a special excursion on Saturday to enable passengers to take a final trip over the Waverley route to Carlisle before it closes on Sunday.

1969

In 1969 it became apparent that if I had stayed in the Government two years ago and turned down the vacant judgeship I should by now have finished up in the House of Lords. The Lord Advocate not having been able to find a seat in the Commons was given a life peerage. No doubt it would have been enjoyable, and a more entertaining life than that of a Court of Session judge—not that I was at all discontented with that. I was pleased to find myself dealing with the case of a paraplegic who had suffered practically the same injury as the unfortunate Mrs McCallum whose case had caused so much trouble the year before. I was able to award a large sum of damages, saying politely but firmly that I agreed with the juries in the McCallum case and giving good reasons for the conclusion, which I did not express in quite these terms, that the Inner House decisions had been ridiculous. An appeal was marked but not persisted in. It was reported; and I had no doubt that along with the other propaganda to which the McCallum case gave rise would have its effect in making sure that the injustice perpetrated on Mrs McCallum would not be repeated. The war in Vietnam continued; but it seemed to me that within the limits of what was politically possible for him President Nixon did not do too badly. He was a practical man, and I was sure he would get America out of the war if he could achieve that result without too obvious an appearance of total defeat. In home politics, the tragedy of Mr Wilson was that he had deprived us of a socialist alternative. In all the major issues the policy of the two parties was to all intents and purposes the same. The whole climate of public life was wrong, with its emphasis on finance and profit and productivity, its contempt for any other kind of values, its determination that to him that hath should be given. There were glimmerings of a reaction against these attitudes, but it was hard to see how we were to escape from them. My Employers Liability Act, to reverse the House of Lords decision in Davie v. New Merton Board Mills—*after many vicissitudes—became law.*

January 4th

To Waverley for the excursion. I was at a table in a saloon carriage with a master from Winchester and a young electrician from Dumbarton, both railway enthusiasts, and we carried on a lively discussion throughout the journey, about the history of all the branch lines, long since closed. There have been letters of protest in the *Scotsman* about this excursion, from Borders people who had been fighting for the retention of the Waverley route, and the train was halted at Millerhill while two police officers made a show of searching it, a phone call having been received at police headquarters that a bomb had been planted on board. The line from Carlisle to Newcastle was new to me; and it was a very successful tour on a lovely bright day—a perfect day for seeing the countryside.

January 16th

H.M. Advocate v. Lesslie. A well-known Dundee psychopath named Shields, a nasty-looking customer, had been drinking with his friends Roger and Gibb in Roger's house and said he had fallen asleep. The next thing he remembered was walking up the road to his daughter's house with his two children, aged two and three, with serious head injuries and his face covered with blood. His skull behind the left ear had been fragmented and required a major neurological operation. Roger and Gibb gave evidence that Lesslie had been in the house when Shields was sitting in the bed and had gone over and hit him on the head with an axe. They denied having witnessed any fight or struggle, but as both had been drinking steadily from nine in the morning till late evening—Gibb said he had had ten bottles of wine—they readily agreed that their recollection might be faulty. Their evidence about who was present at any time, and every other surrounding circumstance, was hopelessly confused, and their readiness to agree with anything put to them made their evidence a tangle of absurdities. Roger insisted that Lesslie had barged in, uninvited, but agreed that Lesslie had been staying in the house with him for the past fortnight. He was not however expecting him back that night. When I asked why, his reply was that Lesslie had been apprehended. We continued with this rubbish until I called a halt for the day.

January 17th

The Lesslie case: his story was that Shields had attacked him—not with the axe, which he maintained was standing in the fireplace and remained there—but with a hammer. Lesslie managed to take the hammer from Shields, and to protect himself struck Shields twice with it on the head. Both it and the axe were found by the police, not in Roger's house but in Shields', lying on a chair. How they got there was a mystery. The blade of the axe was stained with blood, while on the hammer there was only a speck of blood. The jury were out for quite a while before coming back with a majority verdict of Not Guilty. They may have been put against Shields by a violent outburst from him while a young woman who lived near him was giving evidence about some threats she heard shouted in the street. She made some reference to Shields' children, and D.B. Smith, who was defending, was asking her whether the children had not been away from Shields for a time, when Shields jumped up from where he was sitting in the front row of seats and shouted 'None of that, cut that out'. Smith hastily sat down, without pursuing the question any further.

January 21st
A defended divorce out for proof before me today could not proceed because the defender had swallowed a bone.

January 23rd
A case out before me in Procedure Roll: an action by a boy of seventeen who had received an eye injury when playing shinty in the school playground at Spean Bridge. The schoolmaster, it was said, should not have allowed his boys to play shinty without supervision. In any event he knew that Moore had only one good eye and so should not have been allowed to play shinty at all. The defenders say that Moore was an experienced shinty player and played for the school team.

January 24th
Divorces. The pursuer in *Morrison v. Morrison* had had a child, Edward Diamond, before she married the defender in 1961. In August 1963 they had another child, Wendy Morrison, but the pursuer by then had gone back to England and was associating with a man named Barclay there from March 1963. She had two children to Barclay: Angela Morrison in October 1964 and William Barclay in 1965. By the latter date she had gone to Plymouth and was living with a man named Williams, to whom she had a child, Steven Morrison, in 1967. By the time Steven was born she had come back

to her husband, who took her back along with the children and had them all living in family with him—so that he is responsible in law for alimenting all five. The wife was divorcing him for cruelty.

February 1st
Divorces. Caplan was examining a witness from Luton who spoke to the defender and another woman having come from Scotland to live near him, and how he took them to be husband and wife. 'Did they have a baby living with them?' Caplan asked, and the witness replied that the baby had come later. 'Was it just a young baby?' asked Caplan.

February 3rd
Called at police headquarters and recovered ten shillings that Elizabeth had handed in some months ago to the Lost Property Office. She found it in the street, but after handing it in decided that it must be one that she had just dropped herself; so it was not surprising that no one had claimed it.

February 6th
A jury trial. McCluskey opened the case, giving the jury a very clear account of the operation of the drilling rig which caused the accident. Everyone agreed that the drill had toppled over because a compressed-air valve had been opened too wide. The question was whether this had been the fault of the pursuer's mate, Grantham, who had been killed in the accident, or of the pursuer himself. The accident happened away back in 1964, but it seemed to be lucky for the pursuer that it had taken so long to bring it to trial. He led no evidence whatever about the facts of the accident except his own, and if the case had been tried before the Miscellaneous Provisions Bill doing away with the need for corroboration became law I could hardly have refused a motion to withdraw the case from the jury. No such motion was possible today, since corroboration of the pursuer is no longer required. He and Grantham were working alone, so that probably it would not have been possible for him to get corroboration of his story that Grantham had been solely responsible for operating the compressed-air controls. There is an interesting question on the medical evidence about whether the pursuer had a fracture of two cervical vertebrae. He had undoubtedly had a neck injury of some kind, and eight months after the accident dived off a diving board in a swimming bath and so caused a recurrence of his neck trouble. He said that this

had been recommended to him by the National Insurance doctor.

February 7th

The defenders adduced three medical witnesses, who established pretty conclusively that there had been no fracture of the cervical vertebrae. Verdict for the defenders, eight votes to four. The jury may have been prejudiced against the pursuer by his suing for £10,000. The pursuer had come back to court today to hear the end of his case, and I saw him walking across Parliament Square: a lonely, disconsolate-looking figure.

February 19th

Tonight's edition of the Mountbatten story on television. It seemed clear that if Mountbatten had not been overruled at the end of the war, and had been allowed to negotiate the future of Indo-China with Ho Chi Minh in the same way as he negotiated with the other nationalist leaders in South East Asia, the whole tragedy of Vietnam would have been avoided.

February 21st

A Declarator of Marriage brought by a stout, elderly couple who had gone one day, many years ago, to Kirkgunzeon church to be married. The minister told them he could not marry them, as the bride's mother had pointed out that they had been proclaimed in the wrong parish. So they went home to the farm where they lived and took up house together as man and wife. They had so continued at numerous farms ever since, and everyone they knew supposed they were married. 'We lived very respectably', said Mrs Coltart—and from her appearance it looked very like it. I granted decree of declarator of marriage by habit and repute.

February 22nd

Divorces. In one, there was an adopted child, adopted while the parties were living in Hong-Kong, and the birth certificate narrated that it had been 'Found abandoned outside Mong Kok Ferry Pier'.

February 25th

Mr Nixon on the television news, friendly and chatty, ignoring his escort of police and motor cyclists in order to shake hands with children and other bystanders, and pat their dogs.

March 3rd
'World in Action' tonight had an interesting film about politics in Pakistan, with a young student agitator Tariq Ali making an intelligent, thought-provoking appearance which completely belied the mental picture I had of him from reading about him in the newspapers.

March 4th
Gow, who had been at school at Merchiston and went straight from there to Dreghorn to start his national service, recalled how surprised he was to find that of all those in his hut only he and another Merchistonian wore pyjamas at night.

March 6th
Macdonald said he did his best to provide me with interesting work, but whatever he put out before me seemed to collapse. Wheatley remarked that Birnam had always been lucky in regard to cases settling and giving him a free day. He had been in the habit of coming out through the Conference Room at 10.30 or so when the Division judges were assembling to go into court. Cooper, who was a glutton for work and had probably been there from the break of dawn, no doubt found this irritating. After Mitchell had resigned from being Principal Clerk, and his place was taken by Watson, Birnam on the day that Watson took over finished even earlier. At 10.20 or so he came through the Conference Room in silence, with his coat on, and as he was going out of the door turned and remarked with a smile, 'I think Watson's an even better Principal Clerk than Mitchell'.

March 18th
Cross actions of divorce: *McDonald v. McDonald*. The husband is a joiner in Dunning, who in October 1966 took in a boarder, also named McDonald, a man ten years younger than his wife—he himself being ten years older. Suspecting his wife of misconduct with McDonald, he threatened them with a bush knife, and they went off to stay with the parties' married daughter. The daughter's husband then made her put them out because he could not afford to keep them, and the wife had to go back to her husband. McDonald the lodger gave evidence. He said on the one hand that the husband had gone down on his knees to him in the street in Perth and begged him to come back to Dunning, and on the other hand that the husband kept threatening him with a knife and had offered one fellow £10 to

94

do away with him, another £50 and another £5. There was another quarrel between the parties in February 1967, when the husband would not let the wife go to Perth, and she finally left him after he had poured away a basin of water and torn up a towel, to keep her from washing her face. The wife had amended her defences to the husband's action, admitting adultery with McDonald, but the parties were still at issue about whether the husband should be divorced for cruelty. Smith, who was counsel for the wife, was late in coming in, and I took the opportunity of asking Horsburgh, who appeared for the husband, whether he proposed to spend three days on the academic question of whether his client was to be said to have been cruel. He said he had taken this up with his client, and his instructions had been that he wanted to go on defending, but he would speak to him again. He and the husband retired into the lobby, and after some delay Horsburgh and Smith came back with the information that the cross actions were both to proceed as undefended. This left the question of custody of the children: Audrey, who is nearly fifteen, and Norrie, aged five. Since the break-up of the marriage they have lived with the husband at Dunning. Despite inferior accommodation, I was prepared to give custody to the wife, if that was what Audrey wanted; and according to Maguire, who was appointed by Shearer to report on a motion for interim custody, that was what Audrey did want. I assumed that the wife would marry McDonald and so make a home for the children. McDonald however stated categorically in the witness-box that he had his own life to live and had no intention of marrying anybody; and Audrey, adduced as a witness by the wife, said she had no preference as long as she was not separated from Norrie. She had been at variance with her father at one time, but they had now reached a *modus vivendi*. He had tried to stop the children seeing their mother, but Audrey had gone to see her none the less, sometimes taking Norrie. She had been off school for three weeks to look after Norrie while her father was at work—the woman whom he had employed having left. The husband assured me that he would get another housekeeper, and it looked as if things would be no better in Perth—the wife goes out to work all day in a restaurant. She said her married daughter would help with Norrie, and the married daughter said she would, but as she had just had a baby it looked as if the task of attending to Norrie's welfare would devolve upon Audrey in Perth as in Dunning. The wife was a pathetic figure, with her marriage gone, and McDonald throwing her over.

She had a sense of humour, and I liked her much more than her self-satisfied, opinionative husband. But everybody agreed that Norrie was happy where he was, and Audrey is in the school hockey team and a youth club at Dunning, and presumably all her friends are there. I did not see how I could make any change in custody; and I made it clear that the husband must give the children every facility not only to visit their mother but to spend weekends and holidays with her if that was desired.

In *McCallum v. Paterson*, Sibbald told me, the pursuer had agreed to settle for £10,000: a most unfortunate result, it seemed to me, and one that Wylie should never have allowed.

March 19th
To South Morningside Church hall to address the Mothers and Young Wives Group on the subject 'Seen from the Bench'. We had a lively question time, with questions from the young women including two 'Bring-back-hanging' enthusiasts. The young woman chairman was competent and agreeable, and prayed most eloquently.

March 21st
Presentation of a portrait to Lord Reid: an attractive portrait, characteristic of Reid. Its painter, Sutherland, was present with his daughter, and I was annoyed that when drinks were served after the ceremony the Faculty left them by themselves in a corner with no one to speak to. I joined them and carried on a conversation as well as I could—somewhat handicapped by being unable to remember Mr Sutherland's name and so to introduce them to anyone else. Wheatley and other judges who were standing a couple of feet away ignored our guests altogether. Sorn seemed delighted when I congratulated him on the success of his cows at the Dairy Show.

March 24th
One of the clerks of court rang up, wanting me to take an interdict petition, and I had the hearing in the study when the party arrived about 5.30: an attempt by the parents of a 19-year-old French girl to stop her marriage to a school teacher of 35. It was averred that according to the French code absence of parental consent was an absolute impediment to marriage; but even if it were it seemed to me that what I was concerned with was the law of Scotland, in which parental consent was merely an incident. So I refused interim interdict.

The clerks had written interlocutors granting it, and this had to be altered. The marriage is due to take place at Grantown tomorrow.

March 26th
BBC production of *The Basement*, a play for television by Harold Pinter: not so much a matter of guessing the explanation of what was happening as guessing whether anything was happening at all.

March 27th
McDonald v. McDonald. At Smith's instigation, I declined to deal with an application to modify the husband's liability for expenses, so that if he paid up the whole amount the wife would be able to recover the £14 which had been her Legal Aid contribution; but on reflection I thought that was unfair to the husband, and anyhow rather silly—there was no possibility that he would be able to pay up the whole thing so as to allow the wife to get her £14 back. I told Sibbald to speak to the counsel concerned and have the motion enrolled again, so that I could make a more sensible order. The main business of the day was a declarator of irritancy of a lease, against the tenant of Broomly House, Dun, who in 1954 got the assignation of a lease entered into in 1950. In terms of the lease, the tenant accepted the buildings as in sufficient and tenantable state of repair, and undertook to maintain the property, keeping it wind and water tight. He was authorised to carry out improvements provided he got the written approval of the proprietor. The pursuer claims that the defender is in breach of these conditions, and accordingly wants to have the lease declared null and void, and the defender ordained to remove. The day was devoted to the evidence of a surveyor who had examined the property before the action was raised. It was clear from his evidence that the house was far from being wind and watertight. Moreover the tenant had taken down a two-flue chimney stack and replaced it by a single-flue, and had constructed a shower and washplace in an old store in the basement, without getting permission. It looked therefore as if he were in breach of conditions. On the other hand, it became increasingly obvious that the action was something of a racket. The house was an old dower house which had been occupied by the military during the war, and far from being in good condition when the lease was entered into it seemed to have been in a delapidated state. The defender had taken it on at a rent of £30 a year, and with the help of his family had been gradually putting it in some kind of

order. He had worked on a do-it-yourself basis, and it was obvious that in some respects he may have made things worse. It seemed to me however that he had been making a pretty good effort, with very limited resources, and had succeeded in making a reasonably comfortable home for himself and his family. Whether this is a defence I do not know, but when we rose at four, halfway though John Mitchell's cross-examination of the surveyor, my sympathies were all with the defender. Mitchell did very well. His cross-examination was in no way spectacular, but he plodded along patiently, working away at the surveyor's evidence and gradually whittling it down. There have been three families in the house—relatives of the defender's—and the defender had produced a booklet of snapshots taken throughout the years showing them all working and playing about the premises, and what they had done to make it livable and attractive. Despite its deficiencies, it looked rather a nice place.

March 28th
Ridiculous that a case like this should have been put out for the last two days of term, with the result that the case has had to be continued to July.

April 6th
Craigmillar Park: Mr Mactaggart preached about the Resurrection, in his usual undogmatic, 'take-it-or-leave-it' style; indeed he used those very words. One might say that under his regime Craigmillar Park is the agnostics' parish church.

April 10th
London. London birds start singing very early in the morning; they were chirping happily away at five o'clock, long before daylight.

April 22nd
BBC '24 Hours' programme on television: a magnificent performance by Miss Bernadette Devlin, 22 years old tomorrow, and newly elected Civil Rights MP for Mid-Ulster, where she scored a fine victory over the widow of the late Unionist Member. Knowledgeable, courteous, and determined, she made rings round a stupid interviewer, and went on with imperturbable good humour to demolish Mr Chichester-Clark, the Unionist Member for Londonderry, who thought to catch her out with some trick questions. In vain was

the net spread in the sight of the bird. Miss Devlin was a welcome oasis in the barren desert of British politics; she made me feel I should like to start a 'Bernadette for Prime Minister' campaign.

April 24th
Two cases remitted for sentence. The first was *H.M. Advocate v. Watt*, in which the accused had pled guilty to a charge under the Explosive Substances Act of being in possession of six sticks of gel-ignite under circumstances giving rise to a suspicion that he had them for an unlawful purpose. The gelignite was intended for an-other man in London, who required it for some criminal purpose. James Mackay appeared for Watt and put up a tactful and effective plea. He said that Watt had understood that Cooper, the man in London, required the gelignite for removing tree stumps. 'Not Guilty' would not have been the proper plea, because Cooper had no permit for the use of explosives, and Watt in having them in his possession for the purpose of passing them to Cooper therefore had them for an unlawful purpose. The Advocate Depute agreed that Watt was suf-fering from angina, and in view of this, and of the fact that Watt had kept out of trouble for twenty years, I restricted the sentence to four months imprisonment. I thought afterwards that this was probably too lenient, and my doubts were confirmed after the Court rose, when I encountered my old client Mr Greenstein in the lobby and was congratulated by him on my humanitarian view of the case. It appeared that Bruce was a business associate of his. I remarked that Mr Greenstein was one of my failures, but this Greenstein repudi-ated with some warmth, saying I had put up a magnificent fight for him and would have been bound to succeed before any other Court. He assured me that he had never stopped being grateful to me for all I had done on his behalf.

May 6th
Finished reading *Gibraltar Besieged 1779–1783*, by Jack Russell. A good chapter about a catastrophically mishandled assault by French and Spanish forces in which they threw away their chances of vic-tory—to the discomfiture of successive British Governments, who have had to cope with the Gibraltar problem ever since.

May 7th
Municipal election results—not such a disastrous election for Labour

as was generally expected. In Edinburgh another of the old-gang 'Progressives' has been knocked out by a *soi-disant* Conservative. The Edinburgh Conservatives have included in their official programme some criticism of the Progressives' habit of giving themselves and their friends the big contracts for Corporation work, and if they continue to prosper at the expense of the Progressives it may result eventually in a better type of Council.

May 9th

Mr Braggins, in filling up a form about his accident for his insurance company, gave as the explanation of the accident that it was a slight sideways collision in a storm of hail and rain. Not surprisingly, they have written back asking for particulars of what happened, and for a diagram. In reply he has cut a tiny piece, about an inch square, from an Ordnance plan of Edinburgh, showing the Tollcross area, and pasted it in the centre of a sheet of notepaper. In a covering note he says he has nothing to add to what he told them about the accident, except that it happened in a storm of hail and rain. He has made no marking on his little plan, even to show where the accident is sup-posed to have happened. Proof in *Tait v. Sleigh*, a petition for presumption of death of the petitioner's wife. The petitioner was a farmer at Tarves, who married in September 1965. Immediately after-wards his wife became depressed. On 7th December she left the farm in her brother's car to go to the village, and was never seen again. The car was found abandoned a stone's throw from the sea on a rocky part of the coast. A note had been left in the car to the effect that she was sorry to have been a burden to everyone; she hoped his sister would take anything that was of use to her and be a good neighbour to her husband. The husband was petitioning to have it presumed that she died on 7th December 1962—seven years after the date when she was last known to be alive. Relatives had put in Answers agreeing that death should be presumed, but claiming that the appro-priate date at which she should be presumed to have died was the actual date of her disappearance—before the passing of the Intestate Husbands Estate Act, so that they would be entitled to share in her estate of £4,000. Bruce appeared for the petitioner, and put up a good argument, which I was impressed by until Hope replied for the respondents. An interesting debate, and most helpful to have two good counsel who had taken the trouble to look up all the authorities and were able to present an excellent argument. It soon turned out that there was no real answer to Hope's argument.

May 12th
To Muirfield for the Bar Foursomes. It was a long time since I had
had a golf club in my hand, but I played not too badly. Lunch is
entirely self-service now, and I helped myself to a big plateful of
soup, two good helpings of very nice tongue, a plate of raspberries,
custard and trifle, and oatcake and butter. It was worth the fifteen
shillings I had to pay for it, plus fifteen shillings for my partner's
lunch, but a green fee of £2 was rather a shock.

May 14th
Finished reading *The Gardeners of Salonika*, by Alan Warner. For
three years after landing in 1915 the allied expeditionary force accomplished nothing. But then it got a new commander, General
Franchet d'Esprey, and some exciting concluding chapters tell how
in sixteen days from the start of his planned offensive Bulgaria was
suing for peace and the army was on its way to Budapest. It seems a
pity that it could not have been done sooner, and that the force was
kept starved of men and material for three long years while lives were
being squandered endlessly on futile offensives along the stalemated
Western front.

May 15th
In one of the reparation cases which had settled, the pursuer was
called Buggy. Sibbald had told me yesterday that it was a dermatitis
case, and though I had not been sure that he was serious it appeared
that this was right. *Sloan v. Sloan*: the husband defending the wife's
action only on custody of the two children, a boy of twelve and a girl
of eleven. There was a suggestion that at one time the wife had been
drinking and keeping late hours, so as to be an unsuitable guardian
for children. She had been putting obstacles in the way of her husband's seeing them, and I had some difficulty in getting her to tell
the truth about this; I pointed out to her that it was just making
things difficult for me when she gave false evidence, and she eventually owned up. I did not think that her being a liar necessarily unfitted
her to have custody of the children—it was no doubt her determination not to lose them that had led her into it—and the issue was
concluded when the boy himself appeared in the witness-box: neat,
spruce, well-mannered and obviously anxious to have as little to do

with his father as possible. It was what he was rather than what he said that clinched it—it was plain that the children were not being neglected or badly brought up.

May 16th

Jordan v. Jordan, a dispute about custody of an eight-year-old boy. The wife got custody when she was divorced for desertion but got into financial difficulties and then suffered from nerve trouble. She had discussions with Mr Jordan's new wife, Sylvia, with the idea that custody would be transferred to Mr Jordan, and Sylvia would look after John along with her own boy; but she could not make up her mind, and for a time John was put into a home. The husband put in a Minute for Custody, which was unopposed. There have been difficulties about the wife's access, and as she had now recovered her health she is applying to have John back. It seems that the difficulties about access arose from the idea that John was being upset by visiting his grandmother—and from what I saw of this sentimental, self-satisfied old lady in the witness-box I thought he might well have been. Sylvia was called as a witness for the husband, and seemed a sensible person, anxious to do the best for John. Gill, who appeared for the wife, suggested that I ought to see John. There was some discussion as to when he could be brought in to see me, but on hearing that he got out of school today at 3.30 and was expected to go straight home I said I should go out and see him. At 3.30 I set off for Oxgangs, with Mr and Mrs Jordan in the back of the car and the first Mrs Jordan sitting beside me. Sylvia's father and mother were in the house, having come to see to the children while she and Mr Jordan were at court. John I interviewed in a bedroom, by himself. He would not express any preference, and the interview confirmed my impression that the best course was to leave him where he was.

May 17th

Ten divorces. In one there had been a cross-action—today abandoned —in which there were odd averments on both sides. The wife averred that in the winter of 1958 he had induced her to drink some Polish vodka. She collapsed, and on gaining consciousness found herself in the boot of her husband's car. She again lost consciousness, and on coming to her senses found herself naked on the sands at Gullane. The husband on the other hand averred that he had discovered a man named Andy hiding in the house in a state of undress. He had found photographs in the house showing the wife in a state of undress engaging in unnatural activities with an alsatian dog. She was called upon to state the name and address of the photographer. In another of today's cases the parties had been married in a Sikh temple, and three years later went through a ceremony of marriage in a registry office. The husband left the pursuer a month later. I asked her why they had bothered to go through a ceremony of marriage if he was just going to leave her and if, as she said, their life together had been unhappy. She said he had wanted to regularise the position before he left.

May 20th

A proof: *Pullar v. National Coal Board*. The pursuer, a developer in Michael Colliery, slipped on a rail and fell, and a hutch coming behind pinned him between itself and a girder. He sustained a severe injury to his spine, leaving him paralysed from the waist down—in practically the same condition as Mrs McCallum. He has had to found on some far-fetched grounds of action: breaches of two sub-sections of the Mines and Quarries Act and a common-law case based on the management's negligence in not having a system of belling off the haulage when a man has to go in front of a hatch to open a ventilating door. As the pursuer in evidence disclaimed any intention of opening the door, this case may not help him much. Mackenzie-Stuart appeared for the pursuer, Malcolm Morison for the defenders. The pursuer was cross-examined at considerable length, and at about 12.45 was succeeded in the witness-box by the neurologist Phillip Harris. There were two agreed medical reports, and Mackenzie-Stuart accordingly said he could be very short with Harris, and as he had an appointment at 1.30 he hoped I would agree to take his evidence before lunch. Morison got up and intimated that of course he could not promise to be brief; I merely said he would no doubt do his best. He wanted to cross-examine on how the injuries had been inflicted, to try to show that the pursuer had been hutch-riding, but he did not get much out of Harris. Actually he was not particularly long, and we adjourned for lunch at 1.20 with Harris' evidence concluded. We had more witnesses in the afternoon, and started a new one about 3.30. Just after four, when Morison was cross-examining, he intimated that that would be a good point to stop. I replied that I had no objection to finishing the witness's evidence if Mr Morison wanted—to which Morison replied that he did not want to finish it today. I waved him on, ignoring his protests that he would take at least half an hour. In fact he took only twenty minutes, and I congratulated him on taking less time than he had indicated. Sibbald took me to task for sitting late, saying it caused some inconvenience to Parliament House staff. I did not take this very seriously.

May 21st

To Holyrood at 8.15—Nancy in a very attractive green dress that she had got in a boutique in Rose Street. The banquet was served with extraordinary expedition; I helped myself to small portions, but two of the courses were whisked away before I had time to finish. The Queen proposed the toast of the Moderator of the General Assembly—no one proposed 'The Queen'. I left the table with Sir Martin Charteris, to whom I recalled our jeep trip at Balmoral. He clearly remembered it, and remarked that Shackleton had been there—these Court people all have amazing memories. I asked Cobbald the significance of the big key embroidered on the tail of his evening coat. He said it dated from Saxon times, and signified his right as Lord Chamberlain to open any door of the Palace. Had a word with the young Lady in Waiting, Susan Hussey—not exactly pretty, but strikingly handsome and agreeable.

May 23rd

I had had a summons to attend a meeting of the Privy Council at 12.40—odd in being at Holyrood and in having a judge at it instead of a member of the Government. I had thought it might be some special occasion, with a number of judges present, but it turned out to be a perfectly ordinary meeting. We went straight through to lunch. I was set next the Duke of Edinburgh, but he directed his attention to the lady on his other side and during the first half of the lunch did not speak to me at all. This suited me, as I was fortunate in having Susan Hussey on my other side and found her a very delightful companion. Being still inexperienced in the art of carrying on a conversation and eating at the same time, I landed in the same trouble as at the banquet and got very little to eat—I was too busy conversing to attend to the food, and found everyone else finished and the next course coming when I had hardly started. But that was a minor consideration. After lunch I walked through with him to the drawing-room, where the Queen joined in our conversation. She had visited the Free Church Assembly this morning, and everyone seemed to think had had an exceptional success with them. She insisted that she had not gone all the way with them, but had maintained her own point of view. The Moderator in his reply had acknowledged that the Crown was exposed to pressure from many different directions—'a polite way', said the Duke, 'of referring to my playing polo on Sundays'. There had been some doubt about procedure, and the Queen gave an extremely funny imitation of someone—I think the Moderator —standing in front of a microphone giving his address and at the same time saying 'Sit down' to her out of the corner of his mouth. They seemed to be genuinely enjoying themselves, and when an equerry intervened to remind the Queen that she had an appointment somewhere at 2.45 she was quite reluctant to break off. They are having a free day tomorrow, and Budge—who as the Queen's parish minister at Crathie is in residence at Holyrood as chaplain—said he was doing his best to arrange that the family prayers laid on every morning at nine while the Assembly party is at Holyrood would be dispensed with. He was having difficulty about it, in view of a long-standing tradition that the Lord High Commissioner must attend for prayers every day at that hour.

May 28th

The First Division are hearing a reclaiming motion in *McVeigh v. National Coal Board*, and Guthrie remarked to me, quite seriously, that the trouble about reversing my decision was that the House of Lords would quite likely put it back again. Finished the draft of my judgment in Pullar's case. With some dubiety, I have found for the pursuer on his statutory case, and have taken the opportunity of observing that without guidance from authority I should have assessed solatium at a sum approximating to that awarded by the two juries in *McCallum v. Paterson*, but the jury trials as authoritatively interpreted made it necessary for me to restrict this to £9,000— adding that if this meant inadequate awards it was for Parliament to put the matter right. In fact I have made up for it by what I should have regarded as an inflated award for loss of future earnings. I doubt if my judgment is sound on the merits—it seems likely that the section of the Act on which the pursuer founds was not intended to impose any duty on employers—but the opportunity of saying something about the McCallum award seemed too good to miss.

May 29th

Among the motions in my Roll was one for decree in *Macgregor's Executrix v. Menzies Bradley McLean & Co.*, but this morning a Mr McLean turned up in my Court, claiming to be a partner in the defenders' firm and offering to lodge Defences. The Deputy Principal Clerk was excited about this, maintaining that I could not hear Mr McLean, who was neither a party nor a member of the Bar. I said that was all right—I was not really hearing him, only finding out from him what the position was. Gow for the pursuer agreed that the firm should be allowed to put in Defences, and I sent Mr McLean away to see that that was done within seven days. A letter from Mrs Margaret Jordan, in which she told me that she was very disappointed at my decision and gave me reasons for her disappointment at some length.

June 10th

Watt v. Watt. The pursuer gave evidence that the defender had often struck her in the course of arguments. She did not have much supporting evidence, and the defender at first denied ever having struck her. In the end however it appeared that what he meant was that he had not struck her in such a way as he thought would cause serious injury. 'There's no set rules', he said, 'against a blow that doesn't do any harm'.

June 12th

An appointment with the Watt children at 12.30. I found them friendly and forthcoming. It was obvious that they were perfectly happy where they were, and I thought them an exceptionally nice pair—bright, cheerful, intelligent, and apparently in the best of health, though they told me that Carol Ann was off school just now because she was ill. They both giggled when I asked what was wrong with her; they said 'No' when I asked if it was just a way of getting off school. After they had consulted together about whether they should tell me, Eileen said, 'She's got chicken-pox'.

June 19th

In one of today's proofs the adultery which the pursuer founded on had been committed by her husband in the North British Hotel in Edinburgh with Mrs Haggis.

July 9th

From today's *Scotsman*: 'American troops, wearing garlands of plastic flowers, began withdrawing from Vietnam today as military commanders were reported to be anticipating another high point in Vietcong activity . . . The Defence Minister, General Nguyen Pan Vy, told the Americans their departure was a symbol of victory'.

July 10th

A Minute by Mrs Irene Stewart for custody of her nine-year-old daughter Hazel. The Minuter had been divorced on the ground of adultery with her present husband, Mr Hills. When she left her first husband to go to live with Mr Hills, she made no arrangements for the three children, and the husband sent them to his parents at Alyth. Irene came to the house some time later, and took the youngest child, a boy, away with her to Dundee. The husband made no objection, and Irene said in evidence that he had agreed to it because she had told him, falsely, that he was not the boy's father. In 1967 Mr Stewart married again, and the two girls came to live with him and their stepmother, Fiona, in Alyth. A few months later he was killed in an accident. Some time last year, Carol, who is twelve, went back of her own volition to her grandmother, Mrs Isobel Stewart, and has lived with her ever since. Hazel has continued to be with Fiona. Last autumn Fiona married Mr Mackenzie, a man of twenty, ten years younger than herself. Irene was no less dishonest with me than she had been with her husband, and I did not like her at all. She had taken no interest in Hazel, and had not seen her for over three years. She said she saw Carol frequently, but this, as later evidence showed, was untrue. She had never spoken to Fiona, and it was difficult to see why she had chosen now to launch a court application for custody of Hazel, after ignoring her for so long. It seemed to have something to do with Fiona's re-marriage, though there may be some significance in the fact that when Mr Stewart was killed his workmates raised £300 which is held in trust for Hazel and Carol, and from which Fiona is able to make occasional drawings for Hazel's benefit. Mrs Isobel Stewart, called as a witness for Irene, said that Fiona's house in Alyth was spotlessly clean, 'a showpiece', but this she said by way of criticism, not commendation—she did not think it had the atmosphere of a real home, as Irene's house had in Dundee. Mrs Stewart seemed a kindly, amiable old person, but her views on the atmosphere of a real home were suspect—she had thought the same about

Irene's home with Mr Stewart right up to the time of the separation, although it was clear that in fact the marriage by then had completely broken down. Mrs Stewart said that Carol had left Fiona, according to herself, because Fiona went out to dances leaving her in the charge of a schoolgirl who had her boy friends in. Fiona had sat in court throughout the Minuter's evidence, relaxed and unflustered, smiling gently at some of the more poisonous barbs launched against her; and she was the same in the witness box. She had an answer for everything, always a good one, and she was completely candid, admitting the foibles that Cay put to her in cross-examination and making no attempt to offer excuses. She had certainly had a hectic life. She had an illegitimate child before she married Mr Stewart—accepted into the Stewart household, and with her all along. Then within a few months of Mr Stewart's death she had to seek Mrs Isobel Stewart's help in regard to a pregnancy resulting from relations with another man, and on medical advice had an abortion in hospital. The baby she has just had to Mr Mackenzie must have been conceived before she married him. But so far as I was concerned this did not matter in the slightest when set against the obvious fact that she was a warm, colourful, friendly personality to whom Hazel, as everyone agreed, was very much attached. I thought it to her credit too that although, as she said, she was hurt when Carol left her she did not make any fuss about it but let Carol go to her grandmother since that was what Carol wanted. I felt that she would have done the same with Hazel, and that when she spoke of Hazel's attachment to her I could believe her. Her young husband, who gave evidence, seemed a stable, responsible character; and provided that I had power to grant custody to someone who was no blood relation to Hazel I had no doubt that I should prefer Fiona to Irene. If I had had any doubts, they would have been dispelled by Hazel, whom I interviewed in my room. On my own suggestion I saw Carol along with her—I had noticed Carol sitting in court. This turned out to be a good idea: I had only to raise a topic and then let Hazel and Carol talk about it to one another, giving me a very adequate picture of the situation. Hazel, though good humoured about it, was determined that on no account would she leave Fiona and go to Irene, and if I told her she had to do that she would run away. Carol, though she disagreed with Hazel, assured me that Hazel knew her own mind and if she had made up her mind about anything it was no use trying to change her. Carol, when I asked why she had left Fiona, launched out on the orthodox case of the babysitter and Fiona's leaving them alone at nights. 'Oh, she didn't', said Hazel in a horrified tone; and Carol; with rather a red face agreed that 'Margaret' was always there and never had a boy friend in. We chatted about Alyth, and parted with a final friendly warning from Hazel that if I sent her to Irene she would not stay. I saw no reason for keeping them all in suspense, and having heard counsel intimated that Hazel would stay where she was, and that I should give my reasons in writing if anyone asked for them.

July 14th

To Merchiston for the prize-giving—prizes presented by Lord Balerno, whose address was so stupid that it could hardly be called tendentious. His suggestion that the powers that be were determined to drag private schools down to the moronic level on which were all the pupils in local authority schools was received in contemptuous silence even by his Merchistonian audience.

From this month's *National Geographic Magazine*: 'I suggested to Dr William A. Nierenberg, director of Scripps, that there seemed to be an upswelling of interest in the sea by average folk, not just students. "There is a tremendous interest", he agreed. "It is something that has developed rapidly in the past five years. People have gotten emotionally involved with oceans".'

July 15th

A case in the Motion Roll in which the pursuer sought implement of an agreement by the defenders to buy the pursuer's house for £9,500. The defences have been abandoned, and the pursuer got decree for £9,500. This has not been implemented, and today's motion was for an order freeing and relieving the pursuer from all obligations arising under the agreement. That no doubt is the effect in law of what has happened, but as there is nothing about it in the conclusions of the action it seemed to be incompetent. Weir pointed out on the pursuer's behalf that the motion had been intimated to the defenders and was unopposed, and I thought there might be something to be said for the view that if defenders chose to let a motion go unopposed it was not for me to query its competency. So I granted the motion, much to Mr Sibbald's dismay, as he was faced with the task of writing an intelligible interlocutor. When I saw what he had written, I appreciated his difficulty, and began to have doubts of the wisdom of granting incompetent motions. In today's proof the pursuer, sent to Ailsa Hospital to erect an aerial, sues his employers for sending him with a ladder that was not long enough for the job, and the Hospital Board for failure to inspect the ladder. Ross appeared for the employers and Russell for the Board; and when we rose for lunch in the middle of Russell's cross-examination of one of the witnesses Sibbald remarked to me, 'Mr Russell gets very exasperated with you'. 'I get very exasperated with him', I said, to which he replied, 'I can see that too'.

July 16th

Nancy had gone out with Mrs Hunt and the dogs; and shortly after five Mrs Hunt phoned to say that our dog had had a serious accident. Coming through the Hermitage, the dog had jumped into the burn and come right onto a broken bottle which perforated its chest. This had happened near the Blackford Glen end of the path, and Nancy had carried the dog, bleeding profusely, all the way to the mansion house, which is used as a hostel for Scouts. Mrs Hunt had run on ahead, and got the man who looks after the hostel to take out his car and take Nancy to the Dick Veterinary College. I phoned the Dick Vet. Some elderly-voiced person suggested I should come in and give my wife 'support'. From this I thought that the dog was probably dead, but as I was turning into Cluny Gardens a man in another car—the man from the Hermitage—waved me down and assured me that the dog was not dead, and that a vet had been telephoned for to attend at the College. I found Nancy there, with the dog stretched out on a little table, and the vet cutting away at its coat so as to get at the wound. Nancy's clothes were saturated with blood, and though the dog had its eyes open it was lying listlessly. Nancy had had to sit for twenty minutes, holding the bleeding dog, while the College vet was summoned from his home, where he had seemingly gone for tea. The vet said he would have to get a surgeon, and also get some blood put into the dog, if they had any. He told us—as was obvious—that the dog was in a bad way; it had been severely shocked and lost a great deal of blood. He said we could phone tomorrow morning and find out how it was; but we left without much hope of seeing the dog alive again.

July 17th

Phoned the Dick Vet. The dog, I was told, was alive and was being stitched up. If we came for it at four we could take it away.

Decree in ten divorces. In one of them, the pursuer was talking about an argument with her husband, as usual about nothing. He had beaten her up, and 'I woke up unconscious'.

With Nancy to the Dick Vet. at four. We sat for some time before we heard the pattering of feet, and the dog appeared with a young girl. It has a nasty jagged wound on its chest, but seemed remarkably well. Its appetite seemed all right—it was more than ready for a meal.

July 21st

From today's *Scotsman*: 'Edgartown (Massachusetts), Sunday.—A court hearing will be held here tomorrow to decide whether to act on a police recommendation that Senator Edward Kennedy be charged with leaving the scene of an accident. A passenger in Mr Kennedy's car was drowned late on Friday night when the car plunged off a narrow wooden bridge into a pond. Mr Dominic J Avena, police chief of this Martha's Vineyard community said: 'I really believe the accident was strictly accidental''.

August 5th

Oswestry. We went into the church after breakfast to have a look at it, and encountered the vicar, who said they had a good congregation but as they all insisted on sitting in the fringes of the church it always seemed small to visiting preachers. He had urged the worshippers to come to the front, but all that happened was that they moved a little way along the seat.

August 17th

Read out to Nancy some questions in a quiz in today's *Sunday Express* intended to discover how well you know your husband. One of the questions was: 'What quality in a woman charms him most?' Nancy's answer was 'Vivacity'—which I suppose may well be right.

September 7th

Craigmillar Park Church: Mr Mactaggart posed an interesting problem, Does God take a holiday?—and had only a dusty answer.

September 15th

'World in Action' tonight had an effective piece on Northern Ireland, done entirely in poverty-stricken Protestant areas of Belfast. The people, left to speak for themselves, presented a terrifying picture, particularly the women, singing their crazy Orange battle-songs and working themselves into a frenzy against Catholics.

September 25th
John Wheatley was on the television news, speaking about the report of his Commission on Local Government. The Commission has rec-ommended abolition of all Scottish town and county Councils and their replacement by seven regional and thirty seven district authori-ties: a disastrous example of the fallacy of supposing that anything on a big scale must be better than something small. One would have thought that he would have seen plenty of evidence of the absurdity of this conclusion within a ten-miles radius of Edinburgh—by comparing what has been done in housing and town planning, for instance, by places like Musselburgh and Dalkeith, with all the grandiose Edinburgh schemes that have never come to anything.

September 26th
Memorial service to George Montgomery in St Giles'. Dr Whitley's service was dignified but quite artificial—'thy servant George our brother' is a silly way of referring to George Montgomery.

From today's *Scotsman*: 'The Glasgow Procurator-Fiscal, Mr James Tudhope, yesterday described as 'the greatest contempt of court' the action of Mohammed Iqal Saddiqui (34), a Pakistani, who swallowed a razor blade shortly before he was due to stand trial'.

October 2nd
The Court of Session resumed today. We proceeded across to St Giles' for what was described in Clyde's circular to the judges as 'Dr Whitley's Service'. This was a correct designation: the service had all the signs of Whitley's macabre sense of humour. He sat blandly in the pulpit while the assistant read the 59th chapter of Isaiah, about truth failing and judgment being turned away, and justice standing afar off: lies, and false pleas, and adders' eggs. So that there should be no mistake about the meaning, he had it read in some modern version. Ian Robertson, who was sitting next to me, made a remark to me about 'murmuring judges'; and Clyde got the point all right—when we got back to Parliament House he said to me that Whitley always did that: selecting the most offensive passages he could find, and getting his stooge to read them. Clyde had thought of abandon-ing the service, but they had said that if he did Mrs Whitley would

write to the *Daily Express* about it.

Continued proof in *Napier v. John G. Stein & Co.*, adjourned in March so that the pursuer could make a case against the mine oversman. Mackenzie-Stuart put the oversman into the box as a witness for the defenders. Having given away most of his employers' case in cross-examination by McCluskey, he collapsed in the witness box, writhing and moaning. We adjourned for lunch, leaving the oversman in the box to recover.

On television tonight there was a long interview with Ian Smith. Despite a heavy cold, he gave his customarily solid, impressive performance. But the balance was redressed by Maurice Foley. His attempt to say that the sanctions policy might be succeeding was unconvincing, depending as it did on figures that showed a great decline in Rhodesia's exports—another indication of the absurdity of the current craze for measuring a country's prosperity by the amount of goods it sends to other people. But when he came to the wider issues he showed up effectively what a miserable structure of straw lay behind Smith's facade of morality and judgment.

October 3rd

Stirton v. Stirton, the case in which the First Division overturned my decision and allowed the husband to lodge Defences. After many months of delay and expense in adjusting a Record, the husband is now withdrawing the Defences he was allowed to lodge—vindicating my original decision pretty effectively.

October 5th

Craigmillar Park Church: Mr Mactaggart preached on John 2:28. Speaking in defence of young people, he made the point that all twelve disciples were probably under thirty.

October 10th

Hunter, sitting last month as Vacation Judge, ordained a man to appear today to answer a charge of breach of interdict, made by his wife. I had interdicted him from molesting her or calling at her house, and he turned up one night between ten and eleven under the influence of drink and caused some trouble. His explanation today was that he had gone to see about taking out his children. He has eight children, but I thought it unlikely that he would be taking them out at that time of night. I told him to behave himself in future, on pain of being sent to prison if he did not.

October 12th
Merchiston. Rev. J. Stein, a New College student from Linlithgow, gave the address, taking as his text Hebrews 2:18. It was a quaint little revivalist talk; and he made the point that in considering the devil today we should not think of him as a demon with a forked tail and trident but as more like a smiling TV personality.

October 13th
Finished reading Harold Nicolson's *Diaries and Letters 1939–1945*. I had had the idea that there were only two volumes of these diaries, and it was a pleasant surprise to find an intermediate volume; but it is not as good as the other two. Nicolson's conventional enthusiasms and disappointments as the fortunes of war fluctuate seem silly, as also his worry about why so gifted a man as he makes so little impression. With some help from his friends, he comes to the conclusion that he is not sufficiently formidable. This may not be far wrong. The surprising thing is how very seriously those in the know in Britain of 1940 took the possibility that the country would be overrun by the Germans; both Nicolson and his wife carried about with them capsules of poison to be used in the event of their falling into German hands.

October 15th
I incurred a rebuke from Cowie, whom I was trying to dissuade from cross-examining a witness about details of distances and measurements that the witness could not possibly have had any accurate knowledge of. 'If your Lordship', said Cowie, 'would leave me to conduct the case, we should get on faster'.

October 18th
On the road up from Allanton I suddenly came into thick fog. It was impossible to see any distance ahead. At the crossroads at the edge of the moor the figures of two girls loomed up through the fog, standing at the side of the road waving for a lift. The girls were making for Edinburgh, and I said they could get in if they liked but I could not guarantee to get them there. They were nurses in the Western General Hospital, and returning from holiday in Ireland had come off the boat

at Stranraer and been told that this was the best road to Edinburgh. No doubt it was, but whoever had given them a lift had apparently let them off in the fog, without any idea of where they were or much prospect of getting anywhere else. We had the road pretty much to ourselves, and having the advantage of knowing it well I was able to overtake the few cars that appeared in front at a point where I knew the road was straight. By Midcalder it was clearer, and I took my passengers right to the hospital, remarking that I hoped they would look after me well if I had to come into their hospital. One of them said 'We're in the maternity unit'.

October 19th
Braid Church. Mr Smith preached on Matthew 4:4. As always, it was a badly constructed sermon, muffing its points and rambling off into something else just when he was about to make a point; but what he always does is to throw out interesting ideas—he is always on the right tack, and he makes one think.

BBC 2 tonight had an orchestral concert recorded in New York by Leonard Bernstein and the New York Philharmonic Orchestra. Mr Bernstein talked interminably, making silly little jokes, but in the end there was a delightfully spirited rendering of the Allegro from one of the Brandenburg Concertos. Mr Bernstein played the piano part magnificently, and we both thought what a pity it was that when there was something he could do so well he had wasted so much time in talking—which he could not do at all.

October 20th
With Nancy to the Cameo: *Goodbye Columbus*. The affair between the two young people is beautifully done, in its naturalness and gaiety and fundamental innocence, but it seemed to me that the whole thing was spoiled by a cynical ending. Despite its final let down, I enjoyed it, though Nancy did not seem to think there was anything in it. The modern permissive film, with its nudity and love-making, does not appeal to her.

From today's *Scotsman* : 'Rotterdam, Sunday.—The United States aircraft carrier Yorktown and her escort vessel broke off an official visit here so suddenly that about 300 American sailors were believed to be still stranded in Holland today . . . In Washington, informed sources said the US Navy was conducting readiness tests'.

October 21st

A cruelty case in which the pursuer averred that her husband insisted on sleeping with a labrador bitch. Procedure Roll: a young junior, A. C. Hamilton, appeared for the defenders and made two points on relevancy. O'Brien, for the pursuer, was persuaded to put in an amendment. Hamilton moved for expenses; but having upbraided him for raising minor points of relevancy on a general plea instead of specifying beforehand what the defenders' point was and getting it cleared up I made an order for 'expenses in the cause'.

October 22nd

A debate in actions in which a Glasgow man and his daughter claimed damages for an illness they claimed to have suffered as a result of continual dampness in their house, the top-floor flat in a multi-storey block. The point of the case seemed to be that the defenders had failed to repair a leak in a 500-gallon water tank on the roof. Kenny Cameron appeared for the defenders, and argued their plea to relevancy in his usual muddled way. This put the pursuers' junior, Hamilton—the Duke's son, not the Hamilton that appeared before me yesterday—in some difficulty, as he had his argument written out, and it dealt not so much with the points Cameron had made as with those which he ought to have made and which Hamilton had anticipated. Hamilton's speech was brief and quite pleasant, but it was not until his senior, Robert Reid, came to speak that it was possible to find out what the pursuers' case was: that this was a tenancy where the landlord had a duty of maintenance, and the tank was part of the house. He had an averment to that effect, and although Cameron argued that it was ridiculous to say that a big water tank on top of a multi-storey tenement was part of one of the houses in the tenement he had to agree that the pursuers were entitled to a proof of their averment, and seemed quite satisfied to have the pursuer tied down to having to prove that the tank was part of the house.

October 24th

To the bank. I was paying my electricity bill, and in the change got my first 50-pence piece—the coin that is to replace the ten shilling note. I did not have it long, for as I was coming across the pedestrian crossing outside the bank I heard a rattle on the roadway and realised there must be a hole in the trouser pocket. Though I searched all over the crossing and the adjoining roadway, I did not find the ten shilling piece.

October 27th
'World in Action' on ITV tonight dealt with the training of America's special force, the Green Berets—the object apparently being to turn halfwits into lunatics.

November 9th
To Merchiston for the school service: the address given by Rev. Professor T. S. Torrance. He spoke so quietly that it was very difficult to hear what he said. His text was curiously appropriate: 'Why do ye not understand my speech? even because ye cannot hear my word'.

November 13th
I was seized upon by Stevenson to take the rest of this month's Glasgow circuit. Robertson is not to be available next week, and had a case starting tomorrow which he thought might not finish; so I agreed to go tomorrow.

November 14th
High Court: four young men charged with raping Mrs McLaughlan in a wood near Wishaw. Mrs McLaughlan, a 38-year-old woman with six children, living apart from her husband, had gone with some other women to the dancing at Salsburgh miners' club. She was not, she said, at all drunk; she only had six whiskies with lemonade, and a lager, and was enjoying herself, so that when the dancing ended at 10.30 she thought she would like to go on to Barrowland dance hall. She got a lift from a young man, a stranger to her, and set off in the car with the four accused, none of whom she had met before. This was between 10.30 and 11. The next that was known of her was hammering at the door of a house at 1.15 am, without shoes or coat and in a distraught state. She said she had been raped. Mrs McLaughlan was an excellent witness, who gave her evidence clearly and convincingly. All the accused had put in a defence of alibi, but no evidence was led for any of them. Instead I heard argument from the three defence counsel, to the effect that as there had been no corroboration I should direct the jury to acquit. I thought that this argument was probably sound. The only evidence, apart from Mrs McLaughlan's,

implicating the accused was that she had gone off with them in a car intending to go to Barrowland and had arrived instead at a wood near Wishaw; and there was an unexplained gap of about two hours during which anything might have happened. Even if the fact of their all setting off together was corroboration of her evidence that they were all with her in the wood, there was still no corroboration that they had all taken part in the rape. There was ample medical evidence to confirm that she had been raped, but the doctors could not of course say whether more than one man had been concerned, much less all four. It seemed to me however that it would be most unfortunate if I had to direct the jury—just after they had heard clear testimony from Mrs McLaughlan implicating all four accused—that they must find all four Not Guilty. So I refused to withdraw the case from the jury, saying that it was a matter for them to find whether they could draw a corroborative inference from the evidence that had been led; and then when I came to charge the jury I set about getting them to return a verdict of Not Proven. They found the case Not Proven against all four—a satisfactory result.

November 20th
'This Week' on ITV: an excellent programme about Cambodia. It gave a fascinating picture of these happy, laughing people, a delightful combination of simplicity and sophistication. It was distressing to think that the Vietnamese were probably much the same before the American jackboot descended upon them.

November 21st
Undefended divorce proofs. In one of the cases the pursuer had had eight children in nine years, seven boys and a girl. In 1964 she had actually produced two children, one in January and one in December. The cruelty alleged was that he kept going off and leaving her.

November 27th
A reparation proof. I got into an unfortunate altercation with Russell when I asked some questions which according to Russell had destroyed the effect of his re-examination. I said I thought I was entitled to ask some questions to clear the matter up, to which Russell replied that that was so if it was done fairly and not just in support of one side of the Bar. He undertook to put the point again without leading

the witness, and the witness, fortunately for me, gave exactly the same answer as he had given to me.

November 28th
At lunch time there was some talk about a paragraph in today's *Glasgow Herald* reporting that John Mackintosh was to ask some questions in Parliament critical of Court of Session judges, among them a query as to whether undue favouritism might not be shown to advocates who were sons of judges. Seeing Muir Russell in the hall after lunch, I remarked to him that we should get Mackintosh to come into my court and see what sort of treatment a judge's son got.

December 5th
Muir Russell had been in the Second Division yesterday supporting a big jury award, and said he had cited my opinion in *Pullar v. National Coal Board*. Grant had assured him that they had never intended that £8,000 should be the limit for solatium. Divorce proofs on Minutes and Answers out before Cameron: as my case had settled I agreed that one should be transferred to me. It appeared that as soon as this became known counsel got together and settled the matter in dispute.

December 9th
Jury trial: the action by the forestry worker who slipped in the snow on an Argyllshire mountainside and blames his foreman for sending him out to work in snowy weather without gritting the tracks through the forest. It was a case for a short, crisp cross-examination, but Muir Russell appeared for the defenders and the cross-examination was lengthy. Still, he can hardly help winning the case. Bennett appeared for the pursuer.

December 10th
Bennett had apparently decided that the case was hopeless, and addressed the jury very briefly, but that did not deter Russell from going on for half an hour. I charged the jury in favour of the defenders, and after a very short absence they found for the defenders by ten votes to two.

December 12th
A motion for interim aliment in an action of declarator of marriage.

The pursuer avers that the parties were married at Rajpura in the Punjab on Christmas Day, 1957, by a priestess according to Vedic rites, and that the defender, who is a school-teacher in Hamilton and has lost the use of both his legs, refuses to recognise her as his wife. I had been doubtful whether it was competent to grant interim aliment to a woman who was not admitted to be the defender's wife, and the pursuer's counsel was evidently not available. Her solicitor had sent in Vandore, who knew nothing about the case and had no one behind to advise him. I expressed disapproval of this, and got him to drop the motion; I asked him to tell those instructing him that if the motion was re-enrolled I should expect them to be present. 'The trouble is', said Sibbald, 'that by the time the motion comes up again you'll have forgotten about it and calmed down'. Proof in *Dodge v. Dodge*: the pursuer an architect whose wife had gone to live with a Hungarian. The parties were agreed that the three children should go on living with the wife, a student. The dispute was about an aliment claim for two pounds ten shillings for each child. The pursuer said in evidence that he was earning over £2,000 a year, and when Robertson was examining him about details of his expenditure I intervened to ask whether he was saying that he could not afford seven pounds ten shillings a week for the upkeep of his children. He assured me that he was not saying that, but he preferred to pay a smaller sum and make it up by giving the children clothes and suchlike. He seemed a nice, frank man, and I wondered who had advised him to waste his money contesting the case on such an absurd point. Vandore forgot to move for the wife's expenses, so presumably the Hungarian will have to pay them along with the husband's expenses for which he is liable as co-defender. The wife intends to marry the Hungarian, and as they are to get the Dodge children and Mr Dodge is to pay for them it seems fair enough that as things have turned out Mr Dodge will not have to pay expenses as well. Next I had to consider the question of the Hungarian's children, in a divorce action by his wife. The husband wanted to have the children for one weekend each month and a fortnight in the summer; but the wife refused to agree unless it could be arranged that they should not see Mrs Dodge. If the Hungarian and Mrs Dodge were going to be married, this did not seem practicable, but Hope said his client was adamant about it. He asked that that matter should be held over for decision later, but I said I was not going to have the case heard in instalments and if no agreement could be reached about access the divorce would have to be held over too. Faced with this, Mrs Borzsag after some discussion with Hope agreed that the children could meet Mrs Dodge after she and the Hungarian were married. It seemed absurd, as the children go to their father already on Saturdays and of course meet Mrs Dodge. I made an order for the children to go for a fortnight in the summer, for the day on Saturday, but no week-ends. In my final case, the wife had left the husband three months after marriage, and some months before the child was born, and had done her best to prevent the father from ever seeing the boy or even learning of his birth—though the father, a member of a highly respected Aberdeenshire family, seemed to have done everything possible to settle everything amicably. The wife had become a Roman Catholic at her marriage, but then reverted to Episcopalianism, and one of her objections to allowing the father access was that he took the child to Catholic services. One of the conditions agreed was that he would not take the boy to a Catholic church service, except when not doing so would mean that the boy would be left unattended.

December 13th

Finished reading *From the Dreadnought to Scapa Flow,* Vol.3, *Jutland and After*. It includes a series of fourteen sketch plans showing the progress of the battle, and these, with the eminently readable narrative, make the whole picture clear—in particular how far from clear it must have been to Jellicoe and indeed to Beatty. I enjoyed this volume tremendously.

December 15th

Nancy has been complaining, not without reason, about my getting fat.

December 16th

Hunter was recalling an occasion after an All-Sphere Club dinner when he and some others finished up in Alec Thomson's and put through what purported to be an urgent call to R. B. Miller, then Sheriff at Stornoway. Unfortunately he had no telephone in his house, and the message having been received at the Sheriff Courthouse a police van was despatched to bring the Sheriff post haste from his house. As this was in the middle of the night, it resulted in a police enquiry, and a detective-sergeant arrived at Thomson's house. Hunter said that when Miller realised what had happened he had 'behaved very decently' and called off the enquiries. Immediately afterwards, Hunter added, the sergeant was promoted to Detective-Inspector.

December 18th

Sibbald remarked on what a change it was to have a case properly argued—Sutherland is first-rate, and I hardly interrupted at all while Emslie and he were speaking.

December 24th

On television we had the famous old film comedy *Genevieve*: funny in its way, but no substance—not a film to hold one's attention.

1970

In the Court of Session, 1970 was a placid year. Sometimes it was frustrating to be so much divorced from what was going on in the world, but I continued to find it a pleasant, agreeable way of life. During the early months of the year public opinion appeared to be swinging back towards Labour, and when Mr Wilson went to the country in June the opinion polls predicted another Labour victory. But the opinion polls were wrong. In Scotland the Labour voters stood firm, but over most of the country, in every kind of constituency, there was a small but significant swing to the Conservatives: enough to give them a working majority. For Labour, a third successive victory would have had the appearance of endorsing pragmatic politics which fell far short of what should have been expected of a socialist Government; but while in the long run the result might be beneficial to Labour politics, in the short run the country was landed with a doctrinaire Government committed to the theory that the only way to achieve prosperity was by making the rich richer and the poor poorer. What turned the scale, I had no doubt, was the continual rise in prices of commodities to the housewife, and Mr Heath's undertaking that he would be able to end it 'at a stroke'. In the event, the new Government continued the process of putting the price of everything up, while leaving a free field for their profiteering friends. The only semblance of an economic policy consisted of an all-in fight against the trade unions and resistance to every wage claim, while vast increases were readily conceded on salaries of such as doctors and judges. The country was faced with unceasing warfare between the Government and individual sections of workers. The basic mistake they made—one never made by Churchill or Macmillan—was to suppose that nothing had changed since the thirties, and that in a contest between the working people and a Government of the plutocracy the Government was bound to win. It did not work out that way. In the contest with the dustmen they suffered total defeat; and it looked as if the same would happen with the power-station workers if the men's leaders had not taken fright at the extent of their own success. It was not, I thought, only Labour supporters who were beginning to feel that the last Government could not have been so bad after all. Nancy had often spoken of a possible visit to Paris, a city which neither of us had seen, and we spent five days there at Easter. I was rather taken with Paris, and was greatly impressed by the Metro.

January 6th

Fully eight inches of snow had fallen. The milk was frozen solid: big lumps of solid milk in the bottle.

January 7th

Took the car to the shops, where I got a nice little parcel of haddock roe for ninepence. The Mercedes goes quite well in snow. The milk had frozen in the bottles, and pushed the bottle tops upward: each top sitting on a little cylinder of solid milk projecting from the bottle.

January 8th

Eleven undefended divorce proofs. In the first case, the alleged cruelty arose out of the husband's coming home late at night. 'Did that upset you?' asked counsel. 'Yes', said the pursuer, 'it was the cold weather, and he always came to bed with cold feet and put them against my back'. A small, thickset Polish tailor from Dalry Road was divorcing his wife for cruelty. He was voluble and excitable, and spoke bad English in an almost unintelligible accent. 'I think you were married in Poland?' said counsel. 'No', said the pursuer; he had got his wife through an advertisement in the *News of the World*, and had never seen her till she arrived in this country. 'You got married in Scotland?' asked counsel, in some surprise—we had already looked at a large document certifying the marriage, from the Polish People's Republic at Cracow. 'No, no', said the pursuer; it was a 'long-distance' marriage and they were already married when she arrived in Scotland. She had no interest in him, and had married him so as to get a visa. She was a great big woman and sat in his shop making faces at customers. He gave a graphic illustration of the terrible faces she made, and then of her slumping to the floor when she had taken too many drugs. It seemed very doubtful whether they had ever been validly married, but there seemed no harm in granting divorce in case they might have been married.

January 13th

A defender who had been living with another man in England had been brought to speak to the welfare of a child of whom she was to have custody; but two enquiry agents who were to have come from England to speak about the defender's adultery had not arrived. The pursuer was able to give some evidence about this, and I suggested to Shiach that he might get enough from the defender to enable me to grant decree. The defender was quite frank, and the pursuer—a Hungarian who settled here in 1956—was an obviously honest witness; but both Shiach and I were doubtful about whether it was competent to grant a divorce when the parties were the only witnesses. We agreed to take a chance on it, and I granted decree. I found later in looking up the authorities that conflicting opinions had been expressed about this and the point had never been authoritatively decided; so it has been decided now.

January 14th
On television tonight an opportunity to see again the old Danny Kaye film, *Merry Andrew*, with the lovely Pier Angeli as one of the main ingredients in its charm.

January 20th
To the Lyceum: *The Boy Friend*, Sandy Wilson's reconstruction of a musical of the twenties. It was first-rate: gay, colourful and entertaining, with an excellent production by the Lyceum company. They did not guy it, but took the whole thing seriously, making it delightfully funny. It seemed a pity that Edinburgh children had been fobbed off over Christmas with rubbishy pantomimes when they might have had this marvellous show.

January 21st
Lunched at the Barbecue, finding John Henderson, the former Town Councillor beside me at the counter. He spoke in the highest terms of Sheriff K. W. B. Middleton, on the ground that he was always quick in the uptake and regularly took Henderson to task for being unnecessarily longwinded.

January 23rd
Finished reading *The Life of George Crabbe*, by his son, a quaint nineteenth-century biography which tells how George Crabbe left his job when a young apothecary in Suffolk and went off to London with only three pounds in his possession. He seems to have expected to be

supported by the Prime Minister and various members of the nobility, to whom he wrote; and both he and his biographer seem to think it most surprising that none of those distinguished people gave him any reply. But when he was in complete penury a letter to Mr Burke brought a favourable response. Burke not only took an interest in his writings but even took him into his own house, and from then he never looked back.

January 26th

Finished reading *Contempt of Court*, by Alfred Hinds, an account of how the author was sentenced by Goddard to twelve years imprisonment for robbery, and how he devoted most of these years—with the help of several ingenious escapes from custody, and personal appearances in various courts up to the House of Lords—in establishing his innocence, finally succeeding in getting a verdict from a jury in an action of slander against the police superintendent. Assuming that he was innocent of the robbery, as the jury found, one feels sometimes that his misfortunes arose from his own pigheadedness as much as from the stupidity of lawyers and the malice of judges; but there is no getting away from the fact that the stupid lawyers and the malicious judges had a lot to do with it, and that every conceivable obstacle was put in his way by the Establishment, only a piece of luck in the form of the police officer's silly article in a Sunday paper enabling him in the end to vindicate himself. Even then, when in defiance of advice he insisted on having the criminal charge referred back to the criminal courts, a feeble bench of appeal judges refused to admit that anything had gone wrong. I think we should have done a little bit better here but one cannot be at all certain that even in Scotland the same thing could not have happened. Hinds tells his story with amazing good humour, but it remains a shocking story, amply justifying his attitude of 'contempt of court' which gives its title to the book. Considered purely as a book, it is fascinating: interesting, clear, readable and tremendously exciting. The heroes of the story are Hinds and his counsel at the slander trial, Mr Comyn. Such is the compelling force of the book that I followed their fortunes with all the enthusiasm of a complete partisan, and even fore-knowledge of the result did not detract from the suspense of the narrative and the joy of the happy ending. Hinds' pen portraits of the many legal luminaries involved in his case, friendly or unfriendly, are equally delightful. It makes salutary reading for any lawyer, and enthralling reading for everyone.

1970

January 27th

On television tonight a Swedish psychologist who believed that women's capacity for any kind of job was the same as men's, and that women did not go in for certain kinds of jobs simply because people had been conditioned into thinking that those jobs were good only for men. I should have liked to ask her about housebreaking: a career that is open to anybody but attracts hardly any women, though so far as I can see it is left entirely to the free choice of individuals.

January 30th

In a memorandum that the Law Society have submitted to the Law Commission they criticise strongly the low level of damages in serious injury cases in Scotland, and refer at length to *McCallum v. Paterson*. They comment upon my opinion in *Steen v. Macnicoll*, utilising my observation that unaided by authority I should have been inclined· to regard the *solatium* aspect as more serious than loss of earning capacity. They reach the conclusion that civil jury trials should be abolished: a curious remedy to adopt for a situation in which the jury was right and the judges wrong.

February 5th

A proof: the pursuer a garrulous old Aberdonian who in answer to one question put in cross-examination replied that he did not know. 'If I were to tell you the truth about that, I would be telling a lie'.

March 5th

Finished reading *The Frog Prince*, by Stevie Smith, a peculiar collection of poems which have more to them then might at first appear. They are written in simple language, and the effect is sometimes grotesque to the point of absurdity, but sometimes very effective in a macabre, sardonic way. The poems are illustrated by the author's drawings, which like her poems are spare and stark. Some of them seem to have nothing to do with the accompanying poem; others, particularly her weird, hunted-looking animals, provide a wry commentary. None of it is in the least dull.

March 7th

Divorce proofs. An extraordinary mix-up as two enquiry agents proceeded to give evidence about what was evidently a different case. They had been concerned also in today's case, involving a pursuer

127

with the same surname, but not having got up their evidence before coming into court were quite helpless. This case had to be continued so that they might learn up the proper evidence from their reports.

In the afternoon we motored to Balerno and starting at what had been the railway goods depot walked back along the line of the railway, by the Water of Leith. The rails have been lifted and the track levelled, but the stony surface made rough going. A pretty walk.

March 8th

Braid Church: Mr Smith preached a thoughtful sermon on Micah 7:9. The painful woman who thought she should be allowed to give the children's address had unfortunately got her way, and was even more nauseating than I had anticipated.

March 10th

Craig v. Craig, a cruelty action in which the wife left her husband after thirty years of married life. In 1953 he had given her a push, and he admitted that in 1963 he slapped her on one occasion in the course of a quarrel after she came back from the January sale. She always got his wage packet, and on this occasion had bought clothes for the other members of the family but none for him, although as he said she knew he was going about like a tramp. The only other specific allegation was that in 1968 he had thrown butter about the house. This matter remained obscure; all that the pursuer said about it was that she came into the house when her husband was there, and saw the butter was on a piece of paper on the table, not on a plate. The pursuer's main complaint was that her husband would not speak to her. The pursuer was a voluble little woman, and I should not have been surprised if her husband had tired of her talking; but she maintained that for twelve months on end he had never said a word. He denied this, and said all the trouble was caused by his wife's relatives. This too I could well believe, for she adduced a succession of them as witnesses, and it was obvious from what they said that they must have spent a large part of their time interfering in the Craigs' matrimonial affairs. Apart from them, the only witness was the eldest son, now aged twenty-six, who was a most partisan witness and freely admitted that he disliked his father intensely. The reason, he said, was that his father had done things to him that no ordinary father would do. Pressed to elaborate, he gave an example that he professed to remember from the age of six, when his father had tried to enforce an instruction he had from his mother and refused to carry out. The case sets me rather a problem. The obvious thing to do is to throw it out as a lot of nonsense, but it seems a pity to keep the parties together when the marriage is obviously at an end and the only reason for the husband's defending it is the natural one that he does not want to be stigmatised as cruel when there is no justification for it.

March 11th

Cases in the Motion Roll included *Unigate Creameries v. Scottish Milk Marketing Board*, a complicated action about the price of milk sold by the Board to the pursuers for manufacture into butter. The price was to be determined by a formula whereby the price of butter was ascertained each month by taking the average gross realised price per hundredweight of the Board's bulk salted butter, with a proviso that when butter so sold was less than fifty per cent of the bulk butter manufactured the quantity sold should be notionally increased to reach fifty per cent, and the price for the extra amount should be deemed to be the price of the finest New Zealand salt butter in the London Provision Market. A substantial quantity of salt butter manufactured by the Board was upon manufacture placed in 56 lb and 112 lb containers, and the pursuers claim that this was 'bulk salted butter' as distinguished from butter in small packets, and that since the salt butter sold in such containers had been less than fifty per cent of the salt butter manufactured and placed in them the proviso should be applied. The proviso has never been applied, the Board not having accepted the pursuers' contention that the butter in these containers is the quantity of bulk salted butter manufactured by them.

March 12th

A motion in a defended divorce, to take the evidence of a woman doctor in Doncaster. The doctor's husband was ill, and she had to look after the joint practice. A motion had been enrolled to take her evidence on commission, but the defender's counsel would not agree to its being taken on interrogatories, so that counsel and solicitors on both sides would have to go down to Doncaster to take the evidence—at the public expense, as both parties were legally aided. I was told that they were agreed about that, but I demurred to it, and said I should allow the evidence to be taken on interrogatories in the usual way. It was pointed out that there was very little time to prepare cross interrogatories and have the evidence taken, but my answer to that was that they would have to get a move on.

Cameron was lunching with the Outer House judges, and the conversation turned on counsels' earnings as compared with judges' salaries. Cameron remarked that we should all be much better off if we went back to the Bar. I said that in that event we should have to work for our money, but agreed that the Bar was much more profitable—one could earn about twice as much as a judge. Robertson and Fraser protested that this was an exaggeration.

Finished the draft of my opinion in *Craig v Craig*. I have said that my sympathies were all with the defender, but have found the pursuer entitled to divorce on the ground that the excessive taciturnity with which he reacted to interference by the wife's relatives had seriously affected her health. He said himself in cross-examination that he had no use for 'small, crick-crack stupid talk'.

March 13th

We all took our seats in the First Division, so that Clyde could pay tribute to Guthrie, who died on Wednesday. He gave a surprisingly good little address, really about Guthrie. On initial acquaintance, he said, people were often annoyed at his meticulousness, until they found it was due to his genuine desire to get everything right. He always had his own point of view, and in the First Division had been a moderating influence on his more enthusiastic colleagues. But he was always ready to find a compromise if possible, and if they took a different view he never bore them any grudge. As Kissen remarked, it was an interesting sidelight on how the First Division worked.

Ten divorces: Nancy had been amused last night by a Scotticism in the averments in one of them—that the defender had hit the pursuer with a bag filled with messages. This was duly spoken to in evidence, the pursuer deponing that as a result all the messages had got lost.

In the typescript of my judgment in the Craig case, I cut out a rude remark about the pursuer's brother, whom I had described as a pompous witness. This I altered to say that he was a witness confident of his own rectitude. I altered my award of periodical allowance from ten shillings a week to a pound; I thought that ten shillings would look derisory, and as the defender is paying one pound ten shillings under an interim award he should be able to afford a pound. So far as the pursuer is concerned, any award only means that she will get that much less from social security.

March 14th
St Cuthbert's: Guthrie's funeral service. The service ending resound-
ingly with a fine rendering of St George's Edinburgh: 'Ye gates, lift
up your heads on high'.

March 20th
McTurk v. McTurk: a case in which the defender had agreed when
his wife divorced him to pay her one pound ten shillings per week as
aliment for each of the two children. Having since married again, he
was seeking to have this reduced to fifteen shillings. He had been
unemployed for some time, and the Social Security people had agreed
that it was impossible for him to keep up his payments under the
court order. While agreeing not to press him for payment, they had
advised him to come to Court to get the award reduced: a ridiculous
suggestion which meant that he had involved himself in paying instalments of ten shillings to Legal Aid for a year. The husband was a
well-meaning, ineffective sort of man. It was obvious that in starting
a second household he had taken on more than he could manage, but
after his evidence had proceeded for some time his counsel agreed
that the amount should be reduced to one pound for each child. The
husband agreed that he could manage that; I doubt very much if he
will.

March 23rd
An amusing programme on television, 'World in Action' having arranged for Mrs Mary Whitehouse to go to Copenhagen and see the
results of recent Danish legislation making pornography legal. She
walked round with an umbrella and handbag, interviewing leading
citizens—a woman minister, a member of the Government, a crimi-
nologist —all of whom made mincemeat of her muddled protest. She
put it to the minister that what was going on was sin, and was politely
but scornfully asked whether she thought sin should be dealt with by
legislation.

March 24th
A divorce proof. The parties had married when the pursuer was
seventeen and the defender eighteen, and the marriage lasted only for
a year. The defender had been kind and considerate when they were
courting, but after the marriage there had been constant bickering,
with neither prepared to make any concession. If she were reading in

bed and he switched the light off, she would switch it on again; then he would turn the electricity off at the main, and she would get up and turn it on. She thought she was stupid not to have retaliated more when he struck her, and complained bitterly that when at last she lifted a lamp to strike him with it she could not get the lamp to break. As it appeared from the cross-examination that the defender had found another girl and wanted to marry her, I thought I could not be expected to take the defence very seriously. Presumably the argument was really about a claim for periodical allowance of five pounds per week. Before the case was called in the afternoon, Sibbald told me that counsel wanted to see me in the Cedar Room. They wanted to know my intentions regarding the case, and I undertook if the defences were not proceeded with to award three pounds a week. On this basis the case proceeded as an undefended action, and I granted decree of divorce, with periodical allowance of three pounds. Going out into the hall I found Harry Wilson at the fireplace with O'Brien; he said they had just been talking about me, and saying what a good thing it was to be able to go to a judge privately and find out what his views were likely to be.

April 4th

Oatridge point-to-point. Lord Dalkeith, all dressed up to ride in the Open race, stopped me in the crowd to ask what I was doing there. He said he had not ridden for twenty years, and I was on no account to back him. I took this advice, which was good as far as it went, but the horse that I backed was not the winner either.

April 8th

Finished reading *The New Poly-Olbion*, by Andrew Young. It includes a delightful story of how when he was on holiday at North Berwick he fell in love with a beautiful English girl, and prayed that she might fall into deep water so that he might jump in and rescue her. One afternoon as he was going down to the shore he met her coming up, her dress dripping with water. His prayer had been answered, but he had not been there to deal with it.

April 20th

Paris. We walked down to the Jardin des Tuileries. A long line of lights lit up the facade of the Louvre, and Nancy remarked on the debt we all owed to whoever it was that arranged that Paris should not be defended, and so preserved all those wonderful buildings from destruction.

May 4th

Glasgow circuit. *H.M. Advocate v. McIntosh*: a series of charges, mainly of theft of motor cars, to which the accused was prepared to plead guilty. The last charge was to the effect that when two police-men tried to apprehend him he started up the car he was driving and drove off. One of the policemen fell off at the outset, but the other hung on to the door on the driver's side and was carried for 500 yards through Crawford, while according to him the car was being driven at fifty miles per hour and swerved from side to side in an effort to brush him off against a wall. The accused admitted assault on the policemen, but denied that the assault on Murray—the one who was carried through the village—was to the danger of life or that he was guilty of attempt to murder Murray, as the indictment alleged. I charged the jury impartially, and they found the accused guilty of assault to the danger of life, but not attempted murder. This I think was right, in spite of a silly decision by the First Division not long ago when they held a man could be guilty of attempt to murder when he had merely acted recklessly and was not trying to murder anyone. In the next case, *H.M. Advocate v. Ahern*, the accused was a youth of eighteen who had stabbed one of his workmates with a screwdriver. There had evidently been a fight between Ahern and a third youth; Clarkin, the youth who was stabbed, had separated them. Shortly afterwards Ahern had come up to the workplace and pushed the screwdriver through his chest. The blow had penetrated Clarkin's lung and gone through into the heart wall. He was removed to hos-pital, where his life was saved by an emergency operation. The defence appeared to be that there had been a fight between the two lads, in the course of which Clarkin had been stabbed accidentally. This Clarkin denied. The Crown evidence was still being led when we adjourned.

May 5th

Ahern gave evidence in support of his contention that Clarkin had fallen accidentally on the screwdriver which Ahern had happened to have in his hand when they were fighting; and it seemed to me that although quite probably Ahern had stabbed Clarkin deliberately in a fit of anger at the tormenting he got from Clarkin and the others it was most unlikely that he intended to do him a serious injury. The screwdriver was far from giving the appearance of a lethal instrument, and it looked as if it might just have been a threatening gesture which happened to go too far and had the bad luck to penetrate Clarkin's overalls at a vital spot. I charged the jury in favour of acquittal, and got more than I had bargained for: a unanimous verdict of Not Guilty. I had expected Not Proven. Ahern had an excellent background and record, and I had made up my mind that if he were convicted I should put him on probation. In *H.M. Advocate v Mackie*, the principal witness was a policeman named Keenan, who had been driving his car along Possil Road when he saw two men lying on the pavement, with two other men standing over them, striking them with a hatchet and a butcher's cleaver. The two victims had been too drunk to know who or what had hit them—they were two friends named Kilpatrick and Kirkpatrick. They had both been injured, one of them seriously. Keenan jumped out of his car and pushed his way in between the two assailants. One of them threw a lunge at him and knocked him down, and when he got up again the man who took a lunge at him had fled; the only man there was Mackie, whom Keenan apprehended and took into a nearby public house so that he could phone for assistance. He said he had no doubt that Mackie was one of the men who had been wielding the weapons and assaulting the two men. The defence was that Keenan had made a mistake; Mackie had come to Kilpatrick's assistance, they had all been in the Rock Bar farther up the street, and as Mackie and his wife were walking down Mrs Mackie looked back and drew her husband's attention to Kilpatrick lying on the ground, whereupon he had gone across to see what had happened to him and got himself arrested. All the witnesses agreed that Mrs Mackie protested that Keenan had got the wrong man. The only corroboration of Mackie's involvement in the assault was evidence by an inspector and another police officer that when Mackie was put in a police Landrover to be taken to the station he was cautioned and charged, and replied 'They insulted my wife, and that's why I struck them'. This seemed a bit fishy, particularly as when formally charged at the police station Mackie replied that he had nothing to say meantime. I was impressed by Mrs Mackie, who seemed a candid, genuine witness. Mackie denied that he had ever been charged while in the Landrover or had made the reply attributed to him. The evidence ended at 4.30, and having consulted the jury and found that they wanted to go on and finish the case I carried on, and charged the jury after hearing speeches. I covered the ground all right, and was satisfied that it was quite a good charge; but though I intended it to operate in favour of the accused they came back with a majority verdict of Guilty. I had no alternative but to impose a fairly heavy sentence, considering the type of weapon, and with some misgiving about whether we had got the right man sentenced Mackie to imprisonment for 28 months; but the more I pondered the Mackie verdict the more I thought that the jury had been wrong. How could both the assaulted men have insulted Mackie's wife? How did the supposed answer fit in with Keenan's evidence that two men had been committing the assault? Mackie and his wife had admittedly been alone together in the bar. Where did he get hold of the second man? Where did the peculiar weapons come from? Had Mackie, who had no record of violence, gone out with a hatchet concealed in his clothing in case somebody might insult his wife? None of these points was put to the jury by defence counsel, but I ought of course to have put them myself if I had thought about them at the time.

May 6th
Half an hour's delay before starting, because three twelve-year-old boys who were witnesses in today's case were late in turning up. I lectured each of them as he came into the box, so that the first one at least was in a subdued state of mind and when I spoke to him sharply in the course of his evidence was readily persuaded to withdraw his 'don't know' and give an account of what had happened. The accused was a slight, fair-haired boy of sixteen who looked very much younger: a forlorn figure sitting alone in the middle of the dock with a big policeman on either side. The charge was culpable homicide. The victim, an old woman of eighty, had been going down to Copland Road one Sunday morning on her way to 'a wee mission round the corner', as her daughter put it, when O'Brien ran up behind her and pulled her handbag from under her arm. In doing so, he knocked her over, and she fractured her femur and upper arm. She died in hospital a month later. The question was whether the injuries sustained in the fall had caused her death. Professor Forbes and Dr Rintoul maintained that they had; Dr Weir and Dr Imrie said they had not, it being apparent from the post-mortem that she had died of a coronary thrombosis, having successfully survived the shock and other effects of the fractures and subsequent operative treatment. Stewart pressed the culpable-homicide charge with great pertinacity, though at best

for him it seemed that there must be reasonable doubt about the cause of death. I thought it an odd situation to have this little boy—a sneak-thief who would normally have been tried in the Summary Sheriff Court—sitting in the dock in the High Court while counsel and pathologists argued about heart tissues and coronary infarctions and microscopic examinations. Gow defended, contrasting in his usual casual way with Stewart's intensity. There was another charge of breaking into a shop, but the evidence about this was merely that the shop had been broken into, and O'Brien's birth certificate had been found lying inside the broken plate-glass window. The theory was that he had been carrying his birth certificate in order to be able to gain admission to cinemas showing 'X' films, and had lost it while breaking into the shop. It seemed something of a novelty that a housebreaker should leave his birth certificate at the scene of the crime.

May 7th

I had a good audience when I came to charge the jury, all the prospective jurors to be balloted for in the next case having arrived, and quite enjoyed myself. It was obvious that the boy should be convicted of assault and robbery, and that the Crown had not proved culpable homicide, and the jury gave effect to this unanimously. I ordered the boy to be detained for three weeks until a Borstal report could be obtained; and granted Gow's application to have the case certified as one of special complexity justifying additional fees—ironical to think that all the time and ingenuity expended in examining the medical questions in the case arose out of the theft of a handbag which had nothing in it but four shillings and two pairs of spectacles. While the jury were out, I had empanelled another jury and started on the next case, *H.M. Advocate v. Gilmour:* the accused a youth of seventeen who was charged with assault to the danger of life on another youth, McQuade. McQuade was coming down the street after seeing his girl friend home when he was waylaid by two youths, McKenna and Smith. Apparently he has some reputation as a boxer, and laid them both out. McKenna was joined by Gilmour, who came on McQuade from behind. He turned round and saw a knife in Gilmour's hands, with which he stabbed him. I was interested to hear from McKenna and Smith that as soon as they saw blood on McQuade and realised that a knife had been used they were frightened, and ran off and phoned the police. This was rather encouraging—it seemed to indicate that Glasgow youths were at last beginning to realise that the use of weapons would be liable to get them into serious trouble. My charge was entirely extempore, and in some places rather a muddle; but it was adequate to get a majority verdict of Guilty. While the jury were out, we empanelled a jury for the next case, so as to make it unnecessary for those who had not been chosen to come back tomorrow; and when I got back to the robing room I was about to change and go home, forgetting until I was reminded of it that I still had to hear the result of the Gilmour case. I sentenced Gilmour to five years. I travelled back with Stewart and John Smith, who had been defending in today's case. Stewart assured me that we had got the right man in the Mackie case. Mrs Mackie, he said, had made a statement to the police to the effect that she had been insulted in the public house by one of the two victims of the assault.

May 12th

H.M. Advocate v McNeilage: the accused charged with attempted murder of his uncle, Frank Keely, by driving a car forwards and backwards over his body. Keely was a pale, grey, middle-aged man, who gave his evidence very slowly in a low monotone. He agreed that he said in hospital that he had thought McNeilage was trying to murder him, but it appeared from the medical evidence that he was suffering from alcoholic depression. When asked by Gow, who was defending, whether he thought at one time that all his relatives were against him, he replied that he thought the whole world was against him. In hospital he had been violent towards doctors and nurses, thinking they were using him to experiment on. He now thought that what happened on Hogmanay night was an accident, and that was completely borne out by the evidence of all the witnesses. The car had backed, they said, into another car parked in the street and then had driven forward. Keely had fallen underneath. The girls in the car had become hysterical and shouted to the driver to go back, whereupon he panicked and reversed the car over the top of Keely. The witnesses agreed that there was no question of drink so far as the driver was concerned. Nobody suggested there was any hostility between McNeilage and Keely. When five or six witnesses had been led, I asked the Advocate-Depute if he intended to lead any evidence bearing on the charge, which was attempted murder. He said he hoped so, but two witnesses later said he could not proceed with the charge. I directed the jury to return a verdict of Not Guilty, and

caught the 4.50 train to Edinburgh. After an initial feeling of tiredness on the first day, I thoroughly enjoyed my first Glasgow circuit.

May 15th
An action of divorce by a Glasgow master joiner against his Italian
wife. The wife prefers Milan to Glasgow, and at an early stage in the
separation the husband took up with another woman and had a son
by her. Some amusing passages in the wife's letters. 'You have left
me in the most complete abandon, but you have enjoyed your life
with another woman and have with her a boy adultery'. One letter
starts: 'Jim, you are the biggest liar I have never known in all my
life'. The letters are full of complaints about not getting her 'aliments':
'Is your duty to keep first of everybody me'. 'At last, don't forget that
you are now far away from me only 3 hours if I need'.

June 8th
To Ampherlaw—probably for the last time, for Ampherlaw has been
sold on Barney's retiral. Barney gave me an entertaining account of
surgeons and teachers in the medical profession when he was a student. He worked for John Fraser, who was a first-class teacher but
had shortcomings as a surgeon, particularly in diagnosis. His great
regard was for Sir David Wilkie, who he said had all the attributes of
a great surgeon: above all, a proper sense of orientation, so that
whatever the position might be he knew exactly what he was doing.
Henry Wade, with his flamboyant manner, had been treated by the
students as rather a joke, but when Barney as a post-graduate came
back to hear him he found that Wade knew what he was talking
about, compared to people like John Fraser who sounded all right but
might be on the wrong tack. As for Walter Mercer, he thought the
only safe thing to do was to put on roller skates and get as far from
him as possible. He admired Derek Dunlop, who not only had style
but great knowledge and ability as well. He agreed with me that
Crew also had been quite outstanding. Chalmers Watson had been a
crank, but like all cranks he occasionally got on to a good thing—as
in his prescription of cabbage water, which was now widely recognised as sound.

June 11th
'This Week' on ITV: an interview with Mr Wilson by Robert Kee.
Mr Kee was unusually aggressive, and though Mr Wilson kept his

temper it was an unpleasant argy-bargy which I thought would not do him any good. It was probably just as well that Raquel Welch was on at the same time on the other channel.

June 19th
Heath in, with an overall majority of 35: a bitter disappointment for Wilson.

June 21st
From today's *Observer*: 'Richard Nixon has been elected "Churchman of the Year" by the Religious Heritage of America Inc.'

July 2nd
In one of today's divorces, the pursuer's middle name was Immaculata. In answer to a question I put to her, she explained that she had been given the name because she was born on the same day as the Virgin Mary.

'This Week' on television was devoted to funerals of men killed in rioting in Northern Ireland. Their relatives expatiated on what fine, peaceable, friendly fellows they were, who never went down the street without giving away all their money to children for sweets—while meanwhile hard-faced men marched past in the picture, following coffins draped with Orange emblems and the Red Hand of Ulster.

July 9th
Fifteen undefended divorces. When I rose at lunch time, a red-haired, middle-aged woman who had been sitting in court during the forenoon, with some other people, stood up and said, 'I think your Lordship is a darling', in a strong American accent. She added that she was an American, and judges in America were all grim, solemn people, nothing like as nice as I had been. Everybody outside, she said, had told her that Lord Stott's court was the one to go to. I had actually been more than usually lenient this morning, granting decree in one of Ian Ritchie's cases although there had been no proper identification of the defender, and in another case, a desertion one, where the action had been raised before the expiry of the triennium.

July 16th
Commonwealth Games opening ceremony on television from the new Meadowbank stadium, with teams of all the Commonwealth countries

marching past the Duke of Edinburgh: an attractive, friendly spectacle.

July 17th

With Richard to Meadowbank. Admission charges from tomorrow onwards are high: James Leechman, who is taking some friends tomorrow, had paid two pounds ten shillings each for their seats. So I was pleasantly surprised to find that we could get in for two shillings and sixpence each, good seats, right in the front. A colourful spectacle, with competitors of every shade in their bright attire.

July 18th

At Grantshouse petrol was six shillings and eightpence per gallon. I did not stop, and was able to get as far as a garage on the hill down from Tranent before having to fill up. This garage, I remembered, gave a discount of threepence per gallon off the recommended price. These cut-price filling stations are now sufficiently numerous to make it worthwhile to look for them—not that it saves a great deal of money, but I feel that anyone who keeps prices down ought to be encouraged.

July 25th

Kitty Anderson unexpectedly appeared with her poodle and a friend, on their way home to Perth. The cat was in no way perturbed, and played on the carpet with the poodle's lead, without seeming to realise that there was a dog on the other end.

July 27th

Finished reading *Dowding and the Battle of Britain*, by Robert Wright, which tells an absorbingly interesting and quite horrifying story. The author, Dowding's personal assistant during the Battle of Britain, is strongly partisan, but there seems no doubt that the commander whose skilful, untiring organisation and direction of the defence war in the air prevented a German victory was victimised immediately after. It is evident that once Dowding had stood up to Churchill on the question of sending his fighters to France, and alone and single-handed had insisted on keeping enough of them at home, Churchill had no further use for him except to win the battle, and when the battle was won Dowding was expendable. Even at its height he was being pestered about his retiral date; and although Churchill and the Air Ministry may have made a genuine mistake about fighter tactics it is difficult to see any excuse for Churchill's falsification of history in his post-war account. It is some consolation that despite Dowding's own reticence the truth gradually came out, but it remains an outstanding example of official folly and dishonesty.

'Panorama' on tonight's television included a bit about Mrs Margaret Thatcher, the new Minister of Education whose first action in office was to withdraw the Labour Government's circular aiming at plans for comprehensive schools. She is a woman of considerable ability, and put up a strong argument in support of her policy; but it was all pretty synthetic—one felt that what she was concerned with was not children's education but being a Tory Minister.

An advertisement in this week's *World's Fair*: 'Wanted, midget to work in travelling show. Must be small'.

July 29th

James Leechman joined me for an excursion to Cumberland. From Carnforth the line was new to me to Barrow. We had half an hour at Ravenglass before the 2.40 train up the narrow-gauge railway, made up entirely of open carriages; and we were fortunate in having the company of a lively young lady of ten or eleven named Pippa and her elder sister. We had an excellent run up the valley in the toy train— able to pull out fronds of bracken from the line side as the train went along. The heather was out, and at one point there was a lovely scent of bog myrtle. At Dalegarth, the terminus, we walked round the back of the station, where a sparkling beck was coming down through the trees; and on returning to the train found Pippa waving to us to rejoin her. The two-unit diesel train to Carlisle was crowded, but we gradually worked our way back as passengers got out and ended in the back seat with an excellent view of the line. Beyond Seascale it was new to me—a fine view along the line of coast to St Bees Head. Workington must rival any of the Lancashire or Yorkshire towns for the title of the ugliest relic of the industrial revolution; the clear, bright river Derwent seemed out of place in such surroundings. At Carlisle we had a nice dinner in the Crown & Mitre Hotel; and we were in Edinburgh before 11.30.

August 3rd

Bought a sports jacket at Burtons: rather a nice shop. We were served by a pleasant youth with long hair, and there was a pretty, smiling girl in the cash desk. The shop had an old-fashioned relaxed welcoming atmosphere, unusual in these days.

On Blackford Hill we found one or two wild raspberries—surprisingly sweet.

An advertisement in this week's *World's Fair*: 'Wanted Male Midget No Experience Necessary'.

August 8th

Llandudno. We set off in the car for Portmadoc, with the intention of going down the Cambrian coast railway to Barmouth. When Portmadoc came in sight, we saw an enormous queue of cars stretching across the causeway ahead. So I turned round in our tracks, and made for the next station back along the line: Penrhyndeudraeth. In the train we got seats beside a friendly young couple going back with their baby to Wolverhampton after a holiday in a caravan site at Abersoch. The young man was indignant about the poor bus services in North Wales, and the high fares. It was only about five miles, he said, from Abersoch to Pwllheli, but the fare was two shillings and eightpence; it had cost him eight shillings that morning for four of them to get to the station. We had considered Barmouth for our holiday as an alternative to Llandudno, but after one and a half hours at Barmouth were thankful we had chosen Llandudno. Barmouth is a second-rate, down-at-heel seaside resort. Apart from its situation between mountains and sea, there was nothing attractive about it: a long stretch of firm sand, but every hundred yards or so along it a red flag with a warning notice not to 'enter the water at this end of the beach'. These flags and notices actually extended for the whole length of the beach, though apart from the bit at the mouth of the Mawddach estuary it seemed a hard, safe beach. We were able to appreciate what a fine situation Barmouth has, but the town has nothing. On to Machynlleth: a most attractive run—Machynlleth a plain little town, but a nice one, with green country close to the main street on either side. From Portmadoc the run through the mountains—a lovely gorge, a tumbling rocky river, two lakes—was one of the finest roads I have ever travelled. We were back at the hotel at 8.40, and found a nice supper—cold tongue and chicken, with raspberries to follow—all laid out on our table.

August 13th

The valley of the Gwyrfai: a cottage with a notice on the gate to the effect that it was private property but passers-by were welcome to walk through and view the falls: an attractive cascade in a setting of shrubs and trees. There was a collecting box for the Gardens scheme, and a notice telling us there was another garden across the road and inviting us to visit it. This was a wild garden with paths winding up a steep hillside behind the cottage, and a notice at the foot inviting visitors to borrow a walking-stick from the stand at the door. On to Portmadoc and the Festiniog narrow-gauge railway. The carriages are enclosed, and the effect was simply of being in an overcrowded train. The toy train looks quaint from the outside, but inside there was nothing particularly quaint about it except that accommodation was cramped. The doors were all locked before we left. Few of the passengers seemed to have any interest in the railway; their trip on it was merely something to be done. They shut the windows; and the fun and excitement which characterised the Eskdale railway was absent on the Festiniog.

August 16th
To church, where an elderly clergyman preached on Isaiah 40:31. He was ordained, we were told, not long ago, and apart from his clerical status is manager of Boots' Llandudno branch. Perhaps nothing much in his sermon, but it was intelligent and to the point, and preached in a quiet, effective manner.

August 17th
We motored to Llandudno Junction, and took the train to Bangor. In Conway we passed through the derelict railway station—why Conway station should be closed seems a mystery, when it is such a busy place and the station is right in the town. We soon reached the sea, and kept close to it all the way to Bangor. The line from here across the Menai Bridge is closed at present, on account of an escapade by two youngsters who managed to set the bridge on fire. The cathedral, in which a fine organ was playing, was about the only good thing about Bangor.

August 19th
In spite of a half-bottle of wine every night, as well as a meal for the dog, the hotel bill was only £147.16.4: by no means excessive for a comfortable, well-run hotel, where the food was excellent and plentiful.

August 20th
Talking about Elizabeth's 21st birthday, we looked up my diary to

see how I had marked my own, in 1930. I knew that there had not
been any celebration, but I had expected a note to the effect that I
was 21 that day. We were amused to find that this was not even
mentioned; I had finished reading Catullus, and taken my father to
the induction of the minister at West Calder—there was no record of
my having reached the age of 21.

August 25th

The Caley Picture House: *Viva Max*, Peter Ustinov's latest comedy.
There is something very likeable and heartening about most of
Ustinov's films, and this was no exception: the recapture of the Alamo
by a sentimental general and his awkward squad of unarmed, or at
any rate unammunitioned, followers.

August 26th

Oban: the Argyllshire Gathering. Left about four and made for the
station, stopping at a cafe where I had a glass of milk and one small
cake for the rather exorbitant charge of one shilling and elevenpence.
Loch Lomond was looking exceptionally fine today, completely still
with not a ripple on the water. As we came up the Clyde from
Dumbarton, I noticed that the new high-level bridge was almost
complete, only the centre span still absent.

August 31st

Finished reading *Memoirs of a Mendicant Professor*, by D. J. Enright,
short episodes in the author's university life in Japan and at Bangkok
and Singapore, interestingly and amusingly narrated. He seems to
realise that he spends too much of his time complaining about what
everybody else says or does, and in spite of his engaging tolerance
one has the feeling that he has a remarkable capacity for bringing
trouble on his own head. If there is some tactless way of doing a
thing, Professor Enright, one may be sure, will choose that way to do it.

September 6th

With Elizabeth to Charlotte Baptist Chapel, where a crowded congregation gathered to hear their pastor, our friend Mr Prime. He
gave a dissertation on Joshua 22, the subject of which, he said, was
disunity. He went on for quite a long time: interesting and lively, but
extremely odd. Taking it all as literal truth, he drew some quite
sensible lessons from it, but completely ignored the sinister implica-

tions of the Israelites' invasion of Palestine. Then in the middle of
quite a reasonable exposition he would draw attention to the fact that
our enemy was Satan, who was watching to see how he could trip us
up; but on the occasion recorded in Joshua 22 Satan had overreached
himself—his plan to divide Israel had gone astray, and resulted in a
greater degree of unity than before.

September 11th
A Russian film of *Hamlet* on television. It moved slowly, but there
was plenty of rapid motion when rapid motion was required. The
striking thing about it was that it made the plot completely intelligible: there could be no misunderstanding whatever about what Hamlet
was doing or thinking.

September 13th
Craigmillar Park Church. Mr Mactaggart preached. It was different
from last Sunday: the Palestine and Jordan of today instead of the
Promised Land of Joshua, the world and all its problems and how we
should look at them. I felt that he almost went too far in his determination to make his respectable Southside congregation see the other
side of the picture, but it was a thoughtful, courageous, questing
sermon.

September 15th
Richard and I motored to Gullane and had a round of golf. We had
the dog with us, and though it was a nuisance on the tees, having to
be held to prevent it from running after the ball when we drove, it
fully made up for it by its work through the green, quickly finding
Richard's ball on the three occasions when he drove into the rough.
Bought an evening paper: shocked to find that yesterday the price
had gone up another penny, to sevenpence.

September 16th
Finished reading *The Destruction of Dresden*, a grim factual account of
the massacre of 14th February 1945, when in three successive raids in
24 hours the city of Dresden was reduced to ashes, with a death-roll
greater than that at Hiroshima—a significant commentary on the
futility of 'Ban-the-Bomb' propaganda. The first night attack set up
a fire storm which engulfed everyone within reach. Three hours
later, the second attack destroyed fire brigades and others who were

attempting to deal with the results of the first. Then, on the following day, 450 American Flying Fortresses completed the holocaust that British Lancasters had begun; and finally American fighters, flying low over the undefended city, machine-gunned the groups of homeless survivors. The whole thing seems to have come about more or less by accident: a casual Minute by Churchill suggesting that there might be cities in East Germany that could be attacked led to the Air Ministry's instruction for a raid on Dresden, and events then moved on inexorably without its being anyone's business to enquire whether it was really necessary to level such an attack on a fine old city, which had no defences and was of no military or industrial significance.

September 18th
Gullane: a two-ball foursome. We took the dog, and though it was not required often it found the ball at once on the two occasions on which its services were called for.

September 20th
Isobel telling of her experiences with an old lady from Carnoustie who had been spending a few days with her and was liable to get up at three o'clock in the morning and put out one of Isobel's milk bottles, with a note for the milkman to say she was back home again.

September 22nd
A murder trial: *H.M. Advocate v. Forbes*. A succession of young men, members of a bus drivers' darts team, told how they went to the Duke's Head public house to play in a match. Fighting broke out, and the place became a complete shambles. Fighting spread to the street, where two men named Robert Gilroy and John Dick had a fight. Dick was left on the ground, and Gilroy was making his way back into the public house when Forbes, whom he did not know, came out and stabbed him. He shouted to his brother Charles that he had been stabbed. Charles ran out, and thinking that Dick had been the assailant crossed the street to where Dick was lying and kicked him—whereupon the accused came up behind him and stabbed him repeatedly in the chest. Charles Gilroy was dead before the ambulance arrived. Forbes went back into the public house, and was sitting quietly drinking a glass of beer when the police arrived. Five witnesses however identified him as the man who had stabbed the Gilroys,

and a girl who had been with him in the pub gave evidence that when the police made them sit down on a bench he told the other girl who was with them, Alice, that he had a chiv. Alice said, 'Give it to me', and he passed it to her, but when they got up the police found the bloodstained knife down the back of the seat. There were a lot of bloodstains on Forbes' clothes, but as the evidence was that blood was all over the public house that was of no great significance. Forbes said he was a stranger in that public house. The Duke's Head, he said, though well run was always full of criminals; he insisted that all the Crown witnesses were thugs and liars. This was unfortunate for his case, Daiches in cross-examination having been at pains to assure the witnesses that their good faith was not in question, only the accuracy of their identification. The jury were out for only ten minutes, and unanimously found Forbes guilty. Brand, who was conducting the case for the Crown, drew my attention to a schedule of convictions which showed that Forbes had been convicted of murder in 1958. He was sentenced to death but reprieved, and had been released on licence eight weeks before this second murder. I pointed out that for a man to commit a second murder was almost unique in Scotland. Brand said he had no statistics, but in the past it had not been possible for a man to commit more than one murder.

September 23rd
Yesterday's case had given rise to leaders in the *Glasgow Herald* and the *Express*. The *Herald* remarks that 'Yesterday's was one of the shortest murder trials on record in Edinburgh. The prosecution evidence occupied two hours. Forbes, the only witness for the defence, was in the witness-box for 30 minutes, and the closing speeches and Judge's charge lasted for a total of 53 minutes'.

September 25th
Finished reading *Words and Images*, by E. L. Mascall, the kind of book I enjoy: a closely reasoned argument of precise distinctions and meticulous care in the use of words and definitions, employed—unusually—in defence of orthodox theology. The author does not demonstrate that God exists—he does not attempt it. What he is concerned to do is to show that that is a possible topic for reasonable discussion, and his primary aim is to refute a proposition of Professor Ayer's: that a statement cannot be meaningful unless there is a possibility of verifying it by sense-experience. It seemed to me that he demolished

Professor Ayer quite effectively; at all events, he marshals his arguments with wit, good humour, and a great deal of dialectical skill.

October 1st
Parliament House: the opening of the winter session. I had forgotten about the service in St Giles', no circular having been sent round to the judges about it this year—perhaps Clyde thought that if the object was to pray for damnation of the judges, as Whitley seems to suppose, it would be better for the judges to stay away. I arrived in plenty of time to attend, and except for a somewhat tendencious opening sentence this year's order of service was reasonably friendly.

On television an interesting discussion on economics and industrial politics between Crosland and Crossman: a good idea to have two people from the same Party and so get away from the silly argy-bargy about party political points that usually takes place when there is a political discussion. The two participants chatted away in a friendly, convincing way, obviously trying to get at the root of the problem.

October 2nd
A divorce action from Aberdeen. The husband avers that his wife, the defender, is a shrimp packer, to which the answer is: 'Admitted that the defender is a prawn pickler'. In *Chamberlain v. Chamberlain*, the defender worked in Glasgow Corporation Transport. In 1968 he began to stay out at nights, having become attached to another Transport Department employee. He went on holiday with her to Rimini, where two Scottish enquiry agents sent by the pursuer descended upon the couple in their hotel in the middle of the night. It did not seem to have been a particularly exciting marriage, though the pursuer averred that she had given the defender 'encouragement'—by presenting for sixteen years the prizes at the Corporation Bus Garage's annual social. The wife was a somewhat prim, elderly lady. She had never asked her husband why he was staying out overnight, and when asked why replied that she could not possibly say it in open court—could she be allowed to write it down? We all waited eagerly to see the answer, but all she wrote was: 'When I had asked him questions before on other matters, he told me to mind my own bloody business'.

October 3rd
A desertion case: the pursuer a delightful old fellow of 76. He had

married thirty years ago, and a month later his wife left him 'to go to the toilet' and never came back.

October 6th

A jury trial, *Fraser v. William Beardmore & Co*: the pursuer a nice old fellow, a lorry driver who when stepping round from his cabin to the platform of the lorry slipped on some oil on the coping of the platform. There was no reason why he should not have wiped any oil off his lorry himself, but his case was that the defenders had no system for keeping lorries clean. Ian Macdonald presented the case tactfully, saying that something more was required than simply leaving it to the drivers, but keeping discreetly silent about what that something should be. It was presumed that the oil had fallen on the lorry from an overhead crane, though the pursuer seemed to think it might have come off his own boots. I had no strong views about the case, but thought my charge was rather more favourable to the defenders. The jury however found for the pursuer.

Finished reading *Lytton Strachey*, by Michael Holroyd: a pleasant paradox that one who regarded life as such a bore should have afforded material for so interesting a biography.

A nice programme on the wireless of songs written by Fred E. Weatherly. The words he wrote do not appear to be anything out of the ordinary, but it can hardly be a coincidence that so many of the best of the old drawing-room ballads have words by him. He seems to have had the gift of making all the ballad composers do their very best.

On television we had an hour devoted to Macmillan's premiership and the intrigues which ended in Sir Alec's succeeding him, . with poor old Butler commenting that of course he could not question what was constitutional practice but it had been all 'very quick', and Enoch Powell explaining with acid glee how they had provided Butler with a loaded pistol but how on being told that he might hurt somebody if he fired it, and that it might even make a big bang, he had said 'It's very kind of you, but I don't think I will'. Macmillan himself of course was sheer delight.

From today's *Scotsman* : 'Edward Lochrie (17)…admitted having cannabis at his Stirling flat, and police found four LSD tablets taped to his leg. When he was charged, Lochrie replied: "That's cool, man, but you don't dig our scene".'

October 7th

Cameron, speaking about J. S. C. Reid, recalled how after a consultation in a Revenue case someone had compared him to a man who carefully took a watch to pieces and when he had all the little pieces set out on a table went off and left someone else to put it together again.

October 8th

The cat had taken to occupying the dog's bed during the night, as soon as everyone is out of the way, leaving the dog to sleep on the floor, so Nancy put down a blanket on the floor with the idea that if the dog was turned out of its bed it would have somewhere to sleep. The result has been that the cat has remained happily in its own bed on top of the refrigerator, and the blanket has not been occupied.

A divorce proof: the husband had never worked since the war, explaining that he had developed a neurosis by being sent into Belsen concentration camp under a flag of truce, with medical supplies, and being detained there for three months by Hungarian guards until the camp was liberated. The wife, on whom rested the whole burden of supporting the household, worked in Mossend signal-box, and when she came home after working from 3 pm until midnight her husband would question her as to whether she might have been out with other men, and sometimes lock her out of the house—which must have been tiresome for her after a long day's work. The husband towards the end of the proof suddenly came out with an extraordinary story, never before referred to, about how he had gone to Mossend at midnight and found his wife drinking gin in the signal-box in company with a man.

October 9th

Divorces for cruelty: the pursuer in one a Dundee woman who had had one child to her husband before marriage and one after. A year or two later she gave birth to a black baby, having admitted to her husband that she had been going with a coloured man. The husband came with a knife to the house where she was staying with this man, but he was not at home and the man who got knifed was his brother. The children, she said, were being well looked after, and maintained by the gentleman she was living with—not Abdul Mohammed, who had gone back home, but Mr Conway, who worked in Caledon shipyard and was much attached to her and the children. Mohammed had always intended to go back to Pakistan when he had earned enough money. Despite this lurid history, she was a friendly girl, who told her story in a simple, matter-of-fact way, apparently regarding it as in no way out of the ordinary. A more sophisticated pursuer in one of the other cases—a thin case in which the pursuer's complaint was that her husband, when any crisis happened in their married life, went off fishing, so that she had no one to lean upon. The husband was in the RAF, and a sample of what she complained about was set out in an averment: 'He was disciplined for endangering aircraft while drunk and on another occasion he introduced a wild rabbit to a social function'. Another middle-aged pursuer, who Sibbald afterwards remarked was 'a bit of a character', had been beaten up by her husband even before they were married. He had said he would behave better. I pointed out that she had had plenty of experience, having been previously married and divorced. 'I know', she said, 'and you'll laugh when I tell you this—he didn't drink at all'; she had come out of the frying-pan into the fire.

October 11th
St Cuthberts: Dr Stewart preached a magnificent revivalist sermon on II Corinthians 8:9.

October 14th
A Specification of Documents to be recovered by the pursuer in *Derby v. Scottish Television.* One of the calls was for all film taken on the day of the accident, when the pursuer was thrown from his horse during filming, and objection was taken to this on the ground that the film was not a document or photograph but a moving picture, and there was no precedent for recovering a moving picture under a Specification. I granted the motion, remarking that it was not really a moving picture but a series of still pictures which gave an illusion of movement. Typed out a note for the appeal court on an application by Forbes to appeal against his murder conviction. His ground of appeal is that his counsel had made no attempt to show that the Crown evidence was prejudiced, and I observed that this was correct.

October 16th
A party given by Norman Wylie in the reading-room. A long conversation with Lady Clyde, who told me that her husband had a room at Briglands, their house at Rumbling Bridge, devoted entirely to a model railway.

October 17th

An excursion organised by the Railway Society of Scotland. I sat next an extremely knowledgeable boy from Hyndland, who had an encyclopaedic knowledge of Scottish railways, geographically and historically. He seemed to know where every signal-box and siding had been and what it had been used for, and disclosed the information in a modest, unassuming way: an excellent guide. From Garriongill, beyond Law Junction, the train proceeded up a single-line branch to Morningside. So far as I knew, it had never been used by passenger trains. An old gentleman sitting across the gangway from me assured me that it had, and that at one time it had carried through trains from Bathgate to Motherwell; all that, he thought, had come to an end by 1914. At Morningside there was no platform left. There were the remains of two small buildings where the two stations had been—in line, with the platform continuous. The westmost of the buildings had square chimneys characteristic of these small Caledonian stations; the North British one was of a different design. Returning down the hill to Garriongill, we carried on to Coatbridge, Springburn, Cowlairs, Dalmuir, and the former Balloch line of the LMS to Old Kilpatrick. A platform still remained from what had been a big station, Dalmuir Riverside. Some local children who clambered up on the platform, bewildered at seeing a passenger train in the station and swarms of men pouring out of it, put worried questions to us: 'What's wrong, mister? How did the train get there?' From Clydebank Dock Junction, where there was a twenty minutes stop, we headed for home.

November 6th

A string of cases in the By Order roll. The pursuer in *Miller v. Scottish & Newcastle Breweries* was in the Thistle Inn when a disturbance broke out. The defenders' manager and bouncer seized him and threw him down the stairs, so that he fell and fractured his skull. He sues on the ground of assault, or alternatively of negligence in their carrying out their duty of putting him out. The pursuer in one of this morning's divorces maintained that her husband had put rat poison in her apple tart. When asked how she knew, she said it had turned blue. I suggested that if my apple tart turned blue I should not immediately conclude that there was rat poison in it, but she said that she had had the poison in the house and had seen in the instructions that it turned things blue. Anyhow, the police had taken it away. Her counsel asked her if the police had reported that it had rat poison in it. She replied that they had never reported anything, and when further asked if anyone had eaten the apple tart said her husband had.

December 1st
Women Artists' exhibition—bought two pictures: an oil painting by Louise Annand of a Scottish mountain scene cost forty pounds; a small water-colour of an Islay sea loch, by Marjorie Aitken, cost eight pounds eight shillings.

Finished reading *To Whom it may Concern*, a book of poems by Alan Ross. They show a keen sense of observation and an interesting use of words, plus that indefinable touch of magic which makes poetry.

December 3rd
Emslie was speaking about a consultation he had once had in a case about Esk Valley sewers, in which O'Brien had been brought in as junior at the last minute. O'Brien, he said, had seemed completely apathetic and obviously took a despondent view of the case—finally observing that as Gordon Stott was on the other side there was no possibility of winning.

From today's *Scotsman* : 'Washington, Wednesday.—The Pentagon said today that American pilots flying reconnaissance missions over North Vietnam will be allowed to retaliate before they are attacked'.

December 4th
Eleven divorces: one in which the pursuer alleged that her husband in order to vex her had kept a spider in a vase in the livingroom and fed it on bluebottles. 'My whole life was shattered', she said.

December 8th
Black-outs all over the country today when electricity had been cut off in consequence of a go-slow 'work-to-rule' of electricity workers in support of their pay claim. The Government with their usual lack of perspicacity had apparently selected this dispute as a show-down, and insisted that no advance was to be made on the existing offer. The effect of the consequent industrial action was sudden and dramatic, with large areas of the country deprived of electricity within a

few hours of the start of the 'work-to-rule' yesterday morning: no heating in houses and schools, traffic lights not working, factories shut down. Tonight, though electricity was still on in Cluny Drive and Braid Avenue, Midmar Gardens was in darkness, and I found Nancy sitting by the fire by the light of two small candles on the coalbox. We had a nice coal fire, so that no heating problem arose, and by putting my papers on the coalbox beside the candles I was able to get on with my work for tomorrow. Power came on again at about 8.30; and I shaved before I went to bed, in case there should be no power available for the shaver in the morning.

December 9th
Electricity was cut off about 7.30 am. I took my shaver in with me, and plugged it into the socket of a reading-lamp in the Cedar Room.

December 10th
No power cut today.

ITV: the Syd Lawrence Band, with a brief interlude by a very funny comedian, Les Dawson: a serious comedian, not a backslapping one.

December 11th
A proof: *Copland v. Copland*. The Minuter had been divorced a good many years ago for adultery with a man named Turnbull. She and her husband had adopted a boy, Russell, who when the husband and wife separated was just a baby. The wife, Janet Copland, took him with her to her sister's house in Edinburgh, but shortly afterwards the husband took the boy to Ayrshire, where he lived with his paternal grandmother. Janet married Turnbull, but this marriage did not last long, and in due course Turnbull divorced her for desertion. Thereafter, she says, she frequently saw Russell at his aunt's—Mr Copland brought him there to see her, and sometimes, she alleged, stayed the night, even after his marriage to the respondent, Margaret. The grandmother had died, and Russell was brought up by Margaret along with a child of her previous marriage and two young children of her marriage with Mr Copland. Janet went down to Southsea, where she obtained employment as a barmaid. She said she had made Mr Copland promise to write a letter to the effect that if anything happened to him Russell was to go to her. Mr Copland was a young man, but in view of his mode of life she was apprehensive about his

future; he drank a lot, and drove a car. Her fears, if she had any, were well founded, for in the summer of 1967 Mr Copland was killed in a motor accident. Janet came to Scotland two weeks after Mr Copland's death. She wanted to take Russell away, but Margaret would not let her. She went back to Southsea and brought a Minute for custody: the Minute with which I was concerned today. Douglas Johnston in Procedure Roll dismissed the Minute as incompetent. This was reversed on appeal to the Inner House; but Janet meanwhile took the law into her own hands. She came to Kilmarnock and having kept watch to find where Russell was likely to be playing carried him off to Southsea. Russell, she said, was delighted, saying how much he loved her and how he wanted to live with her for ever and ever. The following day she was arrested and brought back by police with Russell to Kilmarnock. Tried in the Sheriff Court on a charge of *plagium*—theft of a child—she was acquitted. In October last she remarried, marrying a shop manager eighteen years younger than herself. Willie Walker appeared for her, and Barr for Margaret. Two short letters were produced, written by Russell to Janet in very affectionate terms; she gave evidence that they were part of a series of letters starting with one in which he had told her to write him not at his home address but at the address of another woman in Kilmarnock. Thereafter, when she wrote him at that address, she sent a stamped addressed envelope, and Russell wrote back, writing his letters at the woman's house. The first letter in the correspondence was not either of the two produced, and I asked what had happened to it. She said she had given all the letters to her solicitor. Whitelaw, who was sitting behind Walker, thereupon produced his bundle of letters. Delivering a short homily on the danger of lodging only part of a correspondence, I allowed the bundle to be lodged, and at lunch time took them to the Cedar Room to read. To my surprise, I found that not only was the first letter exactly in the terms that Janet had told us but the two letters that Walker had put in process were by no means the most favourable towards his case; all the letters were in equally affectionate terms, and one of them as well as saying how much he loved Janet, his 'mum', spoke of his dislike of Margaret and how Margaret had been hitting him. It was clear that the letters were all in Walker's favour and had not been deliberately suppressed; but it was rather mysterious that the boy had written in such glowing terms to a 'mother' whom he had hardly seen since he was a baby. When Walker adduced the Kilmarnock aunt to speak about the baby being brought through from Edinburgh, she agreed with me that that was by general agreement, Janet having been consulted about it. Janet's evidence had been that the baby had been taken against her will. Barr however proceeded to cross-examine the witness about it and gave her an opportunity—which she took—to say that Janet had certainly objected at the time when the baby was taken away, and she might have been mistaken in thinking that Janet had agreed. The proof was continued until Wednesday.

After tea I walked down to Morningside with Nancy and the dog, to get an evening paper. There had been some hope of an early settlement to the dispute, through an initiative by Mr Vic Feather who had arranged a formula which would enable the two sides to get together without any overt Government intervention; but owing to the refusal of the management side to put forward any improved offer negotiations had broken down—no doubt to the relief of the Government, who would have been in an awkward position if Vic Feather had been able to achieve a settlement while they were doing nothing. The men are still in a strong position, being able to achieve a vast amount of damage to the economy at negligible cost compared to what their unions would have to pay out if there had been an actual strike. A bizarre feature of the affair is that right in the middle of it, when Government spokesmen were insisting that the 10 per cent offer to the electricians was the most that was possible in the national interest, and that anything beyond that would lead to disastrous inflationary demands, the Prime Minister in the House of Commons announced an increase in salaries of admirals, generals, judges and higher civil servants of up to 25 per cent, intimating however that we had all patriotically agreed that the increases, due to be paid in January, would not become operative until July. Clyde came into the Outer House judges' lunch room on Friday to tell us about this, saying that the Treasury had insisted that he tell them at once that we should follow the lead given by the Lord Chief Justice, with the possible alternative, if we refused, of having no increase. He had therefore taken it upon himself to say that we would concur. I had not been aware of any proposal for an increase, and had no great interest in it one way or the other; but I remarked to Clyde that while I had no objection to what was proposed I objected to giving any indication of support to the bunch of buffoons who were at present running the country. I actually had no idea what my present salary was, and it appeared that Fraser was equally ignorant—it seems that we are getting £9,500 a year, and the proposal is to increase it to £12,000.

December 13th

To church. Mr Bailey explained that the first Sunday in December was usually celebrated as 'Bible Sunday', but as he had not been ready to speak about that subject last Sunday he would make up for his failure today. He then gave an interesting talk about the work of the British and Foreign Bible Society; and having done so said that he had prepared it before attending yesterday's demonstration in the Usher Hall against the sale of arms to South Africa. As a result, he was perhaps a little ashamed of the talk he had prepared, since apartheid in South Africa was based on the Bible. He is an extraordinary man, and despite his anti-Establishment views everyone in the congregation seems to like him. On television Mrs Thatcher was being questioned by some parents. She has come on a lot since she became Minister of Education, in the sense that she is much more careful and efficient in her answers, making sure that she gives nothing away and that she leaves the impression that she understands the opposite point of view. Nancy, who is very anti-Conservative these days, in contrast to practically all our friends and acquaintances, dislikes Mrs Thatcher exceedingly, and went into the garden while the programme was on.

December 14th

Learned with dismay that the Unions had decided to end the work-to-rule and overtime ban unconditionally. A Court of Enquiry is to be set up, but they seem to be prepared to leave its membership and terms of reference to the Government.

December 15th

A cruelty case: the wife complained that when she had saved up to buy a washing machine the defender spent the money on buying a donkey. Among her other complaints was that he had told a meeting of Penicuik Unionists that she was mentally ill.

December 16th

Copland v. Copland. Margaret, as I had expected, was a complete contrast to Janet—her evidence a masterpiece of understatement. Asked whether Russell was happy with her, she replied. 'He's all right'. Asked whether she had had to bear the brunt of looking after Russell all his life, she replied, 'I got on all right'. I thought she had probably been rather strict, but in the straitened circumstances in which the family was left after Mr Copland's death that was probably understandable. I much preferred her to Janet. I was asked by Walker to see the boy, and Barr had no objection. He is just twelve, and proved to be a delightful boy: friendly, frank, uninhibited, not at all shy or diffident about expressing his opinions, but at the same time courteous and reasonable. I thought he did Margaret a lot of credit. As I had been led to expect, he had enjoyed his dramatic trip south, and having been told all the interesting things he was to see at Portsmouth —the beach, Nelson's ship, the nice new house where Janet lived— was disappointed that all he had seen was the inside of the police station. He was keen to go to Portsmouth right away, but had no desire to be separated permanently from Margaret and the children. He urged me to let him spend six months of the year with Aunt Janet and six months in Kilmarnock with his mum, but when I said that would make things difficult so far as his schooling was concerned he saw the point at once. In response to a suggestion that he might stay at school in Kilmarnock and go to Portsmouth for his summer holidays, he asked whether he could not go to Portsmouth during the term and come back to Kilmarnock for his holidays—no doubt because of his eagerness to see Portsmouth as soon as possible. Janet and her witnesses had insisted that he hated Kilmarnock, but he would not have that—standing up for Kilmarnock when I tried to run it down: its museum, where they had just had a display of space ships, the cinema, the baths, places where he played football. He made it clear that the letters to Janet had been written, as I had suspected, at the instigation of Mrs Cran—who had not been adduced as a witness. He had not written any recently because he had not been going to Mrs Cran's house, having quarrelled with his friend Malcolm Cran because he called him an orphan. I said that the difficulty was just the opposite: that so far from being an orphan he had two mothers and the problem was to choose between them. We chatted agreeably together for twenty minutes. I think that in spite of his alternative suggestion the best solution will be to leave him in Margaret's custody and let him go to Janet for holidays.

December 17th
Shearer is hearing the proof in *Derby v. Scottish Television*, and told us about expert evidence he had been hearing on training horses for film work. Some of the horses were so well trained in this kind of

work that when a cowboy charge was being filmed and the director shouted 'Cut' the horses stopped immediately.

December 18th

I had to interview another little boy. When his parents were divorced, it was agreed that the mother have custody and the father have access during the holidays. The boy is at boarding school at Aberlour, the prep school for Gordonstoun; the mother lives at Insch in Aberdeenshire, the father in Edinburgh. Each parent wanted the other to have the boy for the first ten days of the holidays, the question at issue being which was to have him for Christmas. It seemed to me, when the case came up last week, that that was something the boy should decide for himself; and I ordered that the husband should have his ten days from the start of the school holidays last Saturday, and undertook to extend the access over Christmas if the boy told me that that was what he wanted. But when I saw him in the Cedar Room this morning he made it clear that he would prefer to spend Christmas at Insch. He was friendly and intelligent, and obviously knew what he wanted; and I ordered that the father should have access up to 24th December, and the boy would then be with his mother.

December 27th

Campbell Maclean on television, chatting with three other men about ministers. They had an unfortunate start when their programme got mixed up with one showing at the same time in England, with the result that the vision in the Scottish programme was accompanied by the sound of the English one, and we saw the lips of Mr Maclean and his friends moving while we heard Edith Piaff singing lustily. This, it was later explained, was due to a technical hitch.

December 29th

Finished drafting my opinion in *Copland v. Copland*. I have awarded custody to Margaret, but have suggested that if Janet is prepared to pay Russell's travelling expenses there is no reason why she should not have him at Southsea for a substantial part of his holidays.

December 31st

Babes in the Wood, a Victorian pantomime first performed in 1894: witty, bright, colourful, with never a dull moment—a show not to be mentioned in the same breath as the miserable drivel that passes for pantomime at the King's Theatre. The Lyceum Company gave a brilliant performance, led by Una Maclean as a dashing Robin Hood and Russell Hunter showing that it was possible to be delightfully funny without being in the least degree vulgar. A lot of good old songs, and a lively plot.

1971

Under a Government devoted to the welfare of the affluent, at whatever cost to the community or to the concept of a humane, civilised way of life, 1971 was an easy year for the well-to-do, and so it was for me. Though seldom under any pressure of work, I had a sufficiency of congenial employment, and the year so far as I was concerned passed comfortably and uneventfully. In January, while the Government was engaged in an all-out effort to prevent the postmen from succeeding in their claim for a living wage, they found it possible to announce a vast increase in the salaries of judges and other high-paid officers. Unemployment figures continued to mount up; and it was ironical that Britain's favourable trade balance was running at an all-time high in a year when trade and employment had gone from bad to worse: a striking confirmation of the view that Mr Powell and I had always held, that one fares much better when one's trade balance is unfavourable.

January 4th

On television we had one of a series of lectures by Dr John Napier, on variations in species. Among the curious things that he brought to our attention was the difference in people's methods of folding their arms. I had assumed that it was a matter of indifference whether one's left or right hand was on the outside, but found that when I folded my arms my right hand came naturally over the left arm and that it was awkward when I tried to fold my arms the other way round. Nancy found just the opposite.

January 16th

From this week's *World's Fair*: 'Bugg—in loving memory of my dear husband, Charles Bugg, who passed away January 26, 1969. Your name we often mention'.

January 26th

Alex Thomson was recalling an occasion when he had appeared in a civil jury trial before Sheriff Milne in Dumfries. The pursuer collapsed in the witness box, and was being carried out when the Sheriff held up his hand and stopped the cavalcade, saying 'Wait a minute—there's a juryman missing'. Everyone looked at the jury box, where sure enough there was a gap; but at that moment a juryman's head appeared above the front of the box and the man observed, 'I was only tying my shoe lace'. In the hotel lounge after dinner Sheriff Milne appeared and said he had just had a strange experience. He had gone back to court to get his notes, so as to have a look at them in preparation for the morrow, but had found the door locked. Some way along the street he had found a man in uniform, who listened sympathetically to his story but said he was unable to help—he was not a policeman but an SMT bus driver. He suggested that the Sheriff should go to the police station, and the Sheriff thinking this a good suggestion had gone there and found a young officer who was most helpful and had come back with him to the court, with a bunch of keys. But when he tried the door he found it was not locked after all.

February 1st

The postmen's strike is entering its third week. The postmen have been sending volunteers on two days a week to man Post Office counters, without any wages, so that pensioners could get their money, and in view of the use of blackleg labour in some offices are threatening to withdraw this facility. It seemed to me that this would give rise to public annoyance and do no damage to those whom the strikers wanted to get at—just what the Government wanted. I felt that without any strike pay the Union could not win by trying to keep all their people out indefinitely, and that the better course would be to send their counter staff back and let them get paid in the usual way, asking them to contribute towards the hardship fund that has been started for postal workers suffering from the result of the strike. The important thing is surely to stop the mails by keeping out the postmen and the people who move mail from place to place. The maximum of inconvenience would be caused to the Tories' business friends, people in a position to put some pressure on the Government, at the minimum cost. To the average business man, I should imagine, it would not matter in the slightest whether counter staff were there or not. It seemed unlikely that this simple method of minimising their workers' loss had not occurred to the Union leaders, but they are so amateurish and simple-minded that anything is possible, and I felt that at least it would be worth finding out whether they had considered it and what the objections were. I did not think that I could approach any Union people myself, particularly as neither the Union branch office, if it has one, nor the Edinburgh secretary seem to be on the telephone, and any visit by a judge to the office might be noticed by press representatives. So I got on to Ewan Stewart on the telephone, but though professedly sympathetic he insisted that he had no Trade Union connections. He suggested Ronald King Murray. The difficulty was that Murray, like other MPs, would probably be in London. I phoned his house and put my problem to his wife, who was until recently a Labour town councillor. She was even more helpless than Ewan Stewart. The post office workers were manning the counters already, she said—completely missing the point that they were doing this voluntarily, without pay. She was sympathetic towards the strikers, and hoped that they would succeed, but she did not think they possibly could, and there was nothing she could do about it. She thought that the Union leaders must have thought of my point already. Perhaps they have—and anyhow it seemed that my efforts to find out were not going to get anywhere. No doubt Sheila King Murray is right to the extent that if the Union people are incapable of running their strike properly they must just be allowed to have it their own way.

February 2nd

Procedure Roll debate in actions in which nine children are suing for damages in respect of the death of their father and mother in a motor-scooter accident. Horsburgh appeared for the defenders, and argued that the cases were unsuitable for jury trial. He made some verbal criticisms of the pleadings—for instance that the pursuers averred that the defender ought to have seen the scooter, without averring any reason why he ought to have seen it. Since the road was lighted, and the defender's car met the scooter in a head-on collision, it seemed a pretty obvious inference. Next he said that the pursuers were suing for very large sums, and this would, if the case went to a jury, mislead them into making extravagant awards. Such a ground, I pointed out to Horsburgh, depended on the assumption that the jury would be unreasonable. He denied this, and I referred him to his plea in law: 'The sums sued for in this action being substantially in excess of the sums that a reasonable jury properly instructed would award, special cause exists for withholding the case from jury trial'. Since a reasonable jury properly instructed would not award such sums, there could be no danger in remitting the cases to a reasonable jury. Looking somewhat puzzled, Horsburgh went on his last point: that in the case relating to Mrs Gardiner difficult questions of fact and law would arise on averments by the defender that she was at fault in having chosen to ride on the pillion of an inexperienced driver who had not passed a test. Horsburgh referred me to a case in which James Walker had held that similar averments against a pillion passenger were irrelevant, and another case in which Kilbrandon had disagreed with him. Accordingly, he said, there was a question of doubtful relevancy which made the case unsuitable for jury trial. The pursuer however had no plea to relevancy. Horsburgh of course had to agree that in his submission the averments were relevant, or he would not have put them on, and as the pursuers agreed that they were relevant it was obvious that no question arose. Horsburgh having informed me that Kilbrandon's case was against him had not read on to the end of the case, where Kilbrandon stated in the clearest possible terms that such a case was unsuitable for jury trial. Maclean, who appeared for the pursuers, obviously knew this, and when he came to reply he and I skated all round Kilbrandon's case, carefully avoiding coming to grips with it. He put the points against Horsburgh's arguments with his usual competence. The debate lasted almost until one—mostly through my fault, teasing Horsburgh. I said I should give judgment after lunch, and having made some notes during the lunch hour delivered an opinion allowing a jury trial.

February 3rd
On television tonight a 'Man Alive' programme on class distinctions: a well-devised programme about interesting personalities, including the working-class father of the President of the Oxford Union, a highly articulate butler-handyman who knew his place and was perfectly satisfied with it. It seemed to be about two paces behind his master as he went out shooting. Very sensibly he said that his ambition for his son was to see him in No 11 Downing Street, for that was where the real power lay.

February 4th
A cruelty divorce, *Cummings v. Cummings*. The pursuer married at the age of sixteen, and the marriage lasted exactly five months, with intervals while the parties were living apart or the defender was in

gaol. It had been hopeless from the start. The two got married without having arranged anywhere to live, and turned up at the defender's mother's house at eleven at night expecting her to take them in. The defender was drunk, quarrelled with his mother, and got involved in a fight with the man downstairs, during which furniture was thrown all over the house, and his bride, who tried to pacify him, got a couple of punches in the face. He, she and the man downstairs were all taken to the Infirmary in an ambulance; and at 4 am the couple arrived at her parents' house, announced that they were married, and settled there for a week. Thereafter they moved to a room in a house kept by Mrs McCafferty, who gave evidence. In the middle of her examination by McEwan for the defender, she suddenly observed, 'I've got the toothache and I can't stand it any longer'. No one paid any attention to this, and her evidence continued. She claimed that some time after the parties had stopped living with her she saw a woman in a public house with a group of men whom she took to be foreign seamen, because they were not speaking English, and though she did not recognise the woman her husband pointed out to her that it was Mrs Cummings. The room that the parties had in her house had no floor covering and no furniture except two single beds. A pane in the window was broken, and there was no means of heating except a small gas fire which was not working. The defender did not work either. He lived on unemployment benefit, most of which he spent on drink. He was sent a travel warrant to go to Manchester to look for work, but lost it when he was out drinking in a public house. There was not much evidence of violence, but it was obvious that the pursuer's mother was right when she said that he liked to cause trouble wherever he went and the pursuer—quite a pleasant little girl—had had no sort of life with him. She has a baby, born about seven months after the separation, and the real issue seems to be whether the defender is to be allowed access to the baby. A social worker who visited both parents thought that would not be a good idea, and I am inclined to think that she was right.

I got along to the robing-room just after four, and found that Ian Robertson had gone off wearing my jacket, which had my car key in the pocket—there is an absurd system in the robing-room of laying out all our jackets and vests in little piles, and I had noticed that mine was in the wrong pile; but it seemed extraordinary that Robertson had not observed that the jacket he was putting on was much smaller than his. His jacket was far too big for me, and I could not think how he had got into mine. I tried his house two or three times on the telephone without getting any reply, and eventually phoned Nancy, when she had got home from the Marriage Guidance office, and asked her to come in with my spare key. She said she had seen Robertson walking down the Mound with Emslie, and I phoned Emslie and asked if he knew where Robertson had gone. He did: he had gone to the dentist's, in Charlotte Square, and I phoned there, but too late, Robertson having just left. So Nancy had to come in after all.

Miss Robertson had sent along a message objecting to my deleting periods which her typists always put into Opinions after 'Mr' and 'Mrs', and saying that the Civil Service instruction was that these were to be typed 'Mr.' and 'Mrs.' I explained to Sibbald that this was wrong, and showed what was done in Session Cases—relieved to find that, as I had expected, their practice was correct.

February 5th

Cummings had nothing sensible to say for himself, and at the end of his evidence I was about to indicate my views when I was reminded that I had not heard what counsel had to say. As both Gow and McEwan realised, it did not matter what they said; each confined himself to a few brief observations. I took the case to avizandum, but indicated that until the defender learned to drink less and behave more responsibly my view was that the less he saw of the baby the better.

February 15th

Decimal coinage came into operation today. The new bronze coins are stupidly known as pence, although each of them is worth about two and a half times the value of the old penny.

February 25th

Turned the television on for 'This Week': on the new Government Bill to make life difficult for black immigrants. It had the result of putting me into a state of impotent rage, particularly as the Tory spokesman, a right-wing smoothie named Biggs-Davidson, was more adept than usual at putting over the usual cant about its all being in the best interests of immigrants themselves. The Labour spokesman was Merlyn Rees, who was at the Home Office at the time of the Labour Government's disgraceful Immigration Act. David Steel put the liberal case against prejudice and oppression.

February 26th

'By Order' Roll: *McNish v. British Railways Board*, an action by a man and a wife who were going down the stairs to the platform at High Street station in Glasgow, a station which is below ground level, when an eight-years-old girl fell through the glass roof and landed on them. They alleged that the defenders should have taken steps to prevent children getting on the roof.

March 14th

Posted a cheque in payment of my electricity account in the pillar-box in Braid Avenue, to the surprise of an old gentleman who was passing and asked me if collections had been resumed. I told him what the communication was, and that it did not matter how long it remained uncollected. Pillar boxes in Edinburgh throughout the postal strike have mostly been covered up with inverted mail bags, but some unauthorised persons have removed the bags from several in this part of the town, so that there is nothing to prevent one from posting a letter if one chooses. There seemed to be plenty of room in the box. Apart from the electricity account, the only communication which has got through to me since the strike began was a letter from Pike. He handed it to Miss Howat at Deans Yard and it came up in the Lord Advocate's mail bag and was delivered to me at Parliament House.

March 5th

'By Order' Roll: *Isle of Man Bank v. Quinn*, an action by the bank to recover an overdraft of £2,260. The case is rather mysterious, in as much as it is averred and admitted that the law applicable to the contract is that of the Isle of Man, but no one avers what Isle of Man law has to say on the subject. In *Smith v. Smith*, a divorce proof that I continued some time ago because of a difficulty about access to the children, the parties had agreed that the husband should see the children on Sunday afternoons, but the wife in evidence had said that when the children went to see their father he had been drinking and she could not get them to go again. I had indicated that I could not grant decree until this had been cleared up; and the husband today went into the witness box, agreed that he had been drinking when the children came, explained that it was between Christmas and New Year, and said he would not do it again. That satisfied me, but Maclean, who appeared for the wife, said there was still the difficulty that the children would not go. They had been brought to court today, and Maclean and Barr—who appeared for the husband—said they had agreed that if I interviewed the children the parties would abide by any decision I made. So I retired to the Cedar Room, and Fiona and Sandra were brought in—aged twelve and nine. They were determined to have nothing to do with their father, and Fiona argued their case with pertinacity and skill, meeting every point that I put to her. Persuasion, threats, and entreaties were unavailing, and in the end I had to go back into court and tell everyone that my efforts had been a total failure, and that I could not possibly make an order for access. Both counsel assured me that that was quite all right, and that the access provision would be deleted from the Joint Minute.

From Miss Louise Annand:

THE CORPORATION OF THE CITY OF GLASGOW
GLASGOW MUSEUMS & ART GALLERIES
Department of Education
Education Officer: Louise G. Annand, M.A., A.M.A.

Dear Lord Stott,
I had a note from the Society of Scottish Women Artists in December to say that you had bought 'Mount Keen at Easter', and this of course gave me great pleasure.

As the picture was fairly new and had I think been given just a lick of varnish or retouching varnish, it will very likely begin to require varnishing in the course of the next month or two. As I expect you may know, the surface gradually goes dull and the dark colours 'sink', and this is remedied by mastic varnish. It is as well to give the surface a wipe first with a damp smooth cloth to avoid imprisoning any dust. If you have any difficulty in getting this done I will of course be pleased to do it for you at some time suitable to yourself. It is not a lengthy operation. I am sorry that the enclosed card was not sent to you—but we rather gave up trying to post anything. However you might perhaps have time to take a look at the exhibition before it closes?

Yours sincerely

March 19th
A divorce proof. The defender had formed a liaison with one Mrs Macdonald. A letter was produced which Mrs Macdonald had written him. 'My Dearest Dearest Heart, Oh, my darling, I love you so.

Dear one, thank Heaven and all the Saints that I saw you this morning, and again at 5. Oh, darling I really was frantic, you know, I love you so, my beloved. Oh, I love you, dear'. The letter goes on in a similar strain for four closely-written pages. In putting this letter to the pursuer, McGhie asked her, 'Is it in fairly affectionate terms?' There were eleven undefended divorces. The pursuer in a cruelty case, a young, flaxen-haired woman from Glasgow, was persuaded only with the utmost difficulty to give any evidence adverse to her husband. They had separated three years ago, and when asked what kind of married life she had had she replied diffidently, 'I really don't remember much about it'. 'How did your husband treat you?' her counsel asked, to which the reply was, 'Oh, I don't know; I certainly wouldn't say he was cruel to me'. It later appeared that he had knocked her about quite a lot, but she indignantly repudiated the suggestion that she had ever had to consult a doctor. Reminded that she had gone to see one particular doctor, she agreed, but added that had nothing to do with her husband's conduct. She was obviously a thoroughly genuine, likable person, and I did not hesitate to give her her divorce.

March 22nd
From this week's *Hamilton Advertiser*: 'A man...plunged into the River Clyde and swam away as he was helping police with their enquiries'.

March 26th
At lunch, apropos of the news that Sheriff Watt is seriously ill, Hunter recalled George Thomson's observation that there was no moaning at the Bar when any judge was putting out to sea.

March 30nd
From today's *Scotsman*: 'A man spat at the car conveying Prince Charles, Edinburgh Sheriff Court was told yesterday. John Douglas Wilson (40), a motor driver, said that he was spitting at that time anyway and the Royal car "just happened to come round the corner".'

April 2nd
On BBC television tonight there were two films about Vietnam, Dutch and German respectively, giving a horrifying picture of the misery that the Americans have brought to the Vietnamese—not only physical

suffering, but corruption and degradation of the whole life of the country. It is a pity that the two films could not be shown to President Nixon and his friends.

April 3rd

To Cramond, where we had tea in a new cottage teashop opposite the Inn. The charge for afternoon tea was 30p apiece, which seemed excessive; but when the girl came to give us our bill she decided we had not eaten enough, and by calculating the price of the individual items charged us 27p for the two of us. On this basis, I do not think we would have got anywhere near 60p if we had eaten everything on the table; but it suited us.

April 5th

Finished reading *Eton*, by Christopher Hollis. The main conclusions to be drawn from it seem to be that the so-called permissiveness of present-day youth is nothing compared to the depravity and viciousness of their predecessors, and that the Victorian industrialists who made life so terrible for children working in their factories were no more considerate of their own offspring.

April 11th

When I was sitting beside the burn at Blackford Glen, the dog put its ball into the water, and though the water was not so deep as to stop it from getting it out it was unable to find it. The ball was clearly visible on the bottom, and the dog walked right over it, but it works entirely on its sense of smell and that apparently cannot operate when the ball is under water.

April 16th

London. We went to the St Martin's Theatre to see *Sleuth*—Nancy's choice, based on an enthusiastic note in 'Punch' and other enthusiastic notices about the 'Best thriller now on in London', now in its second year. To our astonishment, it turned out to be unmitigated drivel, completely pointless—a long-drawn exchange of puerilities between two men. The ending was as silly as the rest of it.

April 20th

From today's *Express*: 'The latest employment figures show that there are now 814,189 people jobless in Britain and Ulster—the worst total since April 1940. Employment Minister Mr Paul Bryan told angry Labour critics: "Our policy is to bring unemployment down by the success of our policies".'

April 28th
Called at the King's to get seats for *The Merchant of Venice*. A queue at the box office, and progress slow, as only one woman was in the office and attention had to be given to people wanting to book for this week's show which had been advertised to start at 8.05 but had actually started at 7.45—so that prospective members of the audience had to be warned that it was already well under way. It is astonishing that people continue to attend the theatre in face of all the obstacles put in their way at theatre box offices.

April 29th
Johnstone v. Johnstone, an action of divorce on the ground of cruelty. The pursuer was a pleasant, cheery girl who at the age of twenty four had married a man twelve years older than herself. All went well until after six weeks she told her husband that she was pregnant. The defender had a theory that a wife could not become pregnant during the honeymoon, and thought she had invented it in order to get out of going to work. He told her that if she could not work she was no use to him. His objection was pointless, as his wife continued to work almost until the time when the baby was born. There was not much evidence of cruelty, but the husband was an incredibly self-centred person, unconscious of anyone else's feelings or point of view. I could well understand that he must have been an impossible person to live with. He told us that his habit was to go out at nine every evening, to have two pints at a public house, to buy two cans of beer at the grocer's, and then to come home, where he liked to watch two television programmes: 'News at Ten' and '24 Hours'. He preferred to watch them alone, drinking his beer in front of his own fireside. The pursuer agreed that he was never drunk when he came home, but said that by the time he came to bed, sometimes in the early hours of the morning, he was often intoxicated. He made meaningless remarks, and sometimes got up and blundered into the furniture, or into her mother's room when the parties were staying with the wife's parents. He burned the furniture with his cigarettes. She said she was frightened of him when he was the worse of drink; and there was medical evidence that she had lost weight on account of depression.

She left her husband in September 1968, but was persuaded by the priest to go back. Everything went well for a fortnight, but the husband then returned to his old ways, and she finally left in March 1969. Her doctor said it would be bad for her health to go back. The husband, who according to the evidence is a devout Catholic, was I think genuinely astonished at all this; he had no idea that his conduct could be regarded as objectionable, and thought his wife most unreasonable in criticising him. I felt he was genuinely willing to resume cohabitation, but I agreed with one of his aunts who gave evidence that she deserved a medal for putting up with him for so long.

April 30th

A Minute craving that aliment be reduced from three pounds to two pounds and periodical allowance from three pounds to nil. The Rules of Court provide that an application for variation be made by Minute, and I did not think I could vary the awards until Answers had been lodged and we had had a hearing on the Minute and Answers. Bowen asked for leave to reclaim, which I granted, saying I should be glad of an opportunity of expressing my views about Minutes and Answers. I drafted a note and read it on to tape. I have criticised the whole Minute-and-Answers procedure on questions of aliment and periodical allowance and suggested that they should be dealt with summarily, the defender being allowed to give notice of his objection and to appear at the undefended diet of proof and make a short statement of his financial position.

May 1st

Ten divorces. In one of them the evidence came from two English enquiry agents from the 'Expert Detective Agency', and we were all rather surprised when the second witness came in and turned out to be an old lady of 78.

May 2nd

Cramond Church: Mr Maclean preached on Luke 11:27–8—a remarkable sermon, as always, a dramatic tour de force.

May 3rd

Drafted my opinion in *Johnstone v. Johnstone*. I of course found for the pursuer and awarded decree of divorce.

May 4th

An action of divorce in which the defender admitted adultery, alleged to have been committed in a caravan, but had made averments of condonation. Cay appeared for the pursuer, and the defender was supposed to be appearing on his own behalf. He had not turned up when the proof was called, and we carried on without him. When Cay was halfway through the examination of his client Mr Taylor, the defender, appeared. I made no attempt to tell him what had been happening, but invited him to take a seat beside Cay and told Cay to proceed with the examination of the witness. It appeared that the defender was not now seeking to contest the case on its merits but was objecting to the pursuer's crave for a capital sum of £3,000 and periodical allowance of £20 per week. On that, Cay led no evidence at all, beyond taking from one of his witnesses that he admitted that he owned a cottage on the farm and from the pursuer that he had some connection with a motor business. When he had led his two witnesses he proposed to adduce the defender, but the defender said he had no intention of going into the witness-box or giving evidence. He point blank refused to do so, and as Cay told me that he had not cited the defender as a witness it seemed to me that there was no way of compelling him to give evidence. Cay submitted that if the defender was present in court he could not refuse to be adduced as a witness for the pursuer, and that his refusal was in contempt of court. At Cay's request I granted an adjournment for half an hour so that he could see if he might find any authority for his proposition. When the court resumed, I explained to the defender that if he did not give evidence I could not hear him on any matter of fact which had not been spoken to by the witnesses; but having considered the point he decided, no doubt rightly, that in the state of the evidence he would be better to persist in his determination to keep out of the witness-box. Having heard Cay and the defender on such evidence as there had been, I sent for a shorthand writer and gave a brief judgment. Taking, as I said, a broad axe, which was all that one could do in that state of affairs, I awarded a capital sum of £150, aliment of £2 for each of the three children, and a periodical allowance of £3.

To the King's Theatre: *The Merchant of Venice*. It is a bad play, with a meanspirited plot which reaches its climax half an hour before the end, the rest of the play being padded out by a subsidiary plot which has no relation to the main one. Tonight it was made immeasurably worse by the National Theatre company's production. They chose to play it as a farce; and, when they were not clowning, practically the whole company, including Laurence Olivier, were hamming it like second-rate amateurs.

May 6th

Proof in *Allan v. Scott*. The pursuer, who was only sixteen when the accident happened, gave his evidence from a wheel-chair. From his account of the accident it was obvious that it had been caused by the fault of a taxi-driver in driving his car out of the forecourt of a garage into the path of the pursuer's motor scooter. In these circumstances it was inexplicable that the pursuer's advisers, in face of an averment by the defenders that the accident had been caused by the fault of the taxi-driver, had chosen to restrict themselves to a case against the present defenders, who were only marginally responsible for the accident, if at all. It appeared that arrangements for taking away rubble had been pretty haphazard, and that if it had been removed earlier mud and grit might not have seeped down on to the road, but it was all pretty nebulous.

At lunch time Hunter was speaking about Sir Andrew Clark and recalled how when he was appearing with him in the House of Lords and they were waiting in the corridor for their Lordships to come along Clark, on hearing the sound of the lift, whipped off his wig and stood stiffly erect while the judges passed. The reason, Hunter said, was that when he was not wearing a wig Clark was not required to bow to the Lords of Appeal, two of whom had been junior to him at the Bar. On one occasion he had asked Shearer whether he was going to Ascot in the following week, and Shearer having replied with his customary grunt went on to inform him that he always returned all his work during Ascot Week.

Finished reading *Great Western Branch Line Album*, by Ian Krause, an excellent selection of photographs but depressing to look through with the realisation that most of the lines would never see a train again.

May 7th

Speeches in yesterday's case. Sutherland, who appeared for the pursuer, explained that the taxi-driver was dead and so was his wife, and as he had no executors or representatives it had not been possible to raise an action—though he agreed with McArthur, for the defenders, that the main blame for the accident lay on the taxi-driver. Both counsel, as well as a third who had been brought in, agreed that nothing can be done. It seemed an extraordinary state of affairs; and though I do not know what the answer is it seems incredible that a pursuer who has been injured by a properly insured motor vehicle should be left without a remedy merely because the owner-driver has died without leaving any representative. I think there may be sufficient in the evidence to allow me to find for the pursuer against the present defenders, but it is a difficult case, and perhaps rather hard on them to be saddled with such a big claim for an accident for which they were very little to blame.

May 11th

Parliament House: I came prepared to deal with four divorces, but, just before the Court sat, George Macdonald asked me to take Emslie's jury trial and leave him free to deal with an interdict. Ewan Stewart appeared for the pursuer, and apart from the pursuer's evidence led only one witness, who rather contradicted the pursuer. Jauncey asked me to withdraw the case from the jury, citing a peculiar case in the First Division recently where they overturned James Leechman for proceeding on the Law Reform Act and seemed to say that although the Act said the rule of law about corroboration should no longer apply corroboration might still be necessary. It seemed nonsense to me; and I refused Jauncey's motion without comment. After lunch we had speeches and my summing-up. I did not of course have my usual collection of styles for charging juries, but found I got on perfectly well without them. The jury found unanimously for the pursuer. At lunchtime Hunter had been recalling that Lord Denning when investigating the Profumo case had incidentally to deal with some allegations about the Duke of Argyll's case, and in particular a suggestion that counsel had deliberately pulled their punches—a ridiculous suggestion to make about such a hard-fought case when every punch counted, including any that might happen to be below the belt. Shearer, who had been at one time counsel for the Duke, was sent to London to represent his colleagues and appeared before Denning to be interviewed. Shearer had not been impressed; Balfour, the instructing solicitor, had told Hunter that when Shearer came out from the interview with Denning his comment was: 'The man's a child'.

May 12th

Between the beginning of the University area and Parliament House I carried out a little research by observing what the girls I saw in the street were wearing. Of the total of 31 that I noticed walking in the street, 18 were wearing trousers and 13 short skirts; none was wearing a maxi or a midi.

May 14th

Finished the draft of my opinion in *Allan v. Scott*. I have found for the pursuer, and awarded him £27,500. This includes £14,000 solatium, and it will be interesting to see how the Division, and possibly the House of Lords thereafter, will deal with this attempt to get nearer the jury award in Mrs McCallum's case than the £10,000 which the Division seemed to regard as the limit.

May 18th

Hunter was speaking about his war experiences when serving with a frigate in Iceland waters, and recalled being sent out at full speed from Reykjavik to assist a convoy attacked by U-boats near the Denmark Strait. The U-boats had assembled with the object of attacking warships that were trying to sink the *Bismarck* but an unescorted convoy happened to pass through them and was practically annihilated. The task of Hunter's frigate was to attempt to tow in a big Dutch tanker that had been set on fire and abandoned by most of her crew. Coming up out of the darkness, they saw a submarine closing in with the object of putting the finish to the tanker, and were able to get up unnoticed to a point from which they could fire a couple of shells, which landed close to the submarine. It would not be possible for the submarine crew to see whether the approaching ship was a frigate or a destroyer. Through their binoculars those of Hunter's ship could see men on the conning-tower, obviously discussing what should be done; and they were relieved to see them finally hurrying inside and the submarine submerging. They spent the next fourteen hours searching round for the submarine, and then had to make for Iceland with fuel only to go at five knots. The probable course of the *Bismarck* had been plotted and it seemed clear that the frigate's course would pass close to the *Bismarck's*. Hunter said some betting went on as to whether the *Bismarck* would think it worth while to pay any attention to a solitary frigate proceeding at five knots. At one point they caught sight of the *Bismarck*, hull down on the horizon, but were again relieved to find her going on her way, apparently deciding that the frigate was beneath her notice. Fraser, remarking that at the time he had been fully engaged in the defence of Edinburgh, recalled that his unit, like Hunter's frigate, was armed with what could be called Crimea type guns, including one mounted on an old Albion lorry. Later on, he was serving in Kent. He did not think that his anti-aircraft battery had ever brought down any aircraft, but they had much more success with flying bombs, the course of which was predictable, and many of which had been brought down.

May 26th

Louise Annand had written to say she would like to come and put some varnish on her painting of Mount Keen. She arrived before eight: an agreeable, down-to-earth kind of person.

May 27th

An action of divorce on the ground of desertion: the pursuer 73, the defender 65. The defender had left her husband of her own free will. A defence that she had been justified in leaving him was supported by some rather ridiculous averments, such as that her husband had sold eggs laid by hens belonging to the defender when she wanted to use them for cooking. She had put up with him for 38 years, so that it did not look as if his conduct could have made it impossible for her to live with him. I granted decree of divorce.

May 28th

Twelve undefended divorces. At 12.30 I still had four proofs to do, but at that point Miss Aronson took over, and with her usual competence got all four through by one o'clock.

May 30th

A presentation to Mr Bailey—his last Sunday at South Morningside. Mr Melville made the presentation—a cheque for £75—explaining that the arrangements had been upset by their getting in very much more than they had expected. Mr Bailey replied, saying he had been astounded at how much the people had appreciated him, and had even told him so. His morale when he came had been very low, and we here had given him back his self-respect. He had never experienced anything like it. This was no more than the truth—it is amazing how he gained confidence in himself in the five months he has been here. When he came, he seemed to think he was a complete failure as a minister, and he has suddenly found that he can be a complete success.

June 11th

During lunch Ian Fraser remarked that he had been surprised to find on reading the 121st psalm in the *New English Bible* that the meaning was quite different from what appeared in the Authorised translation, indicating that the psalmist should not lift up his eyes to the hills, since his help came from the Lord. I was much interested to hear this: it confirmed what my father had always said regarding the correct translation of the psalm.

June 16th

On television tonight a film about Dingleton. Being one of the BBC's 'Man Alive' programmes, which are uniformly bad, it did not give much of a picture of Dingleton, but there were interviews with some delightfully down-to-earth old Borderers, male and female, who though classified as mental patients seemed a lot more sensible than the man who interviewed them.

June 18th

A divorce proof in which defences had been abandoned. The pursuer had been writing to the defender in prison about having the house transferred to her name, and there was rather a bad-tempered letter from him, starting off 'I received no stamped addressed envelope, and I have to wait till a Sunday before I can get a letter to answer back, this is Prison not Butlins'.

June 20th

A fee of 31 guineas for a case I had in 1957 that I have no recollection of.

July 1st

A cruelty case in which the defender was an invalid in a wheel chair. I asked about this when the pursuer was giving evidence, querying whether the husband would be capable of assaulting her as she said he did; but she replied that he was quicker in his chair than she was on her legs. I granted decree.

July 4th

From adjoining columns of today's *Sunday Express*: 'Mr Heath tells the shops: Price cuts, please'. 'Because of increasing production costs, the *Scottish Sunday Express* has been reluctantly forced to increase the price of the paper by 1p to 5p'.

July 6th

A divorce proof: a very thin case of cruelty. Besides the pursuer, the only witness this morning was a highly reputable witness who thought the defender must have been drinking because she had seen him in Goldenacre on a Saturday forenoon in an old jersey and slacks, not the proper wear for a business man. By lunch time it must have appeared to the defender's counsel from questions I had put to the pursuer that there was a danger that his client might win; and during the lunch adjournment he got together with the defender and terms were agreed with the pursuer on which the defences would be abandoned and the action proceed undefended.

On Blackford Hill yesterday we had seen a float come for the sheep in the field—it is used regularly for grazing sheep before they go on to the slaughter house—and had watched the efforts of a man and his dog to round up one of the sheep that would not go with the others. It kept dodging round the dog, and even when the man got hold of it refused to budge. Eventually the man, dog and float went off with the rest of the sheep, leaving the one behind. Tonight we saw it still in the field, looking rather forlorn. I suppose it could hardly realise how lucky it has been.

July 7th

On the way out of Dalkeith I picked up two Loretto boys going down for the afternoon to the farm where one of them lived. They had fishing rods with them, but explained that that was simply because they had got the afternoon out on the plea that they were going fishing.

July 8th

Procedure Roll debate: *Gould v. Gould*. Henderson for the defender argued that the action was incompetent because at the time of the divorce, when the pursuer claimed a capital payment from his wife, and the Court was given full information about the parties' assets, the pursuer never suggested that he was the owner of the jewellery that he is now claiming as his property. Lord Johnston, it was said, would never have awarded the pursuer £1,500 if he had made the same averments in the divorce action as he was now making. It seemed to me that while this might be ground for prosecution of the pursuer on a charge of fraud or perverting the course of justice it did not affect the competency of his present action of delivery. If the goods were his, the pursuer was surely entitled to get them from the defender, whatever he might have said or failed to say in the divorce action. Shaffer made a brief reply, and went on to argue that averments about what the Lord Ordinary thought, or what he would have done if he had had different evidence were irrelevant. I thought he was right about this too, though he argued it on the peculiar ground that it would not be competent to lead a judge's evidence. The real ground of criticism obviously was that the averments had nothing to do with the present case. What the pursuer had said or concealed in the previous action was certainly relevant on the question of whether the property was his, but what the Lord Ordinary thought or did about it was a different matter. Henderson had no answer to this, and I indicated that I should repel his plea to relevancy, and refuse to remit the averments about the Lord Ordinary to probation. As Shaffer had succeeded on all the points in the debate, he was prima facie entitled to expenses, but it seemed rather shocking to award expenses to a party whose bona fides was so manifestly suspect. After some argument I said I should hear counsel on the question of expenses again when I had written my Opinion.

Golf on television, with the delightful Huan Lu from Taiwan smilingly raising his little pork-pie hat to acknowledge the greetings of the crowd as he took the lead over a field of highly distinguished competitors. Later we had Mr Heath's ministerial broadcast in support of entry to the Common Market: a propaganda exercise which contrasted strikingly with an interview in a following programme with the Communist Councillor Reid of Clydebank, who though he spoke with restraint and surprising good humour gave the impression of meaning every word he said.

July 9th

I had to deal with Peter Young, a little boy from Aberlour whom I had interviewed at the end of last year. In accordance with a Joint Minute entered into at the time of the divorce, he is due to spend three weeks of his summer holidays with his father, who proposes as he did before to take him to an island in Gair Loch where one Professor McEwan has what seems to be a somewhat primitive holiday cottage. He was unwilling to go, and counsel for both parties invited me to see him again. He put up a good case for himself, telling me how boring and unpleasant it was for him when with his father, and how much he would prefer to remain at Insch and perhaps go with his mother for a holiday in Shetland. When I put it to him that it would be hard on his father if he might not see him again, he suggested that his father might come up during term to Aberlour and take him out for a week-end. As Peter is twelve, I could see no reason why he should not have his own way—which obviously was his own way and not just his mother's—and I withdrew the order for access.

July 12th

Finished reading *Ambassador's Journal*, by John Kenneth Galbraith, an account of the author's two and a half years in India. He recognises, rightly, that in 99 cases out of 100 he is right and most other people wrong, and does not hesitate to say so; and as often as not his assurance and personality are sufficient to get the right thing done. For all that, he never takes himself or anyone else too seriously; and when the best course is to do nothing he is capable of masterly inactivity. The book contains attractive vignettes of people such as a film actress named Angela Dickinson, about whom he goes into raptures.

'Panorama' on tonight's television: first, an interview with Ian Smith, who made rings round a poor boob of an interviewer with a prearranged list of stock questions and total inability to follow any of them up. Second—much livelier—a discussion on the Common Market between Crossman, anti, and Michael Stewart, pro. Crossman in first-rate form left Stewart ploughing along behind, while the two combined to swamp Robin Day out of the picture as he plaintively begged them to 'pass on' to another point. Crossman simply shouted him down, and they went on discussing the point they were interested in. Surprising how few radio and television interviewers realise that it is much more interesting to discuss one topic in depth than to flit superficially from one thing to another. The News included a press conference held by Mr Heath on the same subject, orating meaninglessly on all the things he was 'absolutely certain' about, and looking like a cross between Humpty Dumpty and a tomato.

July 13th

Proof, *Stewart v. Stewart*, concerned the custody of three children: David, aged eight, Philip, aged six, and Gillian, aged four. Mr Stewart, the respondent, had divorced the minuter, Agnes, on the ground of adultery with a man named Wiseman, whom she has since married. When she had gone off with Wiseman in 1969 she had no home to take the children to, and they remained with their father in Ayr. He then became friendly with Wiseman's ex-wife, Mabel, and married her in December 1970. He and Mabel moved into a larger house in Nairn with the three Stewart children and two Wiseman children, Louise and David. In order to avoid having two Davids in the family, David Wiseman's name was changed to Stephen—a name which he himself chose. Meanwhile Agnes and Wiseman moved to Kidderminster. He has a permanent job there, and Agnes feeling that she is able to offer the children a stable home wants custody transferred to her. I was not much impressed by Mr Wiseman, but both Agnes and her ex-husband gave their evidence fairly and reasonably, and I was much impressed by Mabel, who seemed a friendly, sensible person. Everyone agreed that she looked after the five children well and was most capable; and photographs produced gave the impression of a nice family home, with quite a big garden. Mr Stewart has a fishmonger's business, and Wheatley, who appeared for Agnes, argued that it would be better for the children to be with her since she was able to give them her undivided attention, while Mr Stewart conceded that he saw very little of the children except on Sundays. I did not think much of this point; and it appeared that what Agnes was really banking on was an impression she and Wiseman got from David when the children were spending a week-end with them that he would prefer to come and live with her. I had a chat with David in the Cedar Room: a bright, well-adjusted little boy, attached to both his parents and also to Mabel, but he made it absolutely clear that he had no desire to be moved from his home at Nairn. He was quite willing to go to Kidderminster for a holiday, but he was sure all the children were very happy where they were. Out of consideration for the importance of the matter to Agnes, I took the case to avizandum, but it is plain that there is no ground for altering the present arrangements.

July 23rd

I had Dowdall's son take the oath of allegiance before me. I gave him the customary welcome, saying that in a sense his was a formidable task, for we should all be looking to him to maintain the family tradition of distinguished advocacy and indeed to enhance it if that were possible.

1971

July 25th

To church, where a young licentiate preached: one of those self-righteous, unimaginative Christians whose teaching, if it can be so described, bears no relation to everyday life. We must, he said, spare the time to go up the street and down the street to witness for Jesus to an unbeliever. A very attractive young widow sometimes sits in our pew, and as rain was pouring down when we came out of church I thought I could offer to take her home in the car. It turned out however that she lived just across the street.

July 26th

Wheatley was talking about an Irish QC, McSporran, a man of varied talent who was a member of the Stormont Parliament. After Suez, when petrol was rationed, McSporran had occasion to drive into a filling station for six gallons of petrol. He had an allocation of coupons as a member of Parliament, and another for his practice at the Bar. His brother was a doctor and able to spare him some coupons, and his sister was married to a farmer who had plenty of coupons to give away. McSporran ordered six gallons, and asked the boy how many coupons he would have to give up. 'Six', said the boy. McSporran protested that he was not going to hand over six coupons for six gallons, and when the boy persisted drove off without buying any petrol. 'It's not that I don't have coupons', he said, 'But it's the principle of the thing'.

August 3rd

A letter from Jack, the Scottish TUC Secretary, asking whether I would on their behalf conduct the public enquiry which on Anthony Wedgwood Benn's suggestion they are proposing to institute into the history of Upper Clyde Shipbuilders, the latest victim of Government policy. It would have been an interesting assignment, and I was sorry that my position as a judge of the Court of Session made it impossible for me to accept.

August 20th

Vacation Court: *Kelvingrove Conservative and Unionist Association v. Glen.* Kelvingrove and Woodside are to be united into one constituency. The petitioners say that it had been arranged to have a joint meeting of the two Conservative executive committees to discuss the formation of a combined Association. Instead of this, the Woodside

Association resolved to set up a new Kelvingrove constituency association. The old Association is now seeking to interdict the members
of the new one from using 'Kelvingrove Conservative and Unionist'
as their title. I put it to R. E. Henderson, who appeared for the
petitioners, that he had no proprietary right in these words, and that
anyone who chose could call himself the Kelvingrove Conservative
Association; and he had really no answer to this, except to say that it
was an ingenious point but had not been made by the respondents in
their lengthy Answers.

September 1st
Television party political broadcast for Labour—entirely given over
to an appeal for funds. It struck me that at a time when there is so
much unemployment and distress on account of the Government's
policy there might be something wrong with the priorities of a party
which used its fifteen minutes of television time simply asking for
money for itself.

September 4th
We were entertained on television by an extraordinary American film
made in 1959, *Journey to the Centre of the Earth*, in which the Professor, his lady friend and their two faithful followers encounter every
conceivable danger: fire, flood, storm, earthquake, monsters, an attempted murder by a rival scientist. The principal part is played by
James Mason with a deadpan solemnity which is very funny. Whether
the film was meant to be funny is an open question.

September 7th
H.M. Advocate v. Stewart: a man of 27 charged with the murder of a
coal merchant, aged 86, named Devannay. The accused had gone to
Devannay's house looking for drink, and having searched under the
bed and found none struck him over the head with a cooking pot.
Having taken £11 from Devannay's trouser pocket as he lay lifeless
on the floor, he took out Devannay's false teeth to give him the kiss
of life, and when he got no response wiped the blood off his face and
placed a rosary on his chest. There was a second charge that he had
climbed up a rhone pipe into a woman's bedroom and put her into a
state of fear and alarm, but as Stewart was pleading guilty to the
murder charge the Crown did not proceed with Charge 2. We went
on to *H.M. Advocate v. Williamson*, in which a young man is charged

with murdering a six-year-old girl in a derelict tenement. While he was in custody on a charge of breach of the peace, he is said, while his money was being counted at the Bar, to have volunteered the remark, 'I may as well tell you I murdered a wee girl in Brigton tonight'. The police who claimed to have heard this said they then handed him over to the CID for further investigation; and a question arose as to the admissibility of what he said to the CID. I thought the best course was to refuse to admit this evidence, which in any event could add nothing material to what he was already alleged to have said. The effect seemed to be to throw Morton's case into some confusion, and there it rested when we adjourned until tomorrow.

September 8th

Morton had quite a lot of evidence linking the accused with the tenement in which Josephine had been murdered. In view of this, the defence of alibi which had been lodged was obviously no longer maintainable, and indeed when Williamson went into the witness-box he not only said that he had been in the house—he had, he said, been looking for somewhere to sleep later that night—but admitted meeting a little girl with reddish-brown hair and said he had given her a present of Rowntrees' gums. He had then, he said, gone away to the carnival on Glasgow Green, and had not seen the girl again. The jury after a short retiral came back with a unanimous verdict of guilty.

September 9th

H.M. Advocate v. Smith: two youths charged with assaulting another young man, Seaborne, with a razor and bayonet. Seaborne had been at a friend's with two other lads and two girls, Robina and Isobel. They all walked back to Robina's house and stood talking outside. Smith and his companion Todd came along, and Smith accused Seaborne and his friends of making a rude sign to him and Todd shortly before, when they were passing in a taxi. After some exchanges, Smith set on Seaborne, and as they were struggling Todd came forward and slashed Seaborne's face with his razor. A bayonet which Smith had been carrying in his waistband fell to the ground as Seaborne escaped into the house. Smith kept banging at the door to try to get Seaborne to come out, and when this failed Todd proceeded to tear up the next-door fence and throw the palings through the window, breaking two panes. Seaborne decided he would go out, before the place got smashed up. Todd had gone. Smith said something about being sorry for what Todd had done, and wanted to shake hands, but Seaborne was not having any. 'Look at my face', he said. 'It's not an apology I want—I want you in gaol'. Smith thereupon hit him over the head with the bayonet, and he was taken off to the Infirmary. The police rounded up Smith, and went in search of Todd, whom they found hiding behind the bathroom door. He explained that he was running a bath, but as he was standing up on the edge of the bath behind the door this seemed unlikely. Seaborne and his friends turned out to be excellent witnesses, and John Smith, who appeared for his namesake, asked for a short adjournment so that he could consider the position. It looked as if we were going to get a plea, and I thought that if that happened I should have the afternoon free, take the three o'clock train to Balloch, and have a sail on Loch Lomond. But my hopes of this were dashed by Rifkind, an advocate who is a Conservative member of Edinburgh Town Council and was appearing for Todd. His instructing solicitor was Campbell Farrell, and it appeared that nothing could be done until Farrell had been summoned from the Sheriff Court. As a result of their deliberations it was decided to go on with Todd's defence: the familiar one of self-defence and accident. Todd said that his weapon was not a razor but a knife that he used at his work and happened to have with him. When Smith dropped the bayonet Seaborne had picked it up. Todd had taken out the knife to defend himself. Seeing Seaborne attack Smith, he had gone to push him off, with the knife in his hand; and as Seaborne turned round he was accidentally slashed by the knife. Instead of directing the jury that that was no defence in law, I left it to them, observing that even if they believed what Todd had said they would have to think carefully before accepting such a line of defence. It would, I told them, be unfortunate if someone holding a knife in his hands were to be free to set on you—pushing you or whatever it might be—and then if you turned in one direction or another and got cut with the knife to say it was your own fault because if you had not turned in that direction you would not have got cut. The jury returned a unanimous verdict of guilty, and I sentenced both accused to five years' detention.

At the Club I changed quickly; and walked to the station, where I took a day return ticket to Dunoon and train to Gourock. Crossed to Dunoon on the *Iona*, a big car ferry with very little deck accommodation for passengers: a noisy, uncomfortable ship. Despite sunshine and calm sea, I did not enjoy the sail as much as I had expected.

Dunoon seemed completely dead, but it was pleasant there in the evening sun. Supper at the Imperial restaurant—which though it did not look much from the outside provided on excellent meal: good food, well and expeditiously served. Back to the pier for the 7.40 boat, *Queen Mary II*, a commodious, comfortable pleasure steamer which glided quickly through the water with scarcely a sound: the return voyage to Gourock much more agreeable than the outward one.

September 14th

H.M. Advocate v. Crerar, an assault case arising out of an incident in a disreputable part of Glasgow. Kenneth McLeod and Henry McLean were sitting on a low wall at the entrance to the tenement in which McLean lived, watching lightning flashes in a summer storm. They claim that a gang of men came through the close, Crerar among them. Crerar held a knife at McLean's throat, and when McLeod went to McLean's assistance Crerar stabbed him in the side. He ran to his car to let out a savage dog he had in it, but was unable to do so before Crerar and his friends were on to him. In the melee McLean got cut in the face. Crerar's story was that he too was sitting outside the tenement, in the back court, watching not lightning but pigeons. He was set on by McLeod and McLean. There was some defence evidence that McLeod and McLean had been shouting across the street and making rude remarks about Bernadette Devlin. I thought this was possible, but had no doubt that Crerar was the aggressor, and this view was confirmed when I was given a sight of Crerar's criminal record after the jury retired. John Smith made a good speech for the defence, and the jury returned a majority verdict of Not Proven.

September 24th

With Richard to North Berwick for a round of golf on the East course. The course was looking its best, with lovely views of the sea and islands at every hole. Scenically, it must be one of the finest courses in the country.

October 6th

To Gillsland Road to collect Ines and her husband and the children; they are staying in a hotel there. Motored them to Parliament House, where I showed them round before putting them into the First Division courtroom for the installation of two new judges. Kilbrandon has gone to London as a Lord of Appeal in place of Guest, who has retired, and Hunter has been appointed chairman of the Scottish Law Commission, with Alastair Johnston elevated to the bench. An additional judge has been appointed: Harry Keith. After the ceremony I collected my guests and motored them to Lauriston foreshore. The children had never seen the sea except from an aeroplane, and were delighted at going there. After lunch we all climbed to the top of Blackford Hill. I had thought this would not be much of a treat for Swiss children, brought up in the hills; but round about Esslingen they are kept strictly to paths, in recognised Swiss manner, and they regarded a rough hill climb as tremendous fun.

October 9th

Ten undefended divorces. In one, there had been a previous action, heard by Wheatley in 1958. The pursuer, who had married a Pole, had gone with him to Poland and been deserted by him there. Her father had given evidence of her coming home to this country and telling him her husband had left her. Wheatley apparently thought this evidence insufficient; the case had been continued, and later abandoned. The evidence in today's proof was exactly the same, except that the pursuer's father was now dead, so that there was only one witness, the pursuer. I had however a transcript of the evidence given by the father before Wheatley, and granted decree of divorce— there was of course no legal basis for doing so on the evidence of a single witness.

October 12th

Cross actions of divorce: *Runsted v. Runsted.* The wife, the licensee of the Whale Hotel at Eyemouth, claims to have found her husband in bed with one Stephanie Fairbairn, and it was admitted that the husband and Stephanie are now cohabiting. The wife is therefore entitled to her divorce and the marriage is bound to be dissolved; but the husband, not content with that, has raised a cross action on the ground of adultery with an unknown man. I thought it a waste of time and money, and was impatient with him and Stephanie, who gave a lot of highly coloured evidence about Mrs Runsted's goings-on in the hotel. The husband claimed to have seen his wife embracing another man at the Herring Queen barbecue and to have gone home for a camera. His wife obligingly continued to embrace the man until he got back and took a photograph, which was produced and showed an unrecognisable couple, apparently engaged in dancing.

October 14th
Finished reading *Ulysses*, by James Joyce, an extraordinary book, unlike any other I have read. Nothing really happens, and much of it is unintelligible, but I found it interesting throughout. The author has a unique command of language, and writes in a great variety of styles.

October 15th
Worked on my Opinion in *Runsted v. Runsted*. I have assoilzied Mrs Runsted. From today's *Scotsman*: 'John Ritchie (38) was jailed for four years in the High Court in Edinburgh yesterday for . . . stealing a chain saw at Bo'ness. Lord Wheatley told Ritchie he must have an extended period in prison for his own sake'.

October 30th
On television there was an excellent little film of two brothers from a working-class home in Stepney, one of whom had struggled up the educational ladder to win a B.Sc. at the London School of Economics, while the other had left school at fifteen and drifted happily from job to job—cheerful, philosophic, completely unselfconscious. But it seemed sad that the elder brother, an interesting, intelligent personality, should in the prevailing climate of industry have nothing to show for his efforts but unemployment, while his ne'er-do-well, happy-go-lucky brother was building up a good business.

November 2nd
Finished reading *Soldiers*, the controversial play by Rolf Hochhuth on how Churchill and Lord Cherwell arranged the murder of General Sikorski. It is surprisingly effective. The real people who are the characters of the drama are real; the discussion is fair; the argument is powerful. Churchill and the others say things that Churchill and the others might well have said and in the way that they might have said them—heightened no doubt for dramatic effect, since the play is written in what purports to be a kind of blank verse, but still ringing true to a degree most unusual in a fictional work which introduces real public figures. Whatever its merits historically, I found it extremely interesting.

November 8th

On 'Panorama' tonight we had Mr Faulkner answering questions about the position in Ulster. He stood up for himself in his usual forceful manner, but his assertion that they now had the terrorists beaten seemed remote from reality.

November 10th

On television tonight we had the 'Miss World' contest. My favourites, Miss Ceylon and Miss Paraguay, were eliminated in the first round. I rather lost interest in it—though the successful contender, Miss Brazil, was quite a nice girl.

November 12th

Undefended divorce proofs. The defender in one of the divorces was interested in erotic magazines, and had answered an advertisement in one and got a reply from Jane Ford. Miss Ford said she was 22, 'extremely good-looking, long blonde hair, blue eyes, very vivacious, my measurements are 35–22–35, height 5 feet 6 inches with attractive legs made more so with high-heeled shoes and black silk stockings'. She was free on Wednesdays, Fridays 'and of course Saturdays', and would really enjoy herself in being the complete mistress over a nice submissive man. The gift she would expect for this service would be £18 per hour session. She owned a cosy flat in Chelsea, and if he was really interested in being a slave to a beautiful blonde mistress should drop her a line. The defender had kept a copy of the letter he wrote in reply: 'Dear Miss Ford, I thank you for your prompt answer to my reply to your advertisement in M.F. I regret that the services which you have to offer are not quite what I had in mind'. There was also in the productions a long, lurid letter from 'the fabulous Odette (44–26–38)' describing her prowess with two of her male slaves. For this he had evidently paid ten shillings; and Odette offered an even more lurid letter for a pound. I was shown a letter the pursuer had just received from him, saying that if she went on with the divorce he would come to Court for the proof and cut his throat, so we had the court officer in attendance in case anything untoward should happen. He did indeed come to the proof—a small, thin-faced, inoffensive-looking man, who listened to the evidence with a completely impassive countenance, and when I said 'Decree' picked up his raincoat from the seat beside him, put it over his arm, and went out.

November 15th

'World in Action' on television had an interesting enquiry into the effect of uncontrolled doses of aspirin and similar drugs. As I have never taken any in my life, it did not affect me.

November 16th

A jury trial. Apart from the pursuer's evidence, the whole of today's proceedings was occupied by medical evidence. Despite a great deal of argument, and lengthy questioning for the pursuer and defenders, it was obvious in the end of the day that there was no real difference of opinion among the doctors. As usual, they agreed that there was no organic cause for the pursuer's trouble but that it was perfectly genuine so far as he was concerned and would probably clear up when the litigation was at an end. It seemed to me that in most of these neurosis cases all the argument was a waste of time

From today's *Scotsman*: 'The Prime Minister went to the City of London last night and gave an unrelenting message about Northern Ireland. "Terrorism must be brought to an end", he said'.

November 18th

On television tonight there was a short Polish film of the Russian fleet in the Mediterranean: a patriotic film showing how Russian ships and sailors are keeping watch and ward against American aggression. It was just like any other patriotic naval documentary made in any country, but the amusing thing about it was its musical accompaniment: the stirring strains of *Land of Hope and Glory*. I also watched most of the heavyweight fight at Houston, Texas, in which Mohammed Ali defeated another black man, Buster Mathis—officially on points, though it was obvious that Ali could have knocked Mathis out at any time in the last two rounds and refrained from doing so because, as he put it, he didn't have it in his heart to hurt him with his wife and little boy watching. He harangued the interviewers in his usual way in the ring after the fight, saying it was not for him to knock Mathis out just to please a silly gang of spectators who wanted to see blood, and criticising the referee, quite rightly, for not stopping the fight in the eleventh round. If the referee had had any sense, said Ali, that was what he would have done.

November 28th

This morning before getting up I felt a tickle in my throat, and immediately coughed up a large fragment of rough stone. I have no idea where it had come from. It caused no discomfort whatever.

On Sunday mornings we are having Mrs Gaskell's *Wives and Daughters* in six weekly instalments. It is beautifully done, and there is a surprising amount of character and wit in Mrs Gaskell's story.

From today's *Sunday Express*: 'Mr Enoch Powell yesterday said that with every post he received letters from people who agreed, or thought they agreed, with what they understood him to be saying'.

November 30th

Procedure Roll discussion in *Unigate Creameries v. Scottish Milk Marketing Board*. It raises a lot of interesting questions: the real question whether 'bulk salted butter manufactured by the Board' means butter which is in bulk containers when put on the market, as the Board contends, or includes butter that is stored in bulk by the Board though ultimately it is going to be marketed in quarter pound packets. The case was excellently deployed in the opening speech by John Murray for the defenders. Wheatley's reply was less satisfactory, but as his senior is James Mackay there will be no question of my not having the case for the pursuers fully and ably argued.

December 2nd

Chisholm v. Kennedy, an action of damages for slander. The defender was proprietrix of the Cluanie Inn, Glenmoriston. Touring buses stop there regularly for coffee on their way to Kyle of Lochalsh, and the defender was in the habit of using the bus drivers as her messengers to take the hotel takings to the bank at Kyle. The drivers did not get any receipt when they handed in a packet of money; the bank sent a receipt to Miss Kennedy by post. The pursuer, a driver with Highland Omnibuses, says that on 6th August 1969 he called at the Inn with his bus and was given a package by the defender which he handed in at the bank. He was not one of the drivers that Mrs Kennedy regularly employed on this commission; she had never asked him to do it before. On 14th August, a Thursday, he got a message from his inspector at Inverness that Mrs Kennedy had phoned to ask what he had done with the package she gave him on Tuesday of that week. He phoned back as requested and told Mrs Kennedy that the only package he had had from her was on Wednesday of the previous week. She denied that she had given him a package on that day, and insisted that she had given it to him on the 12th and it had not been delivered. She persisted in this accusation to himself, to the police and to his employers, and complained to other bus drivers about what Chisholm had done to her. The defender on Record admitted that she had accused the pursuer of appropriating her package of money and averred that the accusation was true. Her solicitors recently withdrew from the case, and I had been shown a letter from her saying that she would come along today with her witnesses and defend the case herself. Meanwhile however she had been prevailed on to obtain some assistance, and Macaulay appeared on her behalf. The pursuer gave evidence: a prim, self-righteous kind of man but apparently honest. There was evidence from another bus driver that he had walked along to the bank in Kyle with the pursuer on 6th August, and waited outside while he went in, and from a police officer and the bank teller that some days after the 14th the pursuer had approached the officer in the street in Kyle and got him to go with him to the bank, where the teller identified him as the man who had come in with a packet from Mrs Kennedy some day before 8th August. Chisholm was not a customer of the bank, and the teller had never seen him before, so that even if he was mistaken about the date it seemed that he had at some date taken a package from Mrs Kennedy to the bank—which she denies. It appeared from the bank account that there had been no payment in on the 12th, but there had been a payment in on the 6th, described on the pay-in slip as payment 'by messenger'—it is stated in Mrs Kennedy's pleadings that the money that day had been paid in by her son David, who runs the hotel.

December 3rd

The proof continued. Mrs Kennedy was a dour old lady, who had no doubt that Chisholm had taken her money, and was prepared to say anything, however incredible, provided it might fit in with her story. She insisted that she had handed the package over in the presence of an Eastern Scottish driver who was there with a week's tour from Edinburgh. The police after consulting the company's records arranged for a driver named McMorran to call at Cluanie next time he was up; and when confronted with him in the presence of two policemen she said that he was not the man. McMorran gave evidence that up to then he had never stopped at Cluanie, but after calling with the police, and finding that tea there was cheap and good, he stopped quite a lot, instead of at Shiel Bridge. But Mrs Kennedy had meanwhile convinced herself that McMorran was the man, that he had called at Cluanie frequently before the date when the money was handed over, and that he must be in a conspiracy with Chisholm. Since McMorran lived in Edinburgh, was employed by a different company from the company that employed Chisholm, and had so far as could be seen no connection with him, this was a tall story. She did not know who had handed in her money on the 6th. It could have been herself, or any of the bus drivers except Chisholm. She adduced a young girl from the Vale of Leven who had been a temporary waitress at Cluanie in the summer of 1969, and who though she did not know McMorran by name and had never been asked about it till yesterday professed to remember that McMorran's call had been in the first half of August, not the second half. Finally Mrs Kennedy's son appeared to say that he had seen his mother hand the package to Chisholm on the 12th. As nobody had ever suggested that there was any witness to this except the other driver, whoever he may have been, and Mrs Kennedy did not suggest to the police or anyone else that her son had witnessed it, this was pretty obviously an afterthought.

December 4th
Ten divorces. The parties in one of them had been married at the Old Smiddy Inn, Pencaitland, by a minister called Rev. Donald Bump.

December 5th
South Morningside Church: the service conducted by Miss Agnes Forrest, who has just retired from being a medical missionary in Madras. One would think that in the course of twenty years in India and Pakistan she would have found something of interest to talk about, but if she did she kept it to herself, though she spoke at considerable length.

December 6th
Working on my opinion in the milk case: I am dismissing the action, on the ground that the defenders were right in taking 'bulk salted butter manufactured by the Board' to mean butter that was in bulk when it came to be marketed.

December 8th
Finished my Opinion in *Chisholm v. Kennedy*. I had forgotten to take a book to read when I left for Court yesterday, and so whether I liked

it or not had to work on my Opinion in order to occupy myself while the jury in yesterday's case were out; so I had not much left to do. I have found for the pursuer, and awarded him £120.

December 10th

The case of *Deuchar's Tutor v. Johnston*, in the 'By Order' Roll. The pursuer is suing on behalf of his seven-year-old daughter who was injured when she fell off a pony at the Bo'ness gala. The defender, a farmer, had brought two ponies to the gala to be used in the National Coal Board pageant. After the pageant was over, they were used for giving pony rides, under the charge of two young girls. The gala committee had arranged for an aerial display by low-flying aircraft, and as Marion was getting on one of the ponies six aircraft suddenly appeared over the hill and flew low over the park, frightening the pony, which was usually docile, and causing it to rear up on its hind legs. The pursuer says that the defender should not have been giving pony rides when he knew or ought to have known that low-flying aircraft were to give a display.

December 14th

Birley v. Birley, an action of divorce on the ground of cruelty. The defender's agents had retired from the case, and today he appeared on his own behalf and cross-examined his wife at some length. His cross-examination consisted largely of assertions, to which the witness replied by asking him a question designed to show that his assertion must be wrong; but he kept his end up fairly well against her. There was no history of violence, but he had been persistently drunk and made a nuisance of himself in the house to the extent that his wife had finally decided she could not put up with him any longer. Pinkerton having addressed me briefly for the pursuer, I asked Mr Birley if he wanted to say anything. He rather indicated that he did not think it would be much use, and I agreed, pointing out to him that the marriage had obviously broken down and that if he succeeded in his defence he would simply be tied to his wife without any real marriage. He accepted this at once, and I granted decree. The wife was asking for £2 aliment for the child and £5 periodical allowance for herself; and the defender, when I put this to him, said he thought £5 was too much but he was content to leave it to me to decide. I awarded £2 and £3, and everyone went away quite satisfied.

December 18th

To the Lyceum: Brendan Behan's play *The Hostage*, a remarkable extravaganza about the Irish troubles, full of wit and genius, and insight into the extraordinary character of the Irish.

December 19th

Surprised to find I had got myself a mention in the *Sunday Express*. It reported that ten Court of Session judges yesterday morning had disposed of 98 divorce cases. 'Lord Stott dealt with 10 undefended divorces in 70 minutes, in what is believed to be near record time'.

December 21st

On television tonight the BBC had a documentary about Jerusalem. It was a nauseating programme, not through any fault of the film, which was excellently done, but simply because of the nature of the place: swarms of gossiping tourists queuing for tickets for the Crucifixion or the Holy Sepulchre, or for a conducted tour of the Garden of Gethsemane. If one had had any idea of visiting the Holy Land, this film would put an end to it.

December 22nd

Finished reading *Motive for a Mission*, by James Douglas-Hamilton, the advocate who is a son of the Duke of Hamilton and in a specially advantageous position to write about Hess's extraordinary flight to Scotland. He has done it extremely well, and produced a readable, interesting book, not only about Hess and his flight but about the man who seems unwittingly to have inspired it, Albrecht Hushofer. He gives a brilliant account of the dilemma confronting a well-intentioned, intelligent German Foreign Office official after Hitler came to power, and his ultimate destruction.

December 23rd

Lengthy reports in this morning's papers of the decision of the Second Division in *Allen v. Scott*. A curiously constituted court—Walker, Milligan and Fraser—has upheld my decision on the merits and increased the award of damages by £6,000, holding that my figure of £14,000 for solatium was too low. Directly contradicting the decision of both Divisions in *McCallum v. Paterson*, they have held that £20,000 is the appropriate figure for solatium for a paraplegic, and that I should have had regard to awards that had been made in English cases. This of course is very satisfactory, and puts an end to the McCallum doctrine as set out by Clyde, but it is rather hard that I should be the scapegoat and be told that I had followed a wrong approach to the problem—particularly by Walker, who was one of the three judges who overturned the first jury's verdict in Mrs McCallum's case on the ground that an award of £20,000 was grossly excessive. As an article on the centre page of the *Scotsman* puts it, 'it is ironic that the judge they held to have "erred" in not awarding enough was Lord Stott who presided at the second McCallum jury trial and has all along advocated much higher awards'. No doubt I asked for it, by putting in plain language the only possible ratio of the McCallum decisions: that a figure that was reasonable when awarded by judges in England became unreasonable when awarded by a Scottish jury. So stated, it was obviously nonsense, as Fraser observed; and so my ground of judgment could not be right.

December 31st
A letter from Gracie Thomson: 'May I say I thought and so did George that you picked a winner when you got married and time has proved us right'.

1972

*A year of industrial turmoil and ever-increasing disruption in the nation
was for me another quiet year. I was kept fully occupied with congenial
work, and despite the absence of social and public activities seemed latterly
not to have a great deal of leisure—no doubt because of the number of
Opinions I had to produce in the autumn term. If I had been a slower
worker, I thought I might have found it quite heavy going, for I had no
fewer than twenty Opinions to deliver in the course of the term, only six
of them extempore. So I had quite a lot of homework to do, and my
impression that I had not had as much time to myself as usual was
confirmed by finding that I had read only fifty-seven books—the smallest
number in any year since 1958.*

January 6th

Occasionally I get some amusement in undefended divorces by asking some irrelevant question which seems to show that I have some
inner knowledge of the case, so as to lead Mr Sibbald to ask how I
knew about such-and-such a point, and I had a chance to do this
today when the pursuer in an action of cruelty had given evidence
about her husband's assault on her, and was followed in the witness
box by her brother. 'Did your sister', I asked him, 'at one time work
with the police?' 'Yes', he said, 'she did. She was four years with the
Glasgow police'. At the end of the proof Sibbald duly asked whether
I had come across the pursuer some time in Glasgow. I was able to
reply in the negative but to point out that in her evidence she had
said that her husband had struck her 'with his booted foot'—a typical
police expression.

January 11th

A cruelty divorce, *Johnson v. Johnson.* The pursuer in January 1968
was in Stratheden Hospital suffering from delusions in which she
imagined that her husband had given her what I read in the medical
records as 'white rabbits' to make her unconscious. Later I realised

that this was a mistake arising from the doctor's bad writing; what she thought he had given her was 'white tablets'. As she had had six children in the first five years of her marriage, it was perhaps not surprising that she had found things difficult. The children are at present living with the defender and his mother. The pursuer wants to have custody of all of them and brought the two oldest ones, aged fourteen and thirteen, to say they wanted to live with her. Neither would give any reason, except that they liked her better.

January 12th
I concluded the hearing of evidence in *Johnson v. Johnson*, and then at the request of counsel interviewed the four remaining children in the Cedar Room. Apart from the youngest, who had nothing to say, they discussed the situation in a lively, goodhumoured way. All agreed that Thomas (aged nine) wanted to stay with his father. Evelyn (eleven) wanted to go to her mother; and after some cogitation Mary (ten) thought she would like to go with Evelyn. They said that Lynn, the youngest, was always changing her mind, and it did not matter where she went.

January 19th
A man rang up who said his name was Field and he was engaged in security vetting of Lord Wilson of Langside, who has been appointed to the new post of supervisor of Sheriff Courts. Wilson had referred him to me. I ridiculed the idea of a security vetting of anyone who had held office in the Government and had already had access there to far more important secrets, and did not attempt to conceal my view that it was sheer tomfoolery. 'He told me that that would be your view', said Mr Field. I arranged to meet him at Parliament House at 9.30 tomorrow morning.

January 20th
Mr Field duly appeared, and with many apologies extracted from me an assurance that Harry Wilson was not likely to be subject to any subversive pressures such as would induce him to reveal Sheriff Court secrets to Britain's enemies.

January 26th
In the *Daily Record* the whole front page is taken up with two delightful pictures of the Johnson family: Mrs Johnson with the four

children allotted to her, and Mr Johnson with his two. Everyone in both pictures was beaming with obvious pleasure: a singularly happy outcome.

January 27th

H.M. Advocate v. Paul. I refused a request to have the court cleared, and a large audience listened with interest while Elspeth Jaffrey told us of a night in September when she had gone to Bridge of Don barracks with the idea of meeting her boyfriend. After two and a half hours, when he had failed to appear, she set off for home; and when she changed buses at Castle Street another soldier who had been on the first bus got off along with her and pulled her along the street into a multi-storey car park. There he took off all her clothes, and was said to be attempting to ravish her when a police car drove in and broke the party up. Elspeth, who is seventeen, looked about two years younger: a simple-minded, pleasant little girl who gave her evidence mostly in monosyllables, remaining silent from time to time when a question was put until it could be put again in simpler terms. Fairbairn, appearing for Paul, got her to admit that she had had many other boy friends among the soldiers. She insisted that she had not consented to what Paul was trying to do, and I daresay that was true, but if police had not come on the scene and required an explanation I do not suppose we should ever have heard of the matter. Stewart resisted a motion for continuation of bail, but I had no hesitation in continuing it—whether the accused turns up tomorrow seems to me a matter of no importance.

January 28th

The case was resumed—some amusing evidence from two sixteen-year-old girls who like Elspeth were in the habit of going to Bridge of Don barracks in the evening and hanging about at the gate waiting for soldiers. One of them was rather contemptuous of Elspeth because she went with old soldiers like the accused—who is in his early twenties. Apparently any soldier over seventeen is regarded as beyond the pale. The girls gave a different picture from Elspeth's about her meeting with the accused, making it clear that it was on her initiative that he had got off the bus with her. Later there was evidence from a young couple who had heard shouts and screams coming from the car park and phoned the police. It was because of this that the police car had come on the scene, twenty minutes later. The evidence again did not fit in very well with Elspeth's—she had said she had been unable to scream because the accused had threatened to kill her—nor with the evidence of the police, who had not heard a sound while searching through the car park from car to car until one had shone his torch on the naked Elspeth. The accused, a pleasant-looking young corporal of the HLI, who had been flown back from Ulster for the trial, gave his evidence clearly and succinctly: he was a stranger to Aberdeen, and it was the girl who had taken him into the car park, he being the consenting party. The idea dawned on me that the evidence of the young couple could be explained on the theory that it had been someone else they had heard shouting, and this unknown pair had gone off before Elspeth and her soldier arrived. I put this forward as a possibility when I came to charge the jury. The jury were out for no more than ten minutes before coming back with a verdict announced as 'Not proven—by a majority'. This was misleading; I heard that the figures were nine for Not Proven and six for Not Guilty.

February 1st
From today's *Scotsman*: 'Families of the thirteen people shot dead in Londonderry on Sunday said yesterday that none of them was a member of the official IRA or the Provisionals...Several Conservative MPs late last night tabled a Commons motion expressing admiration "for the conduct of British troops in Ulster who under great provocation have maintained the best traditions of the British Army".'

February 3rd
Parliament House. At lunch we were joined by Hunter, who was in great good humour. I happened to remark how curious it was that the Congo, which was the centre of the newspapers' attention a few years ago, had dropped out of the news altogether. Hunter explained that this was because all the people had been killed off. The pygmy inhabitants had been massacred, or more probably eaten.

February 4th
I had thirteen divorces in my Roll for undefended proof, but in *Storrie v. Storrie* I was told that the defender was sitting in court, and at the end of the proof he stood up and said that he could not pay his wife any money. I asked him to come forward, when he said that if I made an order for periodical allowance he would give up his work and she would get nothing. The conclusion was for £7 a week, and I explained to the defender that I had been thinking of modifying this,

but if he was not to pay anything I might as well just grant an order for £7. Faced with this, he said he would pay something; and as he was earning £21 per week it looked as if he could afford something. He is getting married again, and will have another household to keep; but he offered to pay £2 a week, and Cay for the pursuer accepted the offer. When *Brown v. Brown* was called—an adultery case by a husband against a wife—it was pointed out to me that the next case was between the same parties: an action by the wife on the ground of cruelty. The husband's case had been out for proof on a date in March, but the wife's agents, without the authority of anyone acting for the husband, arranged with court officials to have it moved forward to today, when the wife's case was down for proof. The husband had meanwhile disappeared. It seemed wrong that the date for the husband's proof should have been altered at the instance of someone who had no right to interfere; and I said that the case would not be heard until the date in March of which the husband had been notified. Sibbald thought I should continue the wife's case also until March, but as both parties obviously wanted to be divorced I did not see much point in that. The wife had a claim for periodical allowance, but Cay, who appeared for the wife, decided not to ask for any, so that the husband will not have been prejudiced by my having heard his wife's case and granted decree. When his case comes up in March, it will of course be dismissed as incompetent, since there is now no marriage to be dissolved.

February 10th

From today's *Scotsman*: 'Bangkok, Wednesday.—Bombing raids on targets in Laos and Vietnam from the US Air Force base in Southern Thailand were suspended temporarily this morning as the Queen arrived by air from Britain for a one-week state visit'.

February 11th

Parliament House. On going along to the Reading Room I found that all lights had been switched off in support of a Government appeal to save electricity and so relieve pressure on electricity supplies arising out of the miners' strike. Up to yesterday, instructions to the press and broadcasting authorities had obviously been to play down the strike. Nothing much appeared about its effects, either on television or in newspapers. For the four or five weeks it has lasted the idea was obviously to convey the impression that it was having little or no effect, and so discourage the miners, who have had to carry on without any strike pay. It was assumed that sufficient stocks of coal had been accumulated at power stations and suchlike to last for several weeks; and after discussion with Mr Carr the Coal Board this week produced an 'informal' offer to the miners, in reality—as the *Scotsman* alone among newspapers has demonstrated—worse in money terms than the offer made at the outset. The miners rejected it out of hand; and yesterday it suddenly appeared that a fuel crisis was upon us. The miners with considerable ingenuity have not confined their picketing to coal, but with some assistance from other unions have been remarkably successful in preventing essential supplies of oil getting through to power stations. Several have already had to be closed, and others are barely able to carry on. The Government last night announced immediate drastic cuts in electricity supply, which it seems will bring a great part of industry to a standstill, apart from the effect on other consumers. The miners, it appears, are a different proposition from Mr Jackson and his postmen; and the Government in deciding to sit tight and do nothing but prevent the Coal Board from making any offer failed like the foolish virgins to observe that they had no oil in their lamps. I switched the lights in the Reading Room on, and left them on when I went to lunch. Nancy had been intending to go to the Scottish Orchestra concert, but it was cancelled on account of the fuel crisis. When we were just finishing supper, the Leechmans arrived, saying there was a power cut at Barnton which had deprived them of light, and they thought they might as well come and see us. They brought an enormous piece of cod roe. We put on the television for the ITN News: poor, pathetic Mr John Davies bleating away about how the picketing had been quite illegal, what a terrible situation it was, and how he had no idea what would happen if the miners went on as they were doing. Mr Carr has belatedly decided to set up an independent court of enquiry under Lord Wilberforce, and we had a picture of Mr Heath declaiming to some Tory meeting in Liverpool about the wickedness of the miners in not going back to work at once while their case was being considered by the court of enquiry.

February 12th
Electricity was off when we got up, but came on in time to allow me to shave before coming downstairs. There was another cut in the afternoon.

February 13th

From today's *Sunday Express*: 'Mrs Margaret Thatcher, the Education Minister, yesterday called on the miners to return to work. She told a Tory women's conference in Edinburgh: "I know that many, many sets of workers would gladly accept £3 in cash—bringing them up to £23 a week". The one-day conference carried a resolution calling on the Government to continue efforts to abolish poverty'.

February 14th

To town to get a suit at Aitken & Niven's. The Government's panic restrictions on heating came into force this weekend, and there was no heating in the shop, which was very cold.

February 15th

Parliament House was pleasantly warm, not being heated by electricity. The timing of street lamps has gone haywire in consequence of power cuts. We go to bed in pleasant darkness. The lights come on in the early hours of the morning and burn for a good part of the day.

February 16th

The city has been divided into districts, each of which takes it in turn to have a 'high-risk' day. Today was our turn. The electricity went off in the afternoon, and did not come on till shortly after six. I was reading through divorce cases for tomorrow by candlelight when the lights came on. The final cut came about 9.15. I had a bath by the dim light of a big candle that Nancy made out of cooking fat at the time of the last power cuts.

February 18th

When I came out of court at lunch time I was told that the coal strike had been settled, Wilberforce having recommended an award near to what the miners had been asking, and far more than the Government had offered. After lunch it appeared that the rumour of a settlement had been premature. The miners had refused to accept what Wilberforce had recommended, and talks were proceeding with the Coal Board and Mr Carr. It was pointed out with some truth that this *Waiting for Godot* method of wage negotiation had involved the waste of several weeks and that meanwhile the miners had lost quite a lot of money; but I felt that they were chancing their luck in continuing to hold out after winning a complete victory, with a big award backdated to November. Putting on the wireless after we had gone to bed, I was relieved to hear that the mineworkers' Executive had now decided to recommend acceptance. Meanwhile they had had another meeting with Coal Board representatives and had won substantial further concessions. The miners have shown for the first time that doctrinaire, dogmatic government in the interest purely of the well-to-do is no match for organised labour when it is really put to the test.

February 19th

Ten divorces, in one of which the evidence related to an occasion when the pursuer had arrived home unexpectedly in the middle of the night, and after trying his key in the front-door lock went round to the back, where he found another man coming out of the back door carrying jacket and tie. He made the man go back into the house for a discussion, at which they were joined by the pursuer's father and mother. They thought they should have an independent witness and telephoned for their MP, Mr Baxter.

February 27th

Mr Heath gave a short ministerial broadcast on television, on the aftermath of the miners' strike. He assured us that the Government was determined to see that no one would achieve anything through force, but he was unusually subdued—all the bounce seemed to have gone out of him.

March 5th

Started to take the dog down to the pond, but was diverted by a little girl, Jessica, whom I caught sight of outside her house at the corner of Braid Avenue. She came with me to the grass at the foot of Midmar Drive, where we were joined by her older sister and occupied ourselves in throwing the ball for the dog.

March 9th

A cruelty divorce that had been one of Lord Emslie's Roll of undefended proofs for today. It came before me on the Motion Roll on Tuesday, on a motion by the husband to discharge today's diet of proof and allow Defences to be received. This would have meant that a Record would have to be made up, with a delay of twelve to eighteen months, and all the expense and trouble of a defended divorce. So I allowed Defences to be received but refused to discharge the diet of proof and refused leave to reclaim. In this unusual situation, it had apparently been decided to transfer the case from Emslie to me; and after some thought I felt that the best course would be to allow counsel for the defender to appear today if he wished, and cross-examine and lead evidence on the Summons and Defences, such as they were. But when the case was called counsel informed me that the pursuer had agreed to drop her claim for periodical allowance, and that the defences, which had been on the merits, would be withdrawn. It accordingly proceeded as an undefended action in which I heard evidence and granted decree: a complete vindication of my decision to ignore the rules.

March 23rd

Stirling Circuit: *H.M. Advocate v. Murray.* The accused, who is charged with the murder of his wife, Marion, was seen between 8.30 and 9 on the morning of 22nd December outside his house, a two-storey flat in a Council maisonette in Alloa, in an agitated state, saying there was something wrong with his wife. Police and ambulance were sent for, and Mrs Murray was found lying in bed in her nightdress, with two wounds in her head caused by blows from a blunt instrument, and one of her husband's neckties round her neck. Death had been caused by strangulation. One of the ambulance men thought that he could feel a faint pulse still beating when he arrived; and though it seems that this was probably a mistake it is clear that death must have taken place very shortly before. There was a baby in the room, in a carry-cot, and three other children sleeping in another bedroom. No one else was in the house. The accused's story is that he got up soon after 8, leaving his wife sleeping, and left the house at 8.25 to take his employers' van back to the works—he had borrowed it the day before. Halfway into town, he met the van driver coming in his car with another youth to collect the van. The van was handed over to the youth, and the driver gave the accused a lift back to the house—he was meaning to go Christmas shopping with his wife and so was not going to work. He went upstairs to the bedroom and found his wife lying dead. Experiments by the police showed that the accused's expedition with the van could not have taken more than five minutes, and the Crown case seems to be based on the proposition that it was impossible that within the time some unknown stranger could have entered the house, committed the murder, and got away without anyone seeing him and without leaving any trace of his presence. It certainly seems unlikely, particularly as Mrs Murray, so far as all the witnesses knew, had no enemies. On the other hand, everyone agreed that the Murrays were a happily married couple, with no sign of any ill will or enmity between them, that on the previous day they had been on excellent terms and had gone shopping to Glasgow, and that Mr Murray was a quiet, sensible, well-behaved man who had no reason to murder his wife and was the last person in the world one would expect to do such a thing. There was some curious evidence that in order to get off work on the previous day and get the use of the van Murray had told his employer that his wife's mother had just died from a cerebral haemorrhage, and some furniture had to be moved to the house in connection with the funeral; and there was some vague evidence that earlier in the year Murray had told his wife that he was expecting a legacy from his recently deceased employer, the head of a printing firm, who in fact had left him nothing. Both Murray's statements had clearly been untrue—his wife's mother was a witness, and apart from saying that she had never had a cerebral haemorrhage was obviously not dead. But neither of them seemed to have any bearing on the murder. The detective superintendent in charge of the enquiry gave evidence about questioning the accused, and was allowed by Walker, who appeared for the defence, to quote a number of innocuous answers the accused had given; but objection was taken when the superintendent went on to say that he had then put the direct question to Murray: whether he was the person responsible for the injuries to his wife. Walker suggested that I should hear evidence about this in the absence of the jury. I demurred to this, but after quite a lengthy argument, in the jury's presence, I sustained his objection and refused to allow Milligan, the Advocate-Depute, to ask the superintendent what Murray had said in reply.

March 24th

Milligan led a long procession of witnesses, all the people living in the block, to say that they had seen no strangers about on the morning of the crime; but the weakness of that type of evidence was illustrated by the evidence of two of the women, who had been in till well on in the forenoon and had seen nothing unusual—although during that time there had been an ambulance at the house and a resuscitation unit and various police cars, and the woman's body had been carried out on a stretcher. Time was wasted in proving that the husband's finger prints were on an empty milk bottle which was thought to have been the likely weapon. It was obvious that his fingerprints could have been left there while he was handling the bottle in course of having his breakfast. The police doctor gave evidence that wounds on the woman's head had bled profusely before she was strangled, which made it surprising that no bloodstains were found on any of the accused's clothing. Against this, the Crown could lead only some prejudicial evidence to the effect that the household, despite every appearance of affluence, was to some extent in debt. The accused had bought a car on hire purchase and sold it for a small sum without paying up his hire-purchase instalments; and when his wife, who under an assumed name was selling agent for a firm of general dealers in London, got into arrears with her remittances in July of last year he had written to the firm saying that his wife had died eight months before and he would hold himself responsible. When Milligan closed his case, the whole affair seemed to me to be a complete mystery.

March 27th

I left for Stirling in a miniature blizzard of sleet and snow. This morning Murray gave evidence. He had looked a cool customer sitting in the dock, where he followed the proceedings with apparent interest, sometimes making a note with a pencil; and as a witness he was almost too good from a jury point of view: calm, unemotional, intelligent, with an answer for everything. Milligan made a good speech. Walker's reply, I thought, went on too long. He has conducted the case tactfully and well. Some of his questions may have been a little obscure, but as Emslie remarked to me on Saturday his peculiar style of advocacy might be rather effective in a case where it was thought advisable to increase the air of mystery. I charged the jury for Not Proven, but they were out for over an hour, and then returned with a verdict of Guilty, by a majority. Johnston told me that counsel on both sides are agreed that justice had been done; according to their information, there was no doubt that Murray had murdered his wife, the whole thing having been witnessed by their three-year-old son. It had been thought that he was too young to be adduced as a witness.

March 28th

Clyde retired from the Lord Presidency at the end of the term. There was a farewell ceremony which I was unable to attend, being away on circuit, so I thought I should write him a note saying I should miss him about the Parliament House, even if only in the capacity of Oldest Enemy.

From Lord Clyde:

Briglands Rumbling Bridge Kinross 2/4/72
Dear Stott
How very kind of you to write. The actual going was a bit of a jolt after so many years in the saddle, but now that its all over I feel much relieved—I know you and I often disagreed about problems, but I'm happy to think that we never quarrelled about anything.

I know you said 'dont acknowledge' your letter. But I just felt I must say thank you none the less.

Yours ever

April 3rd

To Warriston Crematorium to attend the funeral service of my old Trades Council colleague, James Stewart, who was Lord Dean of Guild at the time of his death: the first Trade Union man to be elected to that office in Edinburgh. During the service I sat next to Forbes Murphy. For once in a way, the service bore some relation to the man. An anonymous minister, who obviously had known Jimmy Stewart well, recited prayers that were appropriate to his life and character, and George Lawson gave a short tribute that was excellent, entirely free from cant or humbug. Murphy told me that his neighbour Lord Avonside was not at all pleased with Emslie's appointment to be Lord President.

April 6th

H.M. Advocate v. Nolan: three youths charged with the attempted murder of a postman named Sked. He had been walking across Portobello golf course late at night on Christmas Eve when he was set on by six teenagers. He gave as good as he got, and had one of them, Shankey, on the ground, when one of the others whipped out a sheath knife and stabbed him four or five times in the chest. He was unable to identify any of his assailants, and there were no eye-witnesses. The Crown had got over this difficulty by putting three of the teenagers—Nolan, Carrol and Shankey—in the dock and using the other three as witnesses. The three all said that the Procurator-Fiscal who came to see them in prison had told them they would only be released if they agreed to give evidence. This I daresay was right enough. Anyway, they kept to their side of the bargain, and gave their evidence freely. They admitted that they had all set on Sked, and said that Nolan was the one who had a knife. Prais, who appeared for Nolan, got one of them to agree that when questioned by the police he decided to say that Nolan was the man who had the knife, and indeed that they had all decided to say that; but when I asked why they had chosen Nolan as the one who had the knife he replied, 'Because he was the one who had it'. When we adjourned for lunch, Nolan decided to plead guilty to assault to the danger of life— the charge of attempted murder being withdrawn—and the other two to assault by punching. I asked Johnston what I should give them. He suggested five years for Nolan, saying I might perhaps think that was rather much, and perhaps twelve months for the others. It seemed to me however that if Edinburgh people were to be protected against this kind of conduct it was necessary to do something pretty drastic, and that even apart from the use of a weapon teenagers should be severely discouraged from setting upon some innocent stranger. So I gave Nolan a six-year sentence, and Carrol and Shankey three years.

April 9th
From today's *Observer*: 'Samuel Smith, 49, a sales director, of Gray's Park, Ealing, was remanded on bail at Camberwell Green Court, London, accused of stealing a stuffed tiger, valued at £500, from Waterloo Station'.

April 16th
Palmerston Place Church: Mr Cumming preached on Psalms 68:18. He is an attractive preacher, with a nice voice and a pleasant way of putting things.

April 17th
Lucerne. Taxi to the Royal Hotel: our taxi-driver discoursed in excellent English on the difference between horse-chestnuts and other chestnuts, and on the different words for them in Swiss-German and classical German.

April 21st
Trolley-bus to the station to join the Hamburg-Chiasso express. We

changed at Bellinzona into the train for Locarno. In the carriage was an old couple with two lovely cats, a white one and a ginger one. They opened the cats' baskets before the train started; and the cats having sat up and looked out lay down to sleep again, making no move to get out of their baskets. Locarno is on Lake Maggiore and there was a pleasant walk along the lake, with shrubs and grass and flowers: wisteria in full bloom. Though the mountain background was perhaps not as spectacular as at Lugano we thought that in some ways Locarno was preferable: not so much traffic, and the lakeside and hillside behind not so much built-up.

April 22nd

Funicular to Sonnenberg: entertained by a boisterous group of middle-aged men who proceeded to sing loudly and lustily during the ascent—a song welcoming the Spring, the song whose tune was used for 'The Red Flag', and one or two others. There seems to be tremendous activity in the building and construction industry in Switzerland just now: new houses, schools, roads and bridges wherever one goes. We had noticed going up the Gotthard line that a great new motorway is being driven up the valley, with massive viaducts and dual-carriage-way tunnels through the rock. In some parts, the road was being covered in, presumably as protection against snow and avalanches, and grass was being sown on the top, forming a carpet of green on top of the rock.

April 23rd

Express to Arth-Goldau, and changed there into the train for Rapperswil. The line wound steeply up the hillside above the wooded glen of a real tumbling mountain stream, with waterfalls and cascades—a highly unusual feature in Swiss scenery. The rapid descent down the green hillside to Lake Zurich must have some of the steepest gradients of adhesive lines anywhere—it seemed to run straight down the slope, regardless of gradient. A *Sunday Times* at Zurich station cost four francs, but included an excellent four-page article demolishing Lord Widgery's whitewashing report on the Londonderry shootings. This article alone was well worth eight shillings.

April 26rd

From today's *Scotsman*: 'A jury at Wakefield, Yorkshire, yesterday found a man not guilty of stealing Cleckheaton railway station'.

April 27th

To town with Pike. We went into what used to be the University Forestry Department so that Pike could see the place where his father used to lecture. It seems now to be part of the department of architecture, but what was odd was that the walls were covered with sexy posters and slogans about sex.

In addition to finishing a Hearing on Evidence, I was supposed to be taking a divorce in which the husband was seeking divorce on the ground of adultery. On Tuesday I dealt with a motion for the wife, to discharge today's diet of proof so that she could proceed with a cross-action on the ground of cruelty, for which she had now been granted legal aid. I refused the motion, and refused leave to reclaim; but the motion had been re-enrolled for today, possibly on the view that I should not be free to take the case and it would be dealt with by some other judge. Disappointed in this, counsel had got together with their clients, and it had been agreed that the wife's action should be dismissed and the husband's proceed as undefended. I accordingly heard evidence and granted decree. I was pleased about this—if the motion to discharge the diet had been granted, as Sibbald assured me would have happened if it had come before some other judge, there would have been the usual delay and expense while a Record in the cross-action was made up and proof heard in the two actions.

April 28th

The judges assembled in the Conference Room to meet the Commission Consultative of the Bars of the European Community: some thirty gentlemen from various European countries who were welcomed by Emslie in an excellent little speech, and then engaged in general conversation with us. The one I was speaking to, from Sweden, spoke impeccable English. I realised after the meeting broke up that I had been conducting my side of the conversation on the basis that his country was in the Common Market, failing to remember that Sweden, so far as I know, is not even a candidate for membership. No doubt he was too polite to correct my mistake.

May 1st

Peebles Hydro for lunch. For a high-class hotel, the charges were surprisingly reasonable: £4.35 for three, including a large carafe of red wine. Television 'World in Action', recording the dockers' reaction to the political tomfoolery of the so-called Industrial Relations

Court in fining the Transport & General Workers Union £55,000 because they could not stop their shop stewards 'blacking' lorries belonging to a small St Helens firm which is fighting the dockers' claim to load containers at the docks.

May 9th

Cameron Miller is anxious to resign his position as Legal Adviser to British Rail in Scotland, and come back to the Bar. He wants to get himself declared redundant. There is some ground for his contention: he has been pretty well redundant since the day he was appointed, there being no need for a Legal Adviser in addition to the Board's Scottish solicitor.

May 10th

Carrol and Shankey are appealing against sentence. Shankey's ground of appeal is stated as: 'I think this was quite a lot for common assault', and Carrol complains, rightly enough, that the three who gave evidence were just as bad as he was and never got punished. They may have some success in their appeals, under the new regime. Douglas Johnston said to me the other day that the First Division in which he was sitting with Emslie and Migdake was the most pleasant Court he had ever sat in. No one interrupted, and the proceedings were conducted with courtesy and understanding. It has been remarked that the silence in First Division hearings is almost uncanny, compared with the hubbub that went on there before.

May 12th

Two divorces where the parties had settled their differences went through undefended. In one of them, *Reid v. Reid*, where the wife was suing her husband, a young doctor, on the ground of adultery, the pursuer was most attractive: a lovely, golden-haired girl with a charming smile. I took three divorces for Ian Robertson, who, as happens not infrequently, had been held up on his Motion Roll. The wife's mother in one of them, being asked what her son-in-law did for a living, replied: 'Nothing—he's allergic to work'.

May 14th

Greenbank Church. Dr Ronald H. W. Falconer preached exactly the kind of sermon one would expect from a former Director of Religious

Broadcasting: well-intentioned, and mildly interesting in the most conventional way.

May 25th
Hamilton v. Grant. The pursuer was using a nail gun to fasten strips of wood to a brick wall. The cartridge exploded, and explosive gases flew up into the pursuer's eyes. Bobby Johnston at the end of the expert evidence wanted to demonstrate something about the working of the gun—which was a production—but the expert in the course of his evidence had taken it to pieces and found he was unable to put it together again. As no one was available who would volunteer to reassemble it we could not have the demonstration.

May 28th
I had been drafted by the Lord President to attend the Assembly service at St Giles' with him and five other judges. Rev. W. M. Dempster preached on Matthew 28:19. It was a harmless sermon: dignified and brief; but seemed a complete waste of the occasion—a crowded congregation, including representatives of every aspect of life in the church and city, and he had nothing to say to them. The judges present afterwards expressed the unanimous view, perhaps slightly exaggerated, that the prayers were the worst we have ever heard. With such a wealth of talent to select from when the Assembly is meeting in Edinburgh, one wonders who selects the people who take part in these Assembly services.

May 30th
Procedure Roll debate in *Duncan's Hotel (Glasgow) v. J. & A. Ferguson.* The pursuers, whose hotel on the upper floors of a building in Union Street, Glasgow, was damaged in the course of reconstruction of the defenders' premises on the ground floor, are suing on the grounds of negligence and nuisance. The defenders have brought in their contractors, Alexander Finlay & Co., as Third Parties, with Baptie Shaw & Morton, the consulting engineers who were advising them. Cullen, who appears for the defenders with James Mackay, opened the debate with an effective speech submitting that the action was irrelevant. He was followed by Edward, for the consulting engineers. McGregor, who appears with Fiddes for the pursuers, had just started when a violent thunderstorm came on. Bobby Johnston complained that owing to the noise of the rain on the roof he could not hear what was

being said; and I agreed to adjourn until tomorrow. I had been told that this debate would take about a fortnight, but it seems obvious that it will finish quite comfortably in the course of a week. I found it interesting.

May 31st
The result of the railwaymen's ballot, ordered by the National Industrial Court, on whether they supported their leaders in further industrial action, was a resounding defeat for the Government, the voters demonstrating by a six to one majority the hollowness of the Government assertion that the Minister had 'reason to believe' that the Union negotiators did not have their members' support.

June 1st
Grieve's installation ceremony: he and Mackenzie Stuart have been appointed to fill vacancies on the bench. 'This Week' on television was dealing with Concorde. It was impossible to comprehend how the British and French Governments could have managed to spend £1,000 million on a single aeroplane: enough to build 2,000 hospitals or replace the whole BOAC air fleet twice over.

June 5th
'World in Action' on ITV was concerned with the fate of mountain villagers of Vietnam, sitting about in despairing wonder while illiterate American louts bombed their lovely country into a desert.

June 6th
Jackson v. Leonard & Partners, an action for payment of fees said to be due to Mr Jackson in respect of civil engineering contracts in Scotland obtained by a London firm of consulting engineers through his efforts on their behalf. Apparently it was agreed that he should receive ten per cent of the contract price payable to the defenders in respect of all such contracts, and he has already received £55,000 from them, simply for taking various architects, local authority representatives and the like out to dinner at places like the Pompadour Restaurant and persuading them to get the bodies they represented to employ the defenders as their engineering consultants on projects for schools, hospitals and other buildings. The letter of agreement, instead of commission of ten per cent, speaks of 'expenses to the limit of ten per cent of the fees received'; but that, it seems, was in order

to conceal from the defenders' professional association that they were employing a commission agent, contrary to the rules of the profession. There is no question of the pursuer's ever having submitted any statement of expenses; he was simply paid a straight ten per cent. In 1967 it appears to have occurred to Mr Leonard, the defenders' senior partner, that they were paying out a lot of money without much justification. A meeting took place between him and the pursuer at which it was agreed that an immediate payment of £8,000 should be made to the pursuer. The pursuer's fees on a strict basis would have been about £15,000. The pursuer says it was further agreed that the defenders would pay him £5,000 per annum until the payments reached ten per cent on all contracts obtained by him. The defenders say this £8,000 was paid and accepted in full settlement. I was rather horrified to think that money from taxpayers and ratepayers was being squandered in providing profits for consulting engineers of such dimensions that they could afford to pay ten per cent of all they got to a spiv like the pursuer, and that it seemed to be taken for granted that the *modus operandi* was to provide lavish entertainment for the architect or other servant of the public body concerned, or for councillors who held office as chairmen of County Council committees. They might be taken for a trip to Stockholm, or accommodation provided for them in a luxury flat in London. There was a letter recording gifts to families and children, and lists of people to whom turkeys were given at Christmas. Despite his supposed reputation as a business man, the pursuer made a poor showing in the witness box. He seemed honest, in the sense that he was unable to appreciate that he had been doing anything reprehensible, and was genuinely indignant at having been cheated out of his just emoluments. His attempts to get back into Mr Leonard's favour were pathetic. Incidentally it appeared from his evidence that when he had taken a party of City Wall Properties people to Stockholm in order to influence them to employ the defenders he had in addition to his fees from the defenders got a fee of £2,500 from City Wall, which he had said nothing about to Leonard. Despite today's slow progress, it did not seem to me that the case would take anything like the four weeks that was prophesied for it; and I have undertaken to go on circuit to Dundee in the week after next.

June 7th
The pursuer was in the witness box all day. In the course of his

cross-examination, Johnston referred to a letter which deals with gifts to officials, and I took the opportunity to warn the pursuer that he did not have to answer any question where the answer might lead to the inference that he had been guilty of criminal conduct. Johnston at once said that he was not suggesting that, but I said that that might be a matter which the court would have to consider, whether he raised it or not. I hoped that when I let the parties see what might be involved they might be induced to settle the case; but we may have to wait until Mr Leonard is in the witness box and gets a similar warning.

June 8th

Not surprised to be asked for a short adjournment, so that counsel could consider the position with their clients; and when we reassembled fifteen minutes later I was told that the case had been settled.

June 9th

A divorce case in which the wife was claiming maintenance for herself and the two children. The husband was already liable for maintaining the child of another woman as a result of the association which had given rise to the action of divorce, and he has now settled down with a third woman, who has borne him three children. It was the usual hopeless case of a well-meaning man asked to provide for three families on one man's pay. He was prepared to offer two pounds a week for each of the pursuer's children, and I awarded her a periodical allowance of two pounds. Both parties seemed pleasant, reasonable people—it was just one of those problems for which there is no solution.

June 19th

From today's *Scotsman*: 'As about 45 firemen, many wearing breathing apparatus, fought the fire and fumes in Grant's store in Earl Gray Street, mother and daughter in a flat above refused to leave their home despite requests to do so from the firemen. Mrs Sheila Black and her daughter Elizabeth (24) said afterwards that they were too embarrassed to come down in the snorkel with a crowd of about 200 watching. Both had just washed their hair and Elizabeth still had her curlers in'.

June 21st

H.M. *Advocate v. Dailly*, a charge of attempted murder. Dailly while

in his sister's house with a young man named Brown had objected to
his sister's proposal to go with Brown's girl friend Ann to a chip
shop. He told them to 'sit down or they would get it'. Brown took
objection to this and started a fight with Dailly, after which Dailly
left. Brown, believing him to have gone to the house of a couple
named Flynn, went there with Ann. It was the middle of the night,
and getting no answer at the door Brown climbed in through a window, and finding Mr and Mrs Flynn asleep in bed wakened Mrs
Flynn and asked if Dailly was there. Dailly had in fact come there
earlier on and been allowed to sleep in the living-room, and as soon as
Brown asked the question ran through and stabbed him repeatedly with
a knife. Dailly conducted his own defence. I suggested that he should
leave the dock and sit at the table; and though Howard demurred,
saying that has never been done, it was done today. Dailly, a young
man with a beard and whiskers, cross-examined with considerable style,
though the proceedings were often slightly comic, particularly as
Dailly always referred to himself in the third person, as 'Dailly'.

June 22nd
Dailly gave a good account of himself in the witness-box. The jury
found him guilty of assault by stabbing, rejecting the charge of attempted murder. Dailly had some previous convictions, and after
congratulating him on the ability with which he had conducted his
case I gave him a sentence of five years. I think that this was perhaps
excessive—it was Brown who had started the trouble and afterwards
went seeking out Dailly. Though self-defence as pled was hopeless,
Dailly may well have been afraid of Brown and gone for him with the
knife rather in desperation than in malice. For that, four years would
perhaps have been enough. Meanwhile, as soon as the jury had retired, we had empanelled a jury for the final case. We sat until 5.30,
in the hope of finishing tomorrow.

Motored to Arbroath, where I had soup and a pie at a snack bar
in the main street—a nice clean place—then motored to the Ness and
walked out along the cliffs. It was an ideal evening for the walk:
bright sunshine with a good breeze, and the Bell Rock lighthouse
standing out on the horizon. I climbed down into Dickmont's Den
and clambered across the boulders into the cave, to a point where I
could see the sea rushing up the long tunnel. I do not think I had
been in the cave since I was a boy.

June 23rd

I asked the jury, when the evidence was concluded, what they wanted to do, and as they all wanted to go on and finish I ordered a break of twenty minutes for a cup of tea, and we then went on to speeches and my charge. The jury were out for an hour, and the Circuit ended shortly after eight.

From Biddy Derham-Reid:

9 Kenilworth Road, Lytham St Annes, Lancashire.
June 27th 1972.
. . . Jane & I motored up to Kyle of Lochalsh on May 26th. It was a day of torrential storms—I have never seen Glencoe like it before—the cars had lights on & the clouds were down in the Glen—and never in my life have I seen so many, many water-falls!! Jane & I both thought of you—& wished you could have been with us. There were small thread like ones pouring down—then enormous ones, which ended up at the Road-side—just boiling. Do you remember kidnapping me one afternoon—to go & see a waterfall—somewhere—you said—near Stirling? & we ended up at Loch Lomond. Anyway—a waterfall anywhere means to me, just you . . .

July 11th

I have instituted the practice of allowing an accused to remain seated while I impose sentence—saying 'Please remain seated' in order to obviate the usual shout from the macer 'Stand up', and the rather awkward arrangement by which the accused has to stand while the judge addresses him. I do not think this had ever been done till I started it at Dundee, but to my mind it is an improvement.

July 24th

We had no *Observer* yesterday on account of a sympathetic strike in support of five dockers imprisoned by Mr Justice Donaldson for picketing a container depot. Today the Scottish papers appeared, though no London papers were published. 'Panorama' on tonight's television was concerned with the industrial crisis. Mr Carr's sneering unpleasantness was more than a match for the simple-minded Mr Prentice, the Labour spokesman on industrial affairs, but the star of the programme was Lord Devlin, who swept aside all the twaddle about upholding the rule of law and said that in this context contempt of court was an absurd concept and the dockers should be got out of prison right away.

July 25th
The *Scotsman* has succumbed to the strike, and we had no newspaper today.

July 26th
The *Scotsman* was delivered this morning, rather to my surprise—no London papers yet being published. We heard on the news that the five dockers had been released, by means of a fiddle whereby it was arranged that the Official Solicitor, without any instructions from the men, and indeed in defiance of their instructions, would make application for their release immediately after a judgment of the House of Lords holding, contrary to what was held by the Court of Appeal, that the Transport Workers Union was liable for the actions of its shop stewards. This enabled Donaldson J. to pretend with some show of plausibility that a new situation had arisen so that the dockers could be released.

August 1st
Finished reading *The French Lieutenant's Woman*, by John Fowles, a beautifully written, most unusual novel, full of odd scraps of interesting information, factual and philosophical. I found it wholly absorbing.

August 8th
Llandudno. Car parking, which at other times is almost impossible, presents no difficulties until about 10 am, and the shops are not nearly so busy as they become later. I bought a brooch for Nancy to celebrate our silver wedding: a rose in silver, for which I paid £8.50. We have apparently exhausted the hotel's supply of half-bottles of hock and tonight had chablis, which we thought rather nice—something like hock, but with a special flavour of its own.

August 10th
St Asaph: the cathedral, though small in comparison with most of the cathedrals, it is quite a gem in its own miniature way.

August 15th
Went down with the dog for Jessica. Megan came out with her, and

we climbed to the top of Blackford Hill. On the way down, the girls got hold of some pieces of cardboard, on which they slid down the grass slope; and we made our way home after a highly successful outing.

Typed out a note on the Murray murder case. When capital punishment was abolished, provision was made that prisoners serving a life sentence for murder should not be released without consultation with the trial judge; but the trouble has been that when release is being considered a good many years after the trial it has been found that the trial judge is not always available. So Emslie has decided that a report should be obtained from the judge at the time of the trial and filed away until the appropriate time. After a resumé of the circumstances, I advised that Murray was not a criminal in the normal sense of the word, and could probably be released at any time without danger to the public.

August 18th
Sitting in the garden with the wireless on—a programme including old English songs—I was delighted to hear them announce my favourite 'Mary Gray of Allendale', which I had not heard for years. It was sung very well.

August 20th
Braid Church. Rev. G. Macmillan, of Portree, preached a fine sermon. He reminded me of Leonard Small: the same voice, but not as harsh, the same logical development, the same down-to-earth phraseology, with every now and then some striking phrase or illustration. He held my attention from start to finish.

August 21st
Elizabeth is going to Liverpool; and as the Beattock line is closed at present during the day to allow electrification work to go on she had to go by Glasgow—trains south from there go by the Dumfries route. I bought her a single ticket, at £4; no suggestion of a higher fare for this longer route. A programme on television about Welsh castles was a complete flop: a lot of Welsh garrulity from Wynford Vaughan Thomas, and hardly a glimpse of a Welsh castle.

August 22nd
Finished reading *Spring Grove*, by Trevor Burgin and Patricia Elwes, in which the headmaster and one of his assistants at a Huddersfield

primary school give a practical account of their work in a school which has immigrant children as fifty per cent of its pupils and where, as the authors put it, 'during the past six years the character of the immigrant population has been enriched by the arrival of increasing numbers of Indians, Pakistanis and West Indians'. One can imagine how differently Mr Enoch Powell would have stated the same fact; and this book shows in the most encouraging way how wrong he is. Unfortunately for the immigrants, and for Britain, the Powells have a lot more influence than the Trevor Burgins; and as the authors point out Huddersfield's high level of employment has assured its immigrant population of a level of security and tolerance which has not been forthcoming elsewhere.

August 24th

Cramond: a coastguard notice on the Yacht Club's notice-board, to the effect that 'a small reward' would be paid to the first person to notify any casualty. We wondered whether a potential casualty would do, or whether one had to wait and make sure that someone was really drowned before rushing to phone the coastguards and claim the reward.

August 31st

We motored to Waverley and bought Nancy's ticket to Cornwall: first-class return, which cost £33.80.

Finished reading *Human Documents of the Victorian Golden Age (1850–1875)*, by E. Royston Pike. The contemporary extracts which make up this volume are not as telling as those in the editors' earlier volume. Except in trades like millinery or dressmaking, where women might be expected to work all through the night, working hours had come down to something like ten a day, with which everyone was satisfied. Would-be reformers were much more concerned with moral dangers to workers where men and girls were 'thrown indiscriminately together', and that women's long hours of work made it difficult for clergymen to see them or converse with them, and did not dispose them to listen to their remarks about their religious duties. All in all, it is still a pretty grim picture. There is a familiar ring about an observation from Connell's iron works, which employed boys of ten from 6 pm to 6 am, and in answer to 'question 7 of the Tabular Form asking for an opinion as to the prohibition of night work by children and young persons' replied: 'It is impossible for us to do so; it would be tantamount to stopping our works'.

September 6th

TUC debate on industrial relations, introduced by Mr Feather in a first-rate speech, in which he made fun of the Industrial Relations Court and its wangling of the law—comparing its failure to hear the Official Solicitor on the Tuesday to a fish-and-chip shop in Barnsley which put up a notice 'No frying tonight'.

September 7th

The TUC debating the economic situation: a lot of tedious repetition but some good speeches, including one by Kendall of the civil servants' union condemning the jargon and gobbledegook of management consultants and time-and-motion experts, and observing that the Civil Service had had to issue a booklet to try to explain it to themselves—an entertaining, witty speech, and tragically all too true. Even more impressive was a modest little speech by a computer designer, showing more in sorrow than in anger how his devices which should have led to a better, easier way of life for everyone had the effect in the existing order of things only of increasing profits and putting workers on the dole.

Elizabeth spent the afternoon in the kitchen, surrounded by cooking materials and utensils, with a Bible and a cookery book open on the kitchen table. She can on occasion bake an excellent cake, just like Nancy's.

September 10th

Morningside Church; Rev. W. C. Thomson. I understood him to say he had come from Dysart, but it seemed to be generally agreed that he is minister of Granton. He appeared to be quite a nice man, but his sermon made utter nonsense of the story of Jacob and Esau. When he read it in the Old Testament lesson, he did so sympathetically and with every sign of understanding, but when he came to preach it was obvious that he had not understood a word of it.

September 11th

A nice long letter from Nancy, who had enjoyed a walk and picnic on Cubert Common. 'I'm not accustomed to this incessant conversation', she says. 'We must lead a very quiet life'. Elizabeth, who read the letter, said it sounded as if she was rather homesick.

September 13th

A High Court sitting to deal with some prisoners remitted for sentence. A poor-looking man with a long record of convictions for theft had broken into a house in Bellshill and got away with £400 worth of stuff, and then for some unknown reason went back to the same house three weeks later and put a brick through a window. He was caught by the householder, and admitted to him that he had done the earlier housebreaking. I imposed a three years sentence, remarking that his record should have suggested to him that as a professional housebreaker he was not in a rewarding occupation. Fraser was charged with uttering two £5 notes that had been forged, and having seven more in his possession. He and another man charged along with him had been going round pubs offering the counterfeit notes and getting change. On a plea on behalf of his co-accused that he had not been in serious trouble before, Sheriff Middleton had dealt with him by way of a fine, and remitted Watson, who had previous convictions for dishonesty, to the High Court. It now appeared that the schedule of the co-accused's convictions had been wrong, and he in fact had a much worse record than Fraser. Fraser, I was told, had agreed to a suggestion made in court that he was the ringleader, because knowing the other man's record he thought that if he was thought to have played a major part the two would be remitted; he hoped to avoid that by taking on the role of principal culprit. As I pointed out to his counsel, all this was not really relevant to the question of what was the proper sentence for Fraser, but as there has plainly been a mix-up I restricted the sentence to two years, the maximum he could have got if he had not been remitted.

Having taken the dog out, I encountered the postman, who was much exercised that some murderess in England had been 'let out on patrol'.

September 19th

Typed out Notes for the Inner House in two criminal appeals. Dailly has put in an appeal against sentence as well as against his conviction, so that I was able to say in my Note that my sentence had been excessive.

September 20th

Vacation Court. An action by a lorry driver employed by the defenders at Aberdeen harbour. When alighting from his lorry, he slipped on a filleted herring, and he founds on the defenders' breach of the

Factories Act in not keeping floors free from any substance likely to cause him to slip.

September 22nd
Vacation Court. An action of interdict against infringement of the pursuers' performing rights. The defender has been playing records of T. Rex, Benny Hill, the New Seekers and Elvis Presley, on a juke-box in his cafe in the Gallowgate, Glasgow, without paying licence fees. The defence is that the cafe building has collapsed, so that interdict is unnecessary.

September 25th
Finished reading *Eamon de Valera*, by the Earl of Longford and Thomas P. O'Neill. There is not a shred of humour in this biography, and it is far too adulatory to be a good one. Much as I have always admired De Valera, I find it hard to accept from his biographers that everything he did was good and wise and right. Even his part in the 1916 Easter Rising, which as appears clearly from the narrative was a fiasco from the start, and which ended with his marching with his men behind a white flag to surrender, is regarded by the authors as a model operation. This is an interesting book in spite of itself—because De Valera lived such an interesting life.

September 26th
Parliament House. I joined the other judges in the procession to St Giles' for the service to mark the opening of the session. Dr Whitley has retired, and the service was conducted by Professor McIntyre from New College. It was all very sedate, and lacked the entertainment value of Dr Whitley's service, with its hymns and lessons about unjust judges and those who grind the faces of the poor.

Home, and took the dog on the hill. Encountered four little girls— Jenny, Fiona, Louise and Annabella—and had a lively time with them and the dog. When I came away, they all came to the top of the steps, and stood there waving and shouting 'Goodbye, Bongo'.

Went through *Hamlet* and extracted lines that have become proverbial or familiar sayings. I found more than seventy—*Hamlet* must have far more 'quotations' than any other play that ever was written.

September 29th
An action by a photographer who submitted colour transparencies to

the defenders for use in pictorial calendars. They undertook that those that were not selected would be returned by registered post. Thirty two transparencies have gone missing; and the defenders in a letter to the pursuer said they had been stored in such a safe place that they had been unable to locate them. The pursuer is seeking to hold the defenders liable for not keeping them safe.

October 6th
Divorce proof in which I granted decree—there was some urgency about getting it through, as the pursuer wanted to re-marry this afternoon.

October 7th
From 'C FA Notes' in this week's *World's Fair:* 'Another member is Mr R. A. Williams, who as he spends much of his time working on lighthouses has little time to visit circuses'.

October 9th
Finished reading *The Poetical Works of Ernest Dowson*. They have a limited range: unrequited love, and the finality of death. But within their limits they are exquisite little poems.

October 12th
Conservative Party conference, on television: an exciting debate on immigration and the Government's decision to admit Asian refugees expelled from Uganda by the racialist president, General Amin. The resolution selected for debate was tabled by Hackney South and Shoreditch Conservative Association; and it turned out—rather, it seems, to the dismay of the Conference organisers—that the president of the Association, who was to move the resolution, was none other than Mr Powell. I did not hear his speech, but I heard the one immediately following, from David Hunt, national chairman of the Young Conservatives. Given this fine opportunity of challenging the Powell doctrine, he took the best possible advantage of it and made a brilliant little speech, saying he did not understand the morality of offering people the protection of a British passport and then when they got into trouble attempting to pretend that it was worthless. A parliamentary candidate from Bedford was equally forthright. It was odd to find youngsters all supporting the official line, with the platform party beaming down on them as they defended the Government against the Powellite attack; and whether by accident or design it

happened that all the speakers called by the chairman on Powell's side had a faintly comic appearance. It seemed that the days were past when Powell could curdle the blood with lurid prophecies of black domination of Britain—even Tory blood.

October 18th
Finished reading *The Art of the Possible*, memoirs of Lord Butler. Despite the occasional dull passage, this is an entertaining book, characteristic of its odd, passionless, idiosyncratic author, and including some amusing anecdotes about Churchill—as when Butler and Halifax were invited to walk up and down in the garden of No. 10 while Winston was rehearsing his speech 'We shall fight on the beaches'. 'There we were, the lanky Edward, the stocky Winston and myself. As Winston declaimed, he turned to us and said, "Would you fight in the streets and on the hills?" Pacific as we were, we warmly agreed, saying "Yes, certainly, Winston", and then continued to walk up and down with him'.

October 20th
The *Journal of the Law Society of Scotland* came this morning; and I was astonished to find when looking through it a curious reference to myself in a topical article over the pen-name 'Pericles': 'There has been a persistent tale that the most brilliant account of Scottish legal life in the twentieth century will come from the pen of Lord Stott, and just as Braxfield and Eskgrove are known to us almost solely through the account of Cockburn so will Clyde and Avonside be presented to the twenty-first century through the mind of Lord Stott'.

October 21st
From today's *Scotsman*: 'The court refused Mr Relino Politti a public-house licence for 209 Fountainbridge after the chief constable said that he had introduced "Go-Go Girls", which had led to overcrowding'.

October 22nd
St Oswald's Church. Dr Stewart, preaching at the church's centenary service, preached an eloquent sermon on II Samuel 3:17–18. The children's address was given by the minister, Rev. C. Murray Stewart, who was obviously a live wire and gave an entertaining, intelligent talk—getting the children to stand up all over the church until their combined ages totalled a hundred, when he drew the appropriate moral.

October 23rd
After tea I set off in the car for the Ayr Circuit, going by Strathaven and Galston.

October 24th
The Provost and magistrates came into the Sheriffs' room to welcome me, and joined with me in deploring the provisions of the Local Government Act, which will put an end to burghs like Ayr by having them swallowed up in some large amorphous district.

October 26th
H.M. Advocate v. Watson. Watson is accused of murdering a boy of sixteen named Wilson. Wilson and his younger brother had gone with another youth named Colville from Ayr to Dalmellington for a Saturday-night party. Wearying of the party, they had come out into the street, shouting gang slogans, and incited a group of local boys to chase them. The boys having run away, they returned to the house where the party was being held, and there Wilson took possession of a lemonade bottle. He and Colville went to look for the boys, Wilson stopping at the corner of the street to smash the bottle against a wall and so provide himself with a weapon. The boys were not to be seen; but while Wilson and Colville were waiting at a bus stop two youths and a girl came down the street. One of the youths was Watson. Watson, it seems, had a scrap with him, and the Crown case is that Watson took out a knife and swung it at Wilson. There was a struggle, in which Wilson tried to take the knife off Watson, and Watson stabbed him repeatedly in the back. The defence case, as presented in cross-examination by Daiches, is that Wilson had stood in the path of the three young people, shouting and swearing at them, and after striking and kicking at the girl got Watson down on the ground. As Watson was lying on his back, with Wilson on top of him, he was so terrified of Wilson that he plunged the knife into Wilson's back. It seems plain that there is nothing to choose between the two sides in this affair and that the best the Crown can hope for is a verdict of culpable homicide. There is a plea of self-defence, and it may well be successful. We had a break at four for a cup of tea; then sat on till 5.40 in the hope of being able to finish the case tomorrow. Unfortunately in this Circuit each of the cases has spilled over into a second day, so that I have had work to do in the evenings instead of having the evening free as happens when each case is completed in a day.

October 27th

An awkward situation arose when I had been in the bathroom, shaving. It has a sliding door, with a luggage stool in the bedroom just beside it. I had been packing my suitcase, and left it on the stool with the lid open, and, when I pulled the door to, the lid of the suitcase had fallen back against the wall, so that when I tried to slide the door open the lid kept it from going along more than about a foot. Try as I might, I could not squeeze out through the space; but luckily the bathroom is just at the bedroom door, and I was able to get my arm out, open the door into the lobby and call to a girl passing by to come in and release me by shutting the suitcase lid. It was lucky too that I was in shirt and trousers.

The first witness today was Watson's young brother, one of the boys chased by Wilson and Colville, who had gone for refuge to the house of Watson's girl friend, a widow named Ruth Frame. The accused was in the house, and after waiting twenty minutes or so to give things a chance to quieten down set off from the house to take his brother home, Ruth coming with them. It was then that they found their way barred by the youths from Ayr, and the fight followed in which Wilson was knifed. Stewart did his best to discredit the brother's evidence in a long cross-examination, but at the end it seemed clear that all the Watsons had wanted to do was to get past on their way home, and the whole trouble arose from the aggressive behaviour of Colville and the Wilsons. The evidence of Mrs Frame was to the same effect. A question has arisen as to how Watson had come to be in possession of the knife which struck the fatal blow: a long kitchen knife which admittedly had come from Mrs Frame's cupboard. The story told by Watson's brother and supported by Mrs Frame was that he himself had taken the knife from the kitchen because he had been frightened of the Ayr boys, and the accused on discovering this as they were coming up the road had taken it from him so that he would not get into any trouble. Mrs Frame had said nothing about this in her statement to the police, and I was quizzing her a little about that, suggesting that it was an afterthought that she and the brother had invented in order to help the accused, when the accused leaned forward from the dock and had a word with Daiches—whereupon Daiches announced that he now had instructions to offer a plea of culpable homicide which the Crown were willing to accept. Presumably the accused, thinking I did not believe the story about how he came to have the knife, had decided that I was against him and that he had better accept a compromise verdict. Actually I was quite sympathetic towards him, and knowing that he had already done three months waiting for the case to come on imposed a sentence of nine months. No doubt he should not have had a weapon of that kind, and when his brother had been chased should have contacted the police instead of trying to deal with the situation himself; but from all accounts he had done the public a service by disposing of Wilson, a tall, powerful youth, and as everyone agreed a most unpleasant character.

October 28th
A case had been transferred to my Roll from Mackenzie-Stuart's—he has been appointed as one of the judges in the European Common Market Court at Luxembourg. Saw from an *Express* that I bought on my way home that yesterday's accused and his girl friend had been pleased with the nine-months sentence. 'Ruth Frame (30) wept in court yesterday when her fiancé was jailed for nine months. But they were tears of joy, not sorrow'. 'Attractive widow Mrs Frame . . . said: "I'm so happy. We will be married when George leaves prison".'

November 1st
To the Crown Office to enquire what the First Division had done about Dailly. They had reduced the sentence from five years to four.

November 3rd
Twelve divorces. In one, there was a letter from the husband asking his wife to meet him in a public house and talk things over. He adds a P.S.: 'You can bring your mother if you want so long as she sits at a separate table'.

November 7th
From today's *Glasgow Herald*: 'Detective Constable John Burns, of Glasgow city drug squad, said there were ten young persons in the basement flat. One young couple were in bed and a number of others were partly or wholly undressed. In the flat he found eleven reefer cigarettes and two pieces of cannabis. He stated: "They told me if I turned to Jesus I would be saved".'

November 9th
Attended in the First Division courtroom for the installation of Brand

as a judge, in place of Mackenzie-Stuart. Ian Stewart has been appointed Solicitor-General in place of Brand.

November 10th
At lunch time there was some discussion of Scots words and expressions, and I told the others about the evidence of an old fellow whose cottage Anne Francis went to for help in my rape case at Ayr. A chap came to the door, he said, and he looked out of the window and saw it was a lassie.

November 17th
Cordiner v. Cordiner, a cruelty action in which the defender had not entered appearance. But when the case was called I was told that the defender was sitting in court, and at my request he came forward, and said the Summons was a pack of lies and he wanted to contest it. I said that as it was a consistorial action he was entitled to come in at any time and defend it; and we launched into the proof, with the defender appearing in person. The pursuer with some encouragement from Smith spoke of the defender's giving her a hammering from time to time during their two years together, and mentioned one or two specific incidents: nothing startling, but no doubt sufficient to entitle her to divorce. The defender however proved to be a cross-examiner of outstanding ability. Without any notes, and never hesitating for a moment, he proceeded to demolish a lot of the pursuer's case, and succeeded in demonstrating that at the dates she had given for some of the incidents they had not even been living in the same house. He got from her that she had never been to a doctor or hospital, or sought help from the police, and an admission that she and her supporting witness, Mrs McGlynne, had been convicted on a charge of attempting to pervert the course of justice. But like many such cross-examinations it was a Pyrrhic victory, for though he showed her up as a muddled and unsatisfactory witness, liable to exaggerate, it all went to confirm my impression that her case was fundamentally sound. I had no doubt that when she said she was afraid of him she was telling the truth. This impression was confirmed when Mrs McGlynne went into the box. She denied that she was frightened when it was put to her by Smith, but gave every indication that she was. Smith got enough out of her to afford corroboration for some of the pursuer's evidence. The Rules of Court provide that where a defender appears without having put in defences the Court shall not

allow him to lead evidence without the consent of the pursuer, but I thought it would be better to have the defender's evidence and allowed him to go into the witness box without asking for Smith's consent. Smith said nothing about it, though he objected when Cordiner proceeded to call another witness. I ruled that the objection came too late; and the evidence turned out to be of no materiality. Cordiner wanted to call yet another witness, but Smith pointed out that the man had been sitting in court; and I, thinking we had had enough, did not allow him to be adduced. Cordiner gave his own evidence quite well, but he admitted having slapped his wife from time to time, and that he might have kicked her. He admitted that he had been in the habit of carrying a knife for use on other people, and made no secret of what we all knew—that he was a well-known criminal with a long record of convictions. His last sentence, from which he must have been released not long ago, was of seven years for attempting to extort £100 from a night club proprietor by threats of burning the place down; and he has also been up on a charge of murder, though it was dropped by the Crown. Smith addressed me briefly, and the defender made an excellent little summing-up on his side. Obviously he has profited from his many opportunities of seeing how a case is conducted. When the defender sat down about 2.30 I sent for a shorthand writer and proceeded to give judgment. I congratulated the defender on his conduct of the case, and agreed that he had brought out discrepancies in the pursuer's evidence, but despite that I preferred her evidence to his—pointing out that her frankness in volunteering the information that her husband was very fond of children, particularly their own child, and had always been good to her, did not sound like the evidence of a vindicative or partisan witness. I was going on to deal with custody when Cordiner got up and rampaged out of the court, shouting that he did not have to stay there to listen to a lot of lies. Sibbald had police in attendance in case any trouble might arise, but I saw no reason why Cordiner should not leave the court. From the point of view of his wife and Mrs McGlynne, it seemed all to the good that he should be off the premises before they came out. But for some reason or other, having gone out at one door he appeared immediately at the other, still shouting at me. I had been going on with my judgment, and told him that if he kept quiet I would say something about access, to which he replied that he did not mind what I said—he would take the law into his own hands. He shouted something to the effect that we should find out what stabbing was—everybody in the court would. 'Nobody in this court will ever sleep in peace'. I told the police to arrest him and take him downstairs, saying I should deal with him at the end of the sitting, and finished delivering my judgment, granting decree of divorce and custody. I said that in view of his present attitude it would be unwise to make any order about access meantime. More trouble then appeared, as Smith rose and said that Mr McGlynne had come into court and was threatening his wife. It had appeared from the evidence that McGlynne was a close friend of Cordiner's, and according to Cordiner Mrs McGlynne had started divorce proceedings against him. I told McGlynne to come forward and warned him against doing any harm to his wife. 'If she comes near my house', he said, 'she's for it. She'll be all right if she keeps away from me'. Having ascertained from him that he and his wife were living apart, I told him to be well advised to keep out of trouble whether she came about the house or not, and though he did not seem to be much impressed I left it at that and went on to the next case. Those who had crowded into court to hear what was to happen to Cordiner had to endure one and a half hours of unmitigated tedium while McEachern led his client laboriously through all the stock evidence of cruelty. It was four o'clock by the time this was disposed of, and Cordiner was brought up, handcuffed to a policeman. I said I had understood him to make threats against anyone present in court, and asked him if he had anything to say. He said he had lost his temper listening to all the lies, and was going on to criticise his wife's evidence when I reminded him that I was not concerned with the evidence in the case but with the threats he had made in court. He had nothing more to say; and observing that I regarded it as a very serious contempt I sentenced him to three years imprisonment. He seemed rather taken aback at this summary justice and said 'Am I not to have a lawyer or anything?' 'Certainly', I said, 'you can consult a lawyer and he will advise you about any remedy that may be open to you'. Sibbald remarked that McGlynne was conspicuously silent as Cordiner was led out.

November 21st

Hunter was mentioning that he had attended a conference of criminologists at the week-end, where, he said, opinion was unanimously against me. But when they realised that it was Cordiner I had been dealing with he felt a change in the atmosphere; the company seemed to be coming round to the view that I might have been right. Ian Robertson said that Bernard Levin had an article about me in the *Times*, which he led me to think was by no means in friendly terms. In the First Division court room Emslie paid tribute to Grant, who was killed in a road accident while driving south in his BMW along the main road near Kingussie on Sunday. Emslie told me that Grant had been a fast driver. On the way home I bought a copy of the *Times*. I expected Levin's article to be offensive, and it certainly was. After pointing out that Edinburgh was noted for its legal absurdities, and that 'the poor devil at the receiving end' was a Mr Cordiner, he narrates some of what Cordiner said; and distinguishing what had happened in the Court of Appeal, where no notice had been taken off the behaviour of a lady who threw her handbag at the judges when her appeal was dismissed, says that Lord Stott 'ordered Mr Cordiner arrested, had him brought handcuffed back into court, and sentenced him to three years' imprisonment for contempt. No doubt it will be said, and on the above evidence no doubt truly, that tribunals such as the Court of Appeal are composed of judges rather more worldly-wise than the justices of the Court of Session in Edinburgh. Certainly one cannot imagine, say, a Goddard on the one hand, or a Denning, say, on the other, doing anything in these circumstances but proceeding calmly to the next case before him'. He hopes that 'Lord Stott's savage reaction—for a reaction, rather than a sentence, is what it was—will receive appropriate rebuke'. After this, it was a pleasant surprise for me on opening the *Glasgow Herald* to find a centre-page article by Watt putting the opposite point of view. Observing that I should no doubt have had in mind Cordiner's arrogant admission that he regularly carried a weapon which he kept 'for other people', and that there has been a threat to a witness by another man, he says that 'during the delivery of judgment, when Cordiner's outburst occurred, Lord Stott treated him with extreme leniency and consideration. The procedure adopted by Lord Stott might be used as a model. Since he is a judge of considerable experience in the criminal as well as in the civil field, a former Lord Advocate, and before that a very busy advocate indeed, he clearly knew how to handle a dangerous situation. When the point was reached for the arrest of Cordiner for a contempt which was blatant and undeniable he did not deal with him immediately, but proceeded calmly to hear another case'. When I had passed sentence, 'there was certainly no question of his having done so in haste or without giving the man every opportunity to minimise his contempt or mitigate the sentence that obviously was coming'. Watt concludes that it might be seen as 'a timely demonstration by the judiciary of its determination to uphold the rule of law in face of a growing tendency nowadays to question its authority'.

November 23rd

Mr Macdonald handed me a letter written to me by Cordiner from prison; he had got it from Cordiner's solicitor, to hand on to me. He says that since he was a child he had always had a temper which not even he could control. 'When I said that the Court was a Kangaroo Court I was not making this remark at you as you in fact did give me a fair hearing as I know you could have let the case go undefended'. He explained that what he was talking about was the refusal of the Law Society to give him Legal Aid, and finishes up by saying he is sorry for his behaviour in Court. I drafted a letter for George Macdonald to write to Cordiner, saying that the matter was out of my hands, but that I had not been particularly concerned with anything he said about me or the Court. What I had been concerned about was his threat to witnesses, and he would no doubt have to satisfy the appellate court about that. I asked Macdonald to add that he could make any use he pleased of the letter.

November 25th

A typewritten letter from an anonymous correspondent in London, reviling me for the injustice I had done to Cordiner. 'It is a pity', writes this somewhat bloodthirsty correspondent, 'you were not in Judge Grant's car'. Cordiner is to appeal to the *nobile officium* of the Court of Session, the appropriate form of appeal against a sentence for contempt in a civil court.

November 30th

O'Brien v. British Railways Board, an action by an Irishman who had hurt his back when working in the signal box at Greenhill Junction. In order to operate the points, he had first to pull a lever which released a lock bolt on the rails, and then the points lever. The lockbar had not been working properly, so that on occasion the points lever would not operate. On 23rd October 1968, having pulled the lever to operate the lockbar he was proceeding to pull the points lever when it suddenly stuck halfway along the line of travel, causing him to lose his balance and sustain an injury which turned out to be a slipped disc. In reply to a call for entries in the Train Register Book relating to the operation of Levers Nos 30 and 32, the defenders had indicated that there were no relevant entries; but the pursuer's solicitors, doubting this, had executed a Commission to recover the books, and had discovered a succession of entries showing there had been constant trouble with the two levers for over a year. In view of what had been discovered, it seemed to me that the defenders had not much left to say for themselves.

December 2nd
Gaumont Cinema: 'The Hospital': a witty, brilliantly directed satire on what goes on in a big American hospital. It never labours a point—you can take it or leave it—and the result is eminently satisfactory.

December 4th
Finished reading *Kim*, by Rudyard Kipling. At first, when the boy sets off to travel through India, I felt it might not be a bad story; but before long I lost all interest in its ramifications. It is a silly book, and to my mind a nauseating one, with its conversation in a mixture of scriptural and babu English, and its author's attitude taking it for granted that there could be no higher ambition for a boy in India than to become a spy for the British Government. It is all distinctly phoney.

December 5th
In *O'Brien v. British Railways* I have found for the pursuer and awarded him £8,500.

December 7th
Custody of a child who had been with one of her parents in Aberdeen but had chosen to go off to the other one in Turiff. The motion was to restore custody to the parent in Aberdeen. 'She who will to Turiff maun to Turiff', I said, refusing the motion.

December 8th
The judges were talking about Manuela Sykes, the Labour candidate who lost to the Conservatives in a by-election yesterday which Labour had been expected to win. 'Well', said Migdale, 'Bernard Levin doesn't like her. That's the only thing to be said in her favour'. 'In

that case', I said, 'she and I—' There was a general laugh, and I did not need to finish the sentence.

A divorce action where the parties had agreed to a Joint Minute whereby custody of the two children was to be awarded to the defender, the wife. I was told however that one of the children had been murdered last week by the co-defender. I allowed the Joint Minute to be departed from, and agreed that meantime the remaining child should be put into the care of the local authority. Coming along the passage, I had observed a large squad of police and prison officers accompanying a man in handcuffs; and when I started my proofs I found that the man was the pursuer in the first case. I was told he was serving a life sentence in England for murder and was regarded as a high security risk. The children of the marriage were with the defender. The pursuer's mother, a funny old Glasgow body who saw the children regularly, was worried about the defender's drinking, but explained that the co-defender was at present 'doing time' and everything would be all right when he came home to the defender in the New Year. I took this to mean that the co-defender, like the pursuer, was in prison, whereupon the witness dissolved into laughter and it was explained to me that she meant he was in the Navy. She promised to keep an eye on the children until then.

December 12th
A defended cruelty divorce. Sibbald observed that so far as he could gather counsel were not keen on having a defended proof and a word from me might settle it. As things turned out, this was unnecessary—the defender failed to turn up.

December 15th
Thomson is head of the Industrial Relations Court in Scotland, and we were talking about the ridiculous case in which Donaldson J. has fined the Engineering Union £50,000 for 'contempt' in refusing to admit Mr Goad to meetings of their Sudbury branch. Industrial action following on this seems likely to stop production of all the London newspapers on Monday. Thomson said the trouble was that trade unions would not come to the court, nor would any employers if they were sensible; and the Government would not come, for after what had happened last time it was dead scared of what might happen if it tried again. So the only people who came to the court were lunatic workmen and lunatic employers.

December 19th

Lucas' Curator v. Young was out for proof: the case of a young girl who was involved in a road accident and suffered severe brain damage. She was in a coma for a long time, and when she came out of it could not speak and gave a good deal of trouble by biting the nurses; and when she was sent to a rehabilitation centre had to be sent home because she got up in the middle of the night and moved the other beds in the dormitory, wakening the occupants. She claims to have been intending to get employment abroad with the World Health Organisation; and when the defenders aver that she had meant to be a missionary and so would have earned a good deal less her reply is that she is and always has been an agnostic. A settlement had been reached, and I was asked to grant decree for £38,000. The list of pursuer's witnesses cited for the proof did not include Miss Lucas herself. Morton told me later that one of her peculiarities was that she refused to answer any questions, so that there was not much point in citing her as a witness.

December 21st

Installation of Wheatley as Lord Justice-Clerk and R. S. Johnston as a Lord Ordinary; he has taken the title of Lord Kincraig. One of my fourteen proofs did not go on, because, I was told, the defender had been murdered last night and her husband the pursuer taken away by the police when he arrived at Parliament House this morning.

'This Week' on ITV was dealing with Ulster from the soldiers' point of view: some surprisingly illuminating comments from the soldiers themselves, including their commander in chief, Sir Henry Tuzo. They all seemed to realise the complete futility of the operations they were directed to carry out.

1973

With Lord Clyde's departure, the Court of Session appeared to have taken a new lease of life, and apart from the vacations I again had quite a busy time—belying my theory that an appointment as Senator of the College of Justice in Scotland is simply a congenial form of retirement. But it was still an interesting and enjoyable way of life. Practically the whole of my autumn term was occupied in one proof. In every other case that I had decided on evidence I had worked from my own notes, avoiding the necessity of a long wait until the shorthand writer's notes had been extended. That had meant that I had myself to take a full note of everything said by the witnesses. In this case however the notes were extended daily as the proof went on, and handed in to me every night. Being thus relieved of the necessity of taking notes, I found the proceedings restful: all I was required to do was to sit peacefully each day from ten to four listening to the evidence. In the course of the year, in addition to run-of-the-mill reparation and divorce actions—including 495 undefended divorces—I had the opportunity of dealing with some knotty legal problems. Politics became more and more depressing as the effects became apparent of the policies of the most incompetent Government in living memory. Towards the end of the year the Government chose to involve itself in a second confrontation with the miners over their current wage claim. This time, instead of a strike, they decided on an overtime ban. The weakness of this type of industrial action appeared to be that so far as industry was concerned it would be slow to take effect, particularly as the power stations—so vulnerable in the last coal strike—had taken care to build up stocks of coal and oil. But the Government solved the miners' problem for them—Mr Heath decreed that the rest of industry must work only a three-day week, so that we had the ironical situation that workers throughout British industry were prohibited from working more than three days a week in order to compel the miners to work more than five. Needless to say, no use was made of the much-vaunted Industrial Relations Act. In the scene abroad, Mr Nixon—having at last got his troops out of Vietnam and accomplished an unprecedented detente with the Communists including a formal visit to China—found himself involved in disaster as a result of the 'bugging' of the Democratic Party's campaign headquarters and the theft of some files from the psychiatrist attending one Dr Ellsberg. These ludicrous incidents, which in this country I would imagine would have been speedily hushed up, were magnified in America to unimaginable proportions, with accusations of a cover-up in which the President was involved, and the institution of criminal proceedings against most of Mr Nixon's closest advisers. He certainly seemed to have surrounded himself with a 'Government' of most unsavoury characters. In summer we had a marvellous holiday at Hornbaek, on the north coast of Zeeland. More by good luck than anything else, we found ourselves in a gorgeous luxury hotel on the very edge of the sea, and with a gloriously warm sea and a week of unbroken sunshine spent most of our days in the sea or in the dunes, in company with a host of golden Danes in scanty beach attire or sometimes with none at all.

January 11th
From Jessica Borley:

> 27 Cluny drive Thursday
> Dear Lord STOTT
> Thank you for taking us out to see Jack and the Beanstalk I thought it was lovely. I liked the twins when they were throwing the Buns at us and the Bit when the Princess married Jack.
> With love

The bit that I liked myself was when Una Maclean's stand-in climbed up the giant beanstalk to the accompaniment of 'Excelsior' sung by the full chorus.

January 12th
Speaking of recent appointments to the Bench, Kissen said that Shearer would have been Lord President if it had not been for the affair of Colin Temple, when he wrote to the employers of one of the witnesses who had appeared before him, suggesting that the man should be dismissed. Kissen said that Wylie had intended to appoint Shearer, but could do nothing for him because of the public outcry that would have resulted. Wylie, he said, was still a close friend of Shearer's and regularly consulted him. Kissen thought that Wylie was an excellent politician. Installation of another new judge: Peter Maxwell, who has

been appointed as an additional judge on account of 'pressure of work in Court of Session'. I had thought that this nonsense would have been put an end to by the new Lord President, who has been active in improving matters in other directions.

January 16th
I was brought in to make a quorum in the Division, with Milligan and Kissen: a reclaiming motion against a judgment by Lord Leechman in *Maclean v. Caldwell's Paper Mill Co.* The pursuer had to drive a thirty-foot crane through Inverkeithing from the defenders' distillery to the mill. For safety reasons, a lorry was attached to the front of it by a tow rope. The pursuer says that as they were going up a steep hill the rope broke. The clutch pedal had been slipping; and when the rope broke he had to grip violently on the pedal and in so doing injured his leg. James Leechman had accepted that the rope had broken and found for the pursuer, assessing damages at £1,200. The only witness who spoke to the breaking of the rope was the pursuer, but as James had found him to be a truthful and reliable witness that should have been good enough. But Clyde and his colleagues of the First Division in a silly case in 1970, *Morrison v. Kelly*, had held that the 1967 Act which purports to do away with the necessity for corroboration cannot be applied if there are other witnesses who contradict or if called might have contradicted the witness the Lord Ordinary has believed, and Lothian, who appeared today with Sutherland for the reclaimers, argued that James was not entitled to proceed on the pursuer's evidence alone since he was contradicted on some collateral matters by other witnesses. I could not see much contradiction, even granted the premise of his argument; we seemed to be agreed that there was not much point in the appeal.

January 17th
When we rose for lunch everyone seemed agreed that, as I suggested, it was a pure question of credibility on which we could not interfere with the Lord Ordinary's judgment. But when Sutherland came on in the afternoon he was obviously swaying my two colleagues his way. His arguments were presented effectively, and it seemed that his skilful sophistries were having some effect.

January 18th
The continued hearing went much better. Milligan and Kissen had

apparently realised that Sutherland's points were not as sound as they had thought. I had reconciled myself to the possibility of having to give a dissenting judgment, and to thinking that it might not be a bad thing—if I were to write a strong dissent, the case would no doubt go to the Lords, and some of the nonsense talked in *Morrison v. Kelly* might well be corrected. But as the case went today it looked as if we were all going to be of the same opinion again. If that is so, I shall be able to agree, without writing any Opinion.

January 19th

A cruelty action in which the pursuer averred that he had come home to find his wife in bed covered with boot polish, which she had applied to her body to make him think she had had an accident.

January 23rd

To Stirling for a sitting of the High Court. The first case was *H.M. Advocate v. Coia*: four charges arising from the theft of a motor car from a car park in Kirkintilloch. Having stolen the car late at night, Coia set off for Dunfermline. A Dumbartonshire police car picked it up on the Glasgow-Stirling road and chased it all the way to Dunfermline. Coia was travelling throughout at 60 to 80 miles an hour, swerving from side to side to prevent the police car overtaking. A Stirlingshire police car, which had taken up the chase, continued to pursue the stolen car northwards on the Crieff road, and was in time to see Coia fail to take one of the sharp corners and plunge through the hedge into a field. When the police arrived there was no sign of Coia. They sent for a constable in the Dogs Department, who came with his alsatian. Having got a scent from the car, it went up on to a disused railway line, followed the track for some way, then came down from the embankment to ground level, crossed two fields, and found Coia lying concealed under the banking of a little burn. This officer paid testimony to the accuracy of the dog's trailing—she had, he said, been operational for six years. I thought there might be a difficulty about the identification of the driver of the car, since apart from the dog no one had identified Coia as the driver. In the event Coia went into the witness box, so no difficulty arose. Apart from theft of the car, Coia was charged with dangerous driving, driving the car at a policeman at Larbert roundabout to the danger of his life, and a second assault by driving the car at the two officers in the police car. The jury brought in a unanimous verdict of Guilty. It appeared from the Social Work department report that Coia had an obsession about cars; he had twice been disqualified from driving, and was constantly getting into trouble by driving cars away. It seemed to me that the sooner he was in a position to drive a car lawfully the better it would be for everybody; so while sentencing him to four years detention I refused to impose any additional period of disqualification, thus leaving him free to drive as soon as he comes out.

January 30th
A fine television play based on the trial which led to the hanging of Derek Bentley. Roland Culver as Goddard, without once going beyond the bounds of credibility, brilliantly demonstrated what a travesty of justice the trial was.

January 31st
Annoyed to find from Milligan that while I was away at Stirling Kissen had changed his mind in *Maclean v. Caldwells* and was now going to reverse James Leechman's judgment. Milligan of course had fallen in with this, so that I shall have to write a dissenting judgment after all. Davidson was telling me about a dermatitis case he had in the Lords, where a judgment of Kissen's, upheld by the First Division, in favour of defenders, had been unanimously reversed. He said that when he was reading the Opinions of the First Division judges to their Lordships he had happened to look up while reading Clyde's opinion and had observed Lord Salmon sadly shaking his head.

February 1st
Working on my Opinion in Maclean's case, I got quite a good Opinion drafted, and was surprised to find when Kissen's came in the bag from court that it seemed a very poor affair: a hotchpotch of criticisms of the pursuer's evidence, with no clear ground of judgment. It will be interesting to see what Milligan produces, particularly if he gets the copy of my Opinion before he finishes his.

February 6th
Sent in a short note on an appeal by Coia against the sentence I gave him at Stirling. His ground of appeal was that the sentence was 'very hard'. 'The judge did not do this case right'.

February 9th

Milligan's opinion in *Maclean v. Caldwells* came in the bag from court. It is a hotchpotch of illogicality; in the end he gives no reason for rejecting James's judgment on credibility. Obviously Kissen had persuaded him to agree to find for the defenders, and he has since been searching for some justification.

February 21st

Some discomfort in my inside.

February 22nd

An unpleasant night. Between four and six the pain eased off, but in the morning it was as bad as ever. I was supposed to be taking a proof, and thought I had better try to go in to Parliament House and see how I felt. But when I had got half into my clothes I gave it up, undressed and went back to bed. Nancy phoned Dr Jamieson, who in turn phoned Mr McIntosh. The two of them said they would like me to go into the Infirmary for a couple of days for a thorough examination. The trouble, they think, lies in the diverticula. By this time I was feeling better, and anyhow was supposed to be going to the Borders on Sunday for the Jedburgh circuit. A compromise was arrived at: that I should go in to court tomorrow, and if that went all right I could go to Jedburgh on Sunday. If there was any recurrence of pain I was to cut Jedburgh out and go into the Infirmary for the examination. George Macdonald however phoned shortly after the doctor had gone and said I must not think of coming in tomorrow. He would see Brown about getting someone else to go to Jedburgh. As there is a civil service strike on Tuesday which will close the Court of Session, I shall have till Wednesday to play about with, and with pain coming on again I was not sorry to take Macdonald's advice.

February 23rd

In the morning I was certainly not well, and I did not demur when Nancy decided to ring Dr Jamieson in the afternoon. He got on to McIntosh, and rang back to say that I was to be at Ward 10 in the Infirmary by 3.30. My bed is just inside the door, open to the centre of the ward but cut off by a solid partition from my next-door neighbour: a good arrangement, giving me complete privacy while allowing me to see what is going on. A wireless was blaring out interminable pop music, but it seems to be right up at the other end and did not worry me.

February 24th

A visit from a Salvation Army lass who came and spoke to me and gave me a copy of *The War Cry*. We had a minor excitement when Ian McLauchlan, the captain of the Scotland rugger team, came in with a broken leg sustained in this afternoon's match against Ireland. Sister Ross said I could have the window above me open if I liked, but Nurse Marshall—a less accommodating person than Sister Ross— said that the window cord was broken.

February 25th

Got up for my breakfast porridge, and thereafter joined in a game of rummy. The four players were on first-name terms: Wayne, Jimmy, Alex and Gordon. I had seen a burly man with a key chain sitting at the fireplace and realised this morning that he was a warder from Saughton who is looking after a prisoner. Which of my fellow-players was the prisoner I did not at first know. I thought it was probably Alex, who like Jimmy had the appearance of a typical young Glasgow keelie. But later I found that the prisoner was Wayne Stratton, who was serving a sentence at Wandsworth and had been transferred to Scotland to stand trial on a Scottish charge: a very different type, with plenty to say and a good opinion of himself. He knew all about everything, including rummy, though in fact he was easily beaten by Alex and Jimmy. An old fellow, Mr Storie, always seems to do the opposite of what is asked of him—lying flat when they want him to sit up, sitting up when they ask him to lie down, and so on. Every mouthful of food has to be fed to him, and as he generally refuses to open his mouth this requires a lot of patience. Sister Ferguson is unable to manage him. 'Open your mouth, Mr Storie', she says. 'I've studied shorthand and book-keeping', mumbles Mr Storie, and closes his mouth firmly. At 5.45 we were invaded by young people from Charlotte Chapel. They handed round hymn-books and asked us to select hymns, for community singing. Luckily there was one old fellow who seemed interested and chose hymns for them—quite a good choice. A girl read a Scripture passage, and one of the youths gave a short exhortation. I had not thought there would be anyone in our ward to whom this kind of thing would make any appeal, but presumably the man who chose the hymns enjoyed it. If it had to be done at all I think they did it as well as possible—it was a pleasant change from the pop music, which was turned off while the young missionaries were in. Scrambled egg for supper. My seat at the table happened to be between Stratton and his warder. Obviously neither knew who I was, and we had a frank, lively argument about how to deal with crime. A Corporation bus tour driver was particularly vociferous; a nurse had to come along and tell us that whatever we were arguing about we should remember there were some people in the ward who were ill. I was impressed by the warder: a fair-minded, level-headed man. Stratton thought that things were much easier for the warders at Wandsworth than at Saughton. There was no flexibility in Wandsworth. A hard and fast line was drawn in everything, and you were never allowed to cross it. It was like a concentration camp. He condemned the probation service, apparently on the ground that the probation officer to whom he had had to report twice a week had failed to fix a time to suit his convenience. I mentioned Cordiner, and the warder observed that he was a most dangerous character. W. M. Reid, the counsel in Cordiner's pending appeal, told me not long ago that his client was enjoying his privileges as a civil prisoner in Saughton and the interest he had aroused in the newspapers.

February 26th

Things that happen here occasionally remind me of the film, *The Hospital*. This afternoon a porter arrived with a wheelchair saying 'Mr Irons for X-ray'. The nurses gazed vaguely round, and told him there was no Mr Irons in the ward. There was Mr McLean. 'Oh, well, Mr McLean then', said the porter, and off went Mr McLean to X-ray. Three probationer nurses assisting Nurse Vetter went off with two syringes in the same dish and failed to remember which injection was for which patient. Nurse Vetter had a bit of trouble sorting this out. But the organisation of the nursing staff is amazing. At each change-over—8 am, 1.30 pm and 10 pm—the relieving staff come in fifteen to twenty minutes before, and there is a conference of nurses at the desk, when the nurse who had been in charge gives a resumé of the position relating to every patient. I kept away from the fireplace to escape from Stratton, who was talking at length about all the places he had been to and the things he had done, without saying anything of the slightest interest. After supper however we had an amusing conversation about his affairs and the sentence he was likely to get in Edinburgh Sheriff Court. When I asked if it was housebreaking he was in for, he denied it—apparently taking the word literally and not in its technical Scottish use. He said he confined himself to places like banks and insurance offices—he did not think it was fair to break into people's houses. The warder was sceptical, and observed that if Stratton kept doing insurance companies it meant that working folk like us would have higher premiums to pay. Although Stratton seemed genuinely anxious to know about his probable sentence, it was extraordinarily difficult to get him to come clean about what he was charged with—it had to be dragged out of him. He seems to have a long record, including escape from Borstal when he was a lad. A crisis arose just after Nurse Marshall took over, alone, for the night. Nurse Vetter's assistant had given a wrong dose to Mr Macmillan, the man in the oxygen mask, and my neighbour, old Mr Fraser, tore off his drip tube as a result of a sudden spontaneous decision by him that he should try to get out of bed. Sister Ross told me she was short-handed in all her twelve wards.

February 27th

Mr Castle was *hors de combat*. His emergency too had been brought on by Nurse Vetter's assistant yesterday. He had come in for a serious operation on which some preliminary work was done when he was in the ward before, four or five weeks ago. The nurse yesterday however had broken through his dressing, and all they had done last night was repair the damage she had done, so as to get him back into the condition in which he could undergo the operation for which he came in. I had two games of cribbage with Stratton. He was a good player, and I had never before played cribbage on the standard of today's play, each player considering what was the best line of play and what would be his opponent's likely response. I pointed out to Stratton that he had failed to mark up a flush of three that he had scored in the play. He rectified this, and shortly afterwards pointed out to me that I had missed something when reckoning up my hand. 'You were honest with me', he said, 'so I'll be honest with you'. 'There you are', I said. 'Honesty for me was the best policy'. The warder, who seemed to be a connoisseur of cribbage, sat beside me and commented on the play. Trolleys came and went as three of our fellow-patients were removed to the theatre and returned in a comatose condition. When they came for the latest admission, we turned to the warder and said, 'That's you—up you get on the trolley'. I have found where the milk is kept, and was able to go along twice to the ward kitchen and help myself. At three o'clock I joined the company round the table, for the last time, for a cup of tea. Another prisoner has come in with his warder: a pleasant, quiet young man with long dark hair who has served one year of a four-years sentence in Saughton—a very different type from the glib, self-assured Stratton. His home is in the Inch housing scheme, and on hearing that I came from Blackford Hill spoke of how much he had enjoyed as a boy climbing about the hill and the Hermitage woods. He seemed to like to stand looking out of the window at the end of the ward towards the traffic and passers-by in Lauriston Place, a kind of view, he said, that he had not had for a long time. Nancy motored me home—after four days' absence which probably made no difference to anyone except the rapist at Jedburgh who had got a ten-years sentence from Brand instead of the five years he would have got from me.

March 7th
The First Division yesterday released Cordiner, having been satisfied, according to the report of Emslie's judgment, that Cordiner was apt to say in anger whatever came into his head, without much appreciation of what he was saying.

March 10th
Wrote a note to Harold Wilson. Roy Jenkins, after causing immeasurable trouble last year by opposing Labour policy on the Common Market—of which he has always been a strong supporter—has now, after the whole thing is finished with and Britain is part of the European Community, re-opened the dispute by an attack on the Party leadership and a self-righteous declaration that he and his friends have alone been consistent. My note consisted of one sentence: 'Why not send Roy to the European Parliament and ask him to stay there?'

March 15th
A cranky woman came to the door wanting to see 'Lord Stout' on a personal matter. I brought her in, and it turned out that she wanted to have a talk with the judge who gave her a divorce in 1970. After looking at me she decided that I was not the judge, and that her solicitor had 'made a blunder' in sending her to me. As it was an undefended divorce, I assured her that whatever judge it was would probably remember nothing about it.

March 30th

Miss Lorraine Campbell, assistant secretary of the Scottish Wildlife Trust, wrote me after seeing my letter in the *Scotsman* about Blackford Hill trees, suggesting that I might like to become a member; and in reply I said I should consider it if she would remind me about it when my next wages payment was due, at the end of March. So she has now sent me a birthday card: a picture of an elephant, and the legend printed inside: 'Of course I remembered!'

April 4th

Put the car through the car-wash at Forrest's. In consequence of the Value Added Tax, which came in on 1st April, they have done away with the 15p car wash, and one now has to pay 20p for wash and wax whether one wants the wax or not. Liberal Party broadcast: worthy, respectable and very dull.

April 5th

My spell of vacation duty began on Wednesday, and this evening an enormous pile of papers arrived for tomorrow's Vacation Court. I worked away steadily on them until supper time, after which Dr and Mrs Rogers came for Bridge. Thereafter I had another half-hour's work to do on the papers.

April 6th

Tonight on television we had a BBC 'Money at Work' programme dealing with VAT, inflation and the Common Market agricultural policy: an excellent programme which pulled no punches. Douglas Jay was the star of the show, with a denunciation of VAT and the Common Market which was extremely entertaining.

April 7th

Richard had been in court yesterday, and said that May had been sitting near him when an interdict hearing was going on, and had observed that I was certain to decide against the pursuers since they were represented by Nimmo Smith.

The Lyceum: John Osborne's *Look Back in Anger*. It is a real play, full of sardonic wit and effective dialogue, and it had a first-class performance by the Young Lyceum Company. Patrick Malahide and Alex Heggie, who had been unconvincing as gentlemen of Verona, were Jimmy Porter and his uncouth follower to the life.

April 9th

The final round of the American Masters tournament was on BBC2 tonight from Augusta, Georgia: a beautiful course, with bright sunshine and all the foliage as green as the fine turf on which the golf was played.

April 10th

Labour Party political broadcast on television had been entrusted to Ron Hayward, the Party secretary. The only possible effect must have been to make anyone who took it seriously decide to vote Conservative. One consoled oneself with the thought that perhaps no one takes these things seriously, but it was pathetic to think that on the eve of critical local government elections this man should have been selected by the Labour Party to speak to the nation on its behalf.

April 12th

ITV programme about Olga Korbut, the delightful little Russian gymnast who won everyone's heart at the Olympic Games: good entertainment, particularly the grim, unremitting training sessions, each girl with her own instructor—solemn, unsmiling, relentless, going through the same routine over and over again without the slightest sign of appreciation. Came down after my bath for the BBC programme on the English local government elections. Knowing the BBC, I had expected it to be useless, but it was far worse than I had expected. Slips of paper were being passed to Alastair Burnett and his two colleagues, obviously giving results as they came in, but it seldom occurred to him to pass them on, simply asking for comments on how things were going—whereupon the commentators said the same things they had been saying for the past half-hour. There was a long interlude when we were favoured with the recording of some debate in Hull Town Council about the need for a bridge across the Humber. When this gave place to two pop-singer guitarists singing about the family I gave up and went to bed.

April 13th

Vacation Court. *David Douglas (Holdings) v. Scottish Daily Record & Sunday Mail*: an action by the company and one of its directors, Wolfson. Wolfson was interviewed about the company's business by a journalist called The Judge who writes in the *Sunday Mail*, in the company's office in Glasgow. He says he took no objection to being interviewed and answered all questions put to him; but as he was leaving after the interview he found that another man who had been present was a photographer. Wolfson refused to be photographed, and covered his head with a coat; but the photographer pursued him along the street and tried to pull the coat away. Wolfson reached the car park and got into his car, and in the course of a scuffle drove the car over the photographer's foot. The *Daily Record* next day had a report of the incident giving no names but referring to a man whom they had been seeking to interview and alleging that after running the photographer down the man had driven off at a fast speed, before the police could be summoned. In fact, according to the petition, Wolfson had gone straight to the police station and reported what had happened. Peter Fraser, who appeared for the pursuers, asked for an interdict against publication in the *Sunday Mail* of any report of the interview or incident so far as reflecting adversely on the company's business activities, on the ground that the *Record* had falsely suggested that Wolfson had been running away and avoiding an interview and it was likely that similar allegations would appear in The Judge's article on Sunday. It seemed to me that the prayer of the petition was too wide, but that there was ground for an interdict against any publication suggesting that Wolfson had been attempting to evade an interview or avoid giving information. The conclusion having been amended to that effect, I granted interim interdict.

April 15th
Seascale. We went down to the beach, and walked southwards along the sand: fine hard sand which stretches for miles in either direction. After dinner we took the dog along the path between the hotel and the railway, and under the line to the beach, where with the tide now full the waves were rippling in under a full moon. The manager was playing away on his Wurlitzer organ in the dining-room. At Moffat I had bought a copy of the *Sunday Mail* and was amused to find a front-page story narrating that I had granted an interdict barring the *Mail* from printing anything about Mr Wolfson's business activities. This of course was inaccurate, and the story as published, suggesting that Wolfson and his company were determined to avoid publicity, was the very thing that I had prohibited.

April 16th
A modest lunch of sandwiches in the Eskdale railway tea-room. At

this time of year the train was made up of covered coaches instead of the open trucks in which I had travelled on previous occasions. This was nothing like the Festiniog's imprisonment system, but a good deal of the fun of the trip was missing when we were not in the open. I had put on my sheepskin jacket for the journey, and when I took it off on getting back to the car we were surprised to see a coat-hanger fall out—without knowing it, I had been wearing under the jacket the coat-hanger it had been on when I took it out of the cupboard at home. We motored back to Seascale. It is odd that in spite of its sandy beach and its situation at the edge of the Lake District no attempt seems to have been made to develop Seascale as a seaside resort. The sea front is completely unspoiled, with no 'attractions' whatsoever—not even an ice-cream parlour. Hotels and boarding houses are few, and nobody seems to advertise bed and breakfast, or rooms to let.

April 17th
The mountain road across Hardknott Pass: a narrow road, very steep, with stretches of 1 in 3 gradient and several hairpin bends. I put the car into first gear, and it climbed easily to a parking place about half way up, where it was pleasant to walk on the mountain turf—a magnificent view all down the valley. The second part of the climb was the worst, particularly as we happened to meet another car practically on a hairpin at about the steepest point. I had to draw into a rocky passing-place and stop; but starting off again on a 1 in 3 gradient was nothing to the Volvo, and after that it was comparatively plain sailing over the top. There was a very steep bit as we came down to Wrynose Bottom, giving the impression that one was going down almost perpendicularly; but on the whole I found the road not as difficult as I had expected. In the guidebook it was described as 'the most difficult motor road in the Lake District'. 'The road is surfaced throughout but is very narrow and even passing places are a tight squeeze'. Cars longer than fourteen feet, it was said, were at a disadvantage; and as the Volvo is fifteen feet long I had been a little apprehensive. But it took the hairpin bends quite easily. I wanted to get to Tarn Hows—a beautiful lake set in a hollow in the hills, where we picnicked on a green hillside looking over the tarn. The road ahead brought us down to Coniston. We followed the bank of Coniston Lake for its whole length, and at Torver turned left for Broughton—where some children were sitting with their feet in the old stocks that still stand there. Tea and a cake in a quaint little shop.

In general, customers are not encouraged in Broughton. Although there seemed to be a high-tea menu, a man who came in and, asked what he would have to eat, suggested pies, was not shown the menu but simply told there was no pies. When he asked for tea cake and sandwiches he was given some ham sandwiches and told there was no tea cake. The little girl who served us was having a contretemps with an elderly man who insisted that he had a regular order for a particular kind of loaf. She kept showing him the same loaf, to which he said 'No', adding 'You've sold it, that's what you've done'. So far as I could understand his dialect, he seemed to be saying that in future he would take his business elsewhere. They would not sell us any milk, and though I got two of the last three pints in the butcher's I was less lucky in trying to get a film for my camera. At the first shop I tried, they hoped to have some in, next week. At the next, though they had some 620 films the date for developing them had passed—the proprietor offered to sell me one for 10p, in the hope that it would turn out all right. As in Seascale, none of the shops has a normal shop door: just a plain door, like the door of a house, which is closed so that they all look as if they were shut. From Broughton we crossed the Duddon and ascending out of the Duddon valley took a road signposted 'Whitehaven by Fell Road—scenic route'. As we came out on the open moorland, we could see masses of white mist swirling across the road ahead, coming from the north, and soon we were right into it: most peculiar, since it did not seem to be wet—I never required to use the windscreen wiper and there was no moisture on the screen— just great wreaths of white driving past us, with visibility down to a few yards. We came out of the mist as abruptly as we had entered it.

April 18th
A lively conversation with a young Lancastrian who now had a tweed manufacturing business at Langholm.

April 19th
Our friend from Langholm told us that police had arrived at the hotel last night after eleven to say that it had to be evacuated, as they had a message that a bomb had been planted in it. The proprietor would not have this, but said they could search the hotel if they liked, and there had been a lot of coming and going along the corridors. It cannot have been a very thorough search—no one came into our room, and we heard nothing.

April 21st
Wastwater. We stopped by the lakeside at the foot of the little glen
where we were on Monday. Snow had fallen, and the mountains
above the lake were white. The sun had come out, and the water was
blue, instead of the sombre dark water which seems to be Wastwater's
normal state.

April 27th
To St Giles' for the Duke of Hamilton's funeral service. Parts of the
service were mildly comical: some weird solo singing to loud percus-
sion music by Patrick Douglas-Hamilton—presumably a relative—and
later a piper processed through the church playing the tune associated with the song about 'toddling with glee to my ain house'.

May 8th
Sitting this week as a member of the High Court, taking Justiciary
Appeals: Emslie, Douglas Johnston, and myself. In *Maxwell v.
MacNeill*, Croan had found the appellant guilty of driving with more
than the permitted level of alcohol in his blood. A police patrol car
had followed the appellant's Mercedes through Bearsden and stopped
it for a random check. The appellant got out, and the two constables,
smelling alcohol in his breath, asked him to take a breathalyser test,
which was positive. He was taken to a police station, where tests
resulted in a finding of 102 milligrammes of alcohol in 100 millilitres
of blood. The validity of all this depended on whether the police had
been entitled to ask the appellant to take the breathalyser test—as
they are if they have reason to suspect that anyone driving a motor
vehicle has consumed alcohol. The police here did not have any
ground for suspicion until the appellant had got out of the car, and
there have been a number of English cases that lay down the proposition that once the driver has got out he is no longer a person driving
a motor vehicle. The Scottish Courts have consistently regarded this
argument as nonsense: the test could not be administered while the
man is actually driving, as it would have to be if one read the section
of the Act literally along the lines followed in England, and in Scotland it has always been held that what the Act is dealing with is not
a man who is driving at some particular moment but one who comes
within the category of vehicle driver. We held that the Sheriff had
been entitled to hold that the procedure had been in order. It was a
pleasant court to sit in. Though George and I put various points to

counsel we gave everyone a fair hearing, and the atmosphere was courteous and friendly. Emslie and I were in complete agreement on all points, and Douglas too agreed with us.

May 10th

A batch of appeals against sentence. An application for leave to appeal by Cairns, the man who got a ten-years sentence from Brand at Jedburgh—the case I should have tried if I had not been ill, involving the rape of a ten-year-old girl. Cairns had come to the premises of the child's father to buy garden produce, and asked the girl if she would like to go with him in his lorry. They told the girl's mother that they were going, then drove into the country and walked to the corner of a field, where the crime was committed. There was no evidence of physical injury, and the crime was rather incomprehensible, as it seemed obvious that it would at once be found out. Cairns was 47, and had an impeccable record; and despite a terribly bad plea on his behalf I managed to get it established that there was no premeditation. We substituted seven years for ten. Next came another of Brand's victims, who had got twelve years for assault with a knife. McBride was said to belong to a gang known as the Mad Squad. Emslie took the view that twelve years went beyond the range of what was recognised as reasonable, even for assault to the danger of life, and we reduced the sentence to nine years. *McGrath v. H.M. Advocate* was the first appeal against conviction: of breaking into the Rob Roy bar in Glasgow and stealing part of the stock in trade. Police went to the premises in response to the ringing of a burglar alarm, and heard someone shout: 'Kick the door in and let me out. The police are coming'. On going round to the back, they found that a hole had been made in the rear wall, and crawling through found themselves in the men's lavatory with the appellant trying to hide in a dark corner. His story was that when he had been waiting at the bus stop outside he was seized by some strangers, who pushed him through the hole into the public house. When brought in today, he said he was not going to persist with his appeal. The same attitude was adopted by the next appellant, who had been convicted of robbing a shopkeeper at Bridge of Dee. He came into her shop with a scarf round his mouth, held a knife at her throat, and got her to give him £8 from the till. At the trial she professed to be able to identify him by the shape of his nose. Jamieson, the next appellant, had been convicted of assault and robbery. He had gone to the house of a man named Prendergast. The house was in darkness, because the electricity had been cut off, but the television was operating by virtue of a lead from the house above. A man McCue arrived and proceeded to threaten Prendergast with a paint scraper. Jamieson was seated in a chair. McCue told him to take the television set. Jamieson demurred, but when McCue said to him 'Do you want a fight?' he picked up the television, and the two walked out into the arms of the police. Morton maintained that Sheriff Peterson had failed to put to the jury a defence of coercion, and referred us to the case of Gordon, reported by Hume, where that defence had succeeded when the house in which Gordon lived had been invaded by Rob Roy with fifteen armed men, who commanded Gordon to come forth with them, threatening to shoot him or cleave him to the teeth. This seemed far-fetched, but Peterson had failed to give any proper direction on art and part, on which the robbery conviction depended. We quashed the conviction for assault and robbery, leaving only the theft of the television, and for the sentence imposed by Peterson substituted a short sentence which meant Jamieson's immediate release. The appellant Druce had been convicted of the reset of two American Express travellers cheques, in the name of one Mr Eccles. He was a Vice-President of the First National Bank, and on reporting the loss had been paid the money for them without question. Lothian argued that Druce himself might have been the thief, and queried whether one could be convicted of resetting goods stolen by oneself. But reset consists in being in possession of stolen goods, knowing they are stolen, and it did not seem to me to matter who had stolen them. We sustained the conviction.

May 11th

A case, in which Campbell appeared, was difficult. Phillips, the appellant, had struck a man named Lopez on the head with a bottle in a street in Port Glasgow. The injuries included loss of an eye. The jury had rejected a plea of self-defence, and Grieve sentenced Phillips to four years detention. He had been dux and sports champion of his school, and a Social Work report bore evidence that he was of a high degree of intelligence and exemplary character. As Lopez seemingly was a very different type, and there had been considerable provocation, we felt that if any of us had been dealing with Phillips in the first place it was unlikely that he would have got four years. But, as Emslie said, there was no ground here for an appellate court to interfere—Grieve had heard the evidence, and we had not—and we refused the appeal.

May 15th

For the past five weeks I have been making a note each morning of anyone I had been dreaming about during the night. These were almost exclusively people with whom I had some personal acquaintance; but on Wednesday night, for no reason that I was aware of, I dreamed about Lord Talbot de Malahide—and in today's *Times* I found Lord Talbot de Malahide's obituary. A strange coincidence.

May 29th

A criminal trial, *H.M. Advocate v. Gray*. The accused is charged with indecent practices with five children and with ravishing one of them: Christine, now aged eleven. The matter came to light when Christine and Bruce ran away from home and having turned up at the house of a school friend of Bruce's asked to be allowed to do some work and earn enough to pay their bus fares to North Berwick, so that they could go back to Dr Barnardo's. Cowie, the Advocate Depute, appeared at first to be suggesting that this was because of their stepfather's conduct, but Gray having been arrested and removed from the house Christine and Bruce ran away again, and repeated the escapade four or five times until the authorities gave in, and they are now back at Dr Barnardo's at North Berwick. Christine, a very competent witness, explained how she and Bruce, aged ten, boarded the North Berwick bus and told the conductress they were from Dr Barnardo's and had forgotten their money, and she allowed them to stay on the bus. It was a tribute to Dr Barnardo's that they had been determined to get back there at all costs. Cowie was excellent—I have never heard child witnesses better handled.

May 30th

The jury found the accused guilty, and I sentenced him to four years imprisonment.

June 2nd

To Mortonhall Crematorium for Alex Sutherland's funeral service— conducted by an old minister who was doddering and slow but seemed to me very good indeed. What he said about Sutherland was eloquent and very much to the point. When I asked afterwards who he was I was amazed to hear that he was John E. Hamilton, now aged 93, the former Labour candidate for East Aberdeen, who used to help us in West Edinburgh and lent us his garden for Labour Party fêtes.

June 5th

H.M. Advocate v. Brady: a respectable-looking, bespectacled young man who was charged with striking a youth named Murray with a tumbler in the Royal Bar, with taking part in a robbery from two men who were taking £2,800 from the offices of Barr's Iron Brew to the bank, and with pretending to the police that his car, which was used in the robbery, had been stolen at the time. On the first charge the main witness was Murray's father, who claimed to have seen Brady strike his son with a tumbler while the son was helping him to his feet when he had fallen on the floor; but as the father agreed that he was blind drunk at the time his evidence may be suspect. The second charge seems to raise a pure question of identification. When the two employees were taking the money to the bank in a padlocked bag, a blue Cortina stopped and two men got out, and having hit the employees over the head made off with the bag. They were pursued by a passer-by, an insignificant-looking little man named Brown, who with commendable courage and resource pursued the criminals along the pavement and got hold of the one carrying the bag. He grappled with him, and although he received some minor injury got the man to drop the money, which was duly returned to Mr Barr. The man, named Ross, was subsequently convicted at the High Court. The other man got away, but a third man, who was driving the Cortina, had got out and joined briefly in the fray before hurrying back to the car and driving off. Nobody had identified him at the time; and when he was put up for identification at a parade—presumably because it was his car that was involved—none of the witnesses picked him out. Brown and Barr's manager, Skinner, who was carrying the money, picked out a man who had nothing to do with the case. Henderson, who was along with Skinner, did not pick anyone out; he said he saw the accused there but did not pick him out because he was not certain. At the end of his evidence it turned out that the man he was referring to was standing at the end of the row—the accused had been standing in the middle. Mr Barr himself, who had come across from his office and seen the assailant walking back to the Cortina, said his back was very like Brady's back—he had been shown Brady when giving evidence at Ross's trial and made this observation at that time. It was Ross's trial that had been Brady's downfall—he was called as a witness, and as soon as Skinner saw him in the court buildings he said, 'That's the man from the car, who attacked us', whereupon despite the failure of the earlier identification parade he was arrested and charged.

June 6th

Police evidence of what Brady was supposed to have said when arrested and charged in the High Court building. Prais cross-examined the police witnesses on whether they should have advised him that he was entitled to have legal advice. 'Surely', said Prais, 'when he was being arrested in the High Court you would have been able to get hold of the odd solicitor here'. 'Yes', said Detective-Sergeant Black, without batting an eyelid, 'you would certainly get the *odd* solicitor here'. The defence evidence was directed towards establishing an alibi: that every Friday Brady went a round of pubs and betting houses with men named Hope and McLaughlin. Hope was a well-to-do heating consultant, McLaughlin a scallywag with a list of convictions, and this curiously assorted trio proceeded each Friday from pub to pub and betting house to betting house, while Hope paid for the taxis and the drinks and gambled away £100 or so each weekend. It was an odd story, but not altogether unconvincing. Ross was adduced to say that Brady was not concerned in the robbery—for which Ross now admitted responsibility after giving evidence at his own trial to the effect that he was an innocent passer-by who had hold of the money bag after wresting it from the robbers.

June 7th

Prais led some more alibi witnesses, and all went well with him until his last witness, an old lady who lives beside Brady's mother and insisted that on the Friday in question Brady was in his mother's house. This might have been an alibi of a sort, but it was dead in the teeth of what the other witnesses had said. It was amusing to listen to Prais desperately trying to break this new unsought alibi. Though it was an entertaining interlude, I did not suppose that anyone would take the old lady seriously. As soon as the jury retired, I started on the next case: two brothers, Robert and Brian Pollock, charged first with murdering a man named Kent, robbing him of a watch and a wallet and throwing him into the Forth and Clyde Canal. Charge two is minor: breaking into a house in Dalmuir and stealing a clock and lighter. Charge three is a second murder—of a man named McKenna in his house in Clydebank. The Brady jury came back with a verdict of guilty of the assault on Ramsay, and Not Proven on the other charges. The first charge was little more than a pub brawl, and I agreed with Prais that if that charge had stood alone Brady would never have been in the High Court. I sentenced him to imprisonment for twelve months—with which he seemed delighted, saying 'Thank you', bowing to me and the jury, and waving to Prais as he was taken out.

June 8th
The Pollock trial was resumed. Witnesses included two flaxen-haired little boys, twin brothers and exactly alike: they looked the same, were dressed in the same way, and gave the same evidence with the same staccato utterance and confident tone of voice. I gave Robertson a lift up, and travelled through with him in the train. Speaking about the two little boys, he remarked jocularly that they had thought it might be one of the Crown's dirty tricks, putting in the same witness twice, under different names. I enjoyed my week, and found Milligan a pleasant companion. His genuine modesty, and lack of confidence in his own judgment, are disarming. He told me a story about R.B. Miller—how when sheriff at Stornoway he had to go to his court at Lochmaddy, and in the days before the inter-island causeway was driven across the ford in a cart. The horse was slow, and he urged the driver to hurry, saying that they did not want to keep the accused man waiting for his trial. 'That's all right', said the driver. 'I'm the accused'. Milligan recalled an occasion in Parliament when some question about teinds was to arise on one of the Finance Bills. Willie Ross made a long, violent speech attacking the Government's proposal and dealing in some detail with teind matters. The minister in charge at the time was Enoch Powell; and according to Milligan Powell made a brilliant reply, showing complete mastery of the subject of teinds and demolishing Ross's argument.

June 11th
The trial was resumed, and the Crown produced their star witness: a man who spoke to a conversation with the Pollocks in which George said 'We done him in', and went on to say in cross-examination that he would not have risked his life by coming to give evidence unless he knew what he was talking about. A succession of girls from the house above that in which old McKenna was murdered included another pair of twins, younger than the little boys we had last week,

and again identical in appearance and manner. It is a curious feature of the case that as an answer to the second murder charge the brothers have put in a defence that the murder was committed not by them but by their father.

June 12th

The trial had livened up, and was especially entertaining when Pollock senior was put into the box. He would have been free to say that he had murdered McKenna, but he insisted that he had nothing to do with it—to the accompaniment of cries from the dock, 'Tell the truth'. Denying that he had been in any way responsible for McKenna's death, he said 'I wish the man would come back from the dead and tell the truth'. At one point he said, 'I'd be telling you a lie if I told you the truth'. But on the whole I thought he sounded fairly convincing.

June 14th

Charged the jury—a lot of ground to cover, and I took well over an hour. Under Charge one, the jury, finding murder Not Proven, convicted Robert of robbery of the watch, and found the whole charge Not Proven as against Brian. On the charge relating to McKenna, they found both guilty of murder. It seemed to me that what the jury had done was absolutely right.

June 19th

Cross actions of divorce, *Kelly v. Kelly*: the husband a psychopathic exhibitionist whose case—based on his wife's feeding him on fish and chips instead of chops and prepared dishes that he preferred—never got off the ground. I thought that I should probably be able to turn down the wife's case as well. She had left him only when the electricity got turned off through a dispute about the bill. According to the wife, he had brought girl friends to the house, including one who slept in the same bed as herself and her husband for three weeks. She rang up her mother to ask her advice about this, but all her mother said was that she had made her bed and must lie on it.

June 24th

Drafted an Opinion in *Kelly v. Kelly*; I am refusing decree of divorce to both parties.

June 26th
Barry v. Barry. The three children—Derek, now aged nine, Alan, aged seven, and Diane, aged six, have been living with the pursuer at his parents' house near Kilsyth. The pursuer's uncle William, MP for West Stirlingshire, gave evidence. Everybody agreed that he and his wife had acted as a moderating influence, and so far as the two younger children are concerned his intervention has been completely successful—the defender collects them every second Saturday, and quite often with the pursuer's consent they have stayed overnight with her. But Derek has steadfastly refused to go.

June 27th
Had undertaken to interview the children, and having discarded my wig and gown went out to the Hall, where I found them. They were unwilling to be detached from their grandfather, but I took them round the Hall, showing them the picture of it in the old days that hangs above the fireplace, and into the Corridor to show them the Flodden pennant. By that time they were willing to leave their relatives, and we all ran along happily to the Cedar Room so that I could have a talk with them by themselves. Derek only smiled and shook his head when I asked him about going to see his mother, but Diane was more forthcoming, agreeing that Derek should come with them and that she would do her best to get him to come. I gave judgment ordering that all three children would spend every second week-end with the defender.

June 29th
A cruelty action by a husband whose wife had tried to commit suicide on numerous occasions. The pursuer seemed a frank witness, and agreed that he had said to his wife, 'Go and jump into the Clyde'; but that, he said, was a common Glasgow expression, and he had not expected her to do it.

July 13th
An undefended action of declarator of the death of James Boyd, formerly manager of a tea estate in East Pakistan, who was last seen alive on 15th June 1971. Guerilla groups operating against the Pakistan Government had blown up the machinery on the estate, and Boyd was abducted by a group of armed men in Pakistan army uniform. He was dragged off towards the border river, where explosions

were heard; it seems that he was shot, and his body thrown into the river. Mr Chakravaty, whose evidence was taken on commission, made some enquiry and learned that one Shri Norander Sirdar had been asked 'to find out the dead body of the late Mr Boyd, but it would not be found as the river was full of water'. I granted decree of declarator.

July 24th

Copenhagen. The new pedestrian precinct is a curious mixture of expensive shops and old-fashioned pornography shows. We had a delightful sail down a canal to the harbour, along the harbour past several big steamers, up the next canal and so back to Kongens Nytorv. Bus to the station for the Helsingor train. Hornbaek: Hotel Trouville—I fixed it up after examining brochures dealing with Zea- land beaches. The hotel is a big new building, with a back entrance opening right on to sand dunes at the sea. After dinner we went out on the dunes, and found a nice sheltered path through masses of wild roses.

July 25th

At Hornbaek there is very little movement of the tides, so that one can bathe, it seems, at any time of day. This evening we had a delightful bathe in a choppy sea, which did not seem at all cold.

July 27th

A nice dinner—the soup always excellent. The pianist is a strikingly handsome young man, with a varied repertoire which he goes through, night after night. We have got to the stage of exchanging smiles with him, which is more than we can say about the residents. The Danes seem to keep very much to themselves: it is rare to find them ex- changing a smile or word of greeting with one another, much less with foreigners like us. Twilight here lasts for a long time, and after dinner we had a lovely walk along the edge of the sea, in the dusk of a balmy evening.

July 28th

Morning on the dunes and in the sea. Most of the people on the beach are bronzed and sun-burned. Bra-less girls are in order—one does not give them a second thought—but they are the exception rather than the rule. Children run about the beach completely naked, and very brown below their flaxen hair. The woods immediately behind could have been in another world: a quiet path which could have been miles from the sea in the heart of a pine forest.

July 29th
Detained in conversation by a drunk man: a grizzled elderly Dane who had been at Scapa Flow and did not seem to think much of 'England'. This was the first indication of drunkenness we had come across in Denmark. When we were sitting in the dunes after our bathe, a completely naked young lady—tall, handsome and beautifully bronzed—came walking past us on her way to and from the sea.

July 30th
Fredensborg Castle, an imposing white building with a big cobbled courtyard, reminiscent of Versailles. Passing a little garden full of odd sculptures of children engaged in children's ploys—eating an ice-cream slider, or feeding a dog—we came into lovely parkland: a stretch of lawn, with fine trees towering up. We made our way into a curious circular hollow, with an obelisk in the middle and dozens of nude statues set out round the hollow in a double circle—apparently of peasants and country people. Coming out of this sombre glade, we reached a rose garden with many different varieties of roses.

July 31st
Stockholm: Park Hotel, where Cook's had booked a room for the 'Stockholm Package' holiday that I brought to their notice. Our 'package' covers only bed and breakfast, and we walked down the street in search of a cafe. Not having a word of Swedish, we did not fare very well. In a big open square there were some fine fountains playing, and a religious pop group rather like the singers from Charlotte Chapel. We saw two or three police cars—not having in Denmark seen a policeman except one standing at the door of his house in Hornbaek, in his shirt sleeves.

August 1st
Dinner in the hotel restaurant. I had never had a dinner for two which, with a half bottle of wine, cost not much short of the equivalent of £10. But it was a nice dinner, beautifully served by an attentive young waiter. A party of young Japanese girls seemed to be having a table d'hôte dinner—twenty or thirty of them. Most of the girls looked completely exhausted or supremely bored and gave no indication of

enjoying themselves. The four men in charge of them seemed cheery enough. After dinner a bus took us across to a quay from which we had a good view of two cruising liners, all lit up from stem to stern. We came back by the Stockholm underground, a new development since I was here before. It must have gone very far underground indeed, for we came up two of the longest escalators I have seen. They switched themselves off as soon as the passengers had got to the surface. A short walk through dark deserted streets to the hotel.

August 2nd

To Saltsjobaden—an excellent seat in the open part at the stern of the motor launch. A beautiful blonde Swedish girl was on board as courier, and the first part of the voyage was marred a little by her descriptions of points of interest, in Swedish, English, German and French, over a loudspeaker so distorted that I could not make out a word she said. But later she gave up, and came and chatted to passengers individually. It was a lovely sail, but in Sweden they do not seem to have the same gift as in Switzerland or Denmark for blending the houses in with the countryside. No doubt the houses are nice to live in, but usually they tend to be rather an eyesore, both the older villas and the great blocks of flats which appear everywhere round Stockholm. However, we were soon out of the town, passing little rocky islands and turning into a lovely wooded stretch. We emerged into open sea in the sense that it was a lovely expanse of blue water, but itself also to all appearance landlocked, a wooded ridge forming the coast on the far side. At Saltsjobaden we lay in the sun among pine trees. The water looked pretty polluted. Saltsjobaden, with its woods and inlets, is a lovely place, but not really a place to linger in. Train back to Stockholm. Tickets had to be obtained at a newspaper kiosk, but when I presented my bus card there it was obvious that the woman had never seen one before. Saltsjobaden was outside its limit of validity, and what I intended was to take a ticket to the first station inside the zone, with the card valid from there. The woman suggested I should produce it in the train. When the conductor came round, he merely looked at the cards and did not charge us anything. At the Hotel Anglais grill we had a good dinner for approximately half what I paid last night at the Park Hotel. After dinner we went to the square where the fountains were. Dancing began on a small wooden platform to the accompaniment of an accordion and a double bass: polkas, waltzes, and round dances of various kinds danced by the public with vigour, to lively, catchy tunes. We were impressed by the skilful way in which almost everyone who took part performed the complicated steps, particularly two middle-aged women dancing together: the only pair which was wholly female. The taller of the two guided her smaller companion round and round the platform with tremendous energy and evident enjoyment—an unusual sight in this country of dour, sombre people.

August 3rd

We made use of our tickets to go for a bus ride. Our road brought us on to one of the great high-level bridges crossing Lake Malar, from which we had a wonderful view along the lake to the city. In the evening we went for an hour's sail round Djurgarden: one of the nicest cruises we have had. Having had a fairly strenuous day, we decided to get back to the hotel and dine in comfort. We shared the restaurant, and the luxury choice afforded by the Park Hotel's menu, with one other couple. As Nancy said, if they brought their prices down a bit they might get a few more customers. The cauliflower soup was delicious, and as soon as we had finished a big bowl of it the waiter appeared with another bowl. No change in the weather—I have practically given up wearing a jacket, and was in trousers and open-necked shirt throughout the day.

August 4th

Visiting the Stockholm cathedral. Our way up the hill passed the entrance to the royal palace: a sentry at the gate lolling about and glancing at his watch in a slightly unmilitary attitude. The cathedral quite small, but richly and attractively ornamented: a huge painting of the Last Judgment occupying the wall in one of the chapels. We strolled through the narrow, shady, deserted lanes of the old town— hardly any pedestrians and no traffic except one taxi which appeared unexpectedly behind us. To the Anglais for dinner of roast chicken. Passers-by in the street included a large number of aimless-looking young people in jeans who seem to be numerous in Stockholm, and in particular to frequent our park. Police cars always seemed to be there, and although at first it appeared that they were simply keeping an eye on the hippies we noticed them today getting them up off the grass and turning them out. It looks as if the Stockholm authorities must be making an effort to discourage these odd young people from descending on the city and making it the centre for their activities—

if activities is the word to use for such a lackadaisical way of life.

August 5th

Morning service in the cathedral: a fine organ, and a big congregation, which joined heartily in the singings. Bishop Ingmar Strom preached on Matthew 17:1–8. He had a pleasant quiet voice, but was an austere preacher, who in the course of a 25-minute sermon only three times made any gesture. I enjoyed the service. The collection was taken up in bags on the end of big poles, like shrimping nets. A boat tour round Stockholm bridges. We had a lively young Swedish girl to lecture us. She told us in conversation that she spoke seven languages, and today she had to lecture in three: Swedish, English and Italian. She was interesting, and her enthusiasm quite infectious. Bus back to the hotel for dinner. On Saturdays and Sundays there is a table d'hôte 'family meal', which attracted more custom than dinner has done. With our half-bottle of hock, we did not get out of it at much under the usual 100kr, but we got three courses as well as the wine and a big glass of milk.

August 6th

We took a bus to the lift that starts from the platform of the Saltsjobaden station and goes straight up to a walkway, level with the top of the cliff. It gave a magnificent view across the water to the city, both on the sea side and on the lake side. We happened to pass a restaurant specialising in fish, where I noticed there was fried herring on the menu, and for our evening meal I thought it would be an agreeable change. Nancy had scampi, and I was served with no fewer than twelve little herring, tasty and beautifully fried. After dinner we walked down to the gardens for a last walk—the end to our holiday, which started so well at Hornbaek. Nancy has never become reconciled to Stockholm and its sombre, unsmiling inhabitants.

August 8th

From today's *Scotsman*: 'A year-long programme of success against terrorism in Northern Ireland has been reported by the province's security forces'.

August 9th

To the bank, so that I could sell back the balance of my Swedish and Danish currency. When this had been done, I was able to calculate the cost of our holiday. The total for the fortnight—hotels, travel, and all expenditure while we were out of the country—came to £377.48. This compared favourably with our Swiss holiday last year: £253.20 for a week. The direct flight to Denmark is a great advantage.

August 11th
Two old Buster Keaton silent films on television. Today they seem quite a lot funnier than the early Chaplins: witty, ingenious, perfectly suited to the artistry of a deadpan comedian.

August 12th
Palmerston Place church. Rev. J. Stanley Firth, minister of St John's, Carluke, preached on Malachi 3:1: a strongly revivalist sermon, and an extraordinary one. He would seize on odd words or phrases in his chapter of Malachi, and expound to us in glowing terms how new life was coming to the church—at one moment extolling the virtues of Palmerston Place's prayer meetings, at the next reading to us a cryptic passage from a missionary pamphlet about souls being redeemed in the Congo. Just when one thought he might be coming to a close, he was seized with some new enthusiasm as he explained to us how he had got a lunatic to cure himself when he visited him in Carluke Hospital.

August 15th
Finished reading *New Lives New Landscapes*, by Nora Fairbrother. This is something almost unique: a readable book about country planning. Every page has some interesting idea, interestingly discussed. The author has a wide range of knowledge and makes excellent use of it in a multitude of allusions which are always illuminating and relevant. She is practical and tolerant, with an understanding of everybody's point of view; and her occasional prejudices make her all the more endearing. It has been a delight to read.

August 16th
A reception in the Upper Hall of the Signet Library to legal delegates attending this week's Commonwealth Universities conference. We pushed through the throng to the far end, where the Vice-Chancellors of Liverpool and Manchester universities had ensconced themselves with their wives on a comfortable settee—an interesting and pleasant pair. Later I was landed with the wife of the High Sheriff of Cheshire. She was a lay magistrate and extolled the unmatched virtues of lay

magistrates' courts, being herself a perfect example of their terrors. Nancy, like most of the ladies, was in a long dress and evidently found the party as agreeable as she looked herself.

August 17th

Jessica is staying with the Macmasters in Comiston Drive, and Mr and Mrs Macmaster were evidently pleased to have the two children go out with me. We motored to Crichton and walked along the hillside to the castle. A woman with four dogs arrived and opened it up. She told us that sheepdogs always had to have single-syllable names for convenience in calling to them. Finished reading *More Collected Poems*, by Hugh MacDiarmid. I think this is the best selection of MacDiarmid's poems that I have come across, displaying not only his immense erudition but his complete command of language— technical terms, proper names, colloquialisms, all are readily absorbed, and yet there is never the slightest doubt that this is poetry. Moreover it is poetry that is about something, something real and important. It is forceful, penetrating, convincing; and though there is an element of doubt in it which I never noticed in earlier collections the conclusion on the whole is surprisingly optimistic. He is a realist, but a realist who can see the ultimate reality behind all the present-day humbug and confusion.

August 25th

From today's *Scotsman*: 'A constable said in Glasgow Sheriff Court yesterday that after speaking to two men who appeared to be kissing in a parked car, one of them said he was a policeman interviewing an informer'.

September 4th

Guided by a note in the *Scotsman* of the time at which the American 'skylab' spectacle was to be visible, I looked out for it tonight at nine and saw it cross the southern sky from west to east, like a small star, except that instead of appearing stationary it moved rapidly across the sky.

September 11th

Finished reading *In My Way*, by George Brown: his political memoirs. I found the book unexpectedly interesting—it rather adds to his stature. He is hopelessly wrong in some things, such as Vietnam and the EEC; but he seems to have realised, as Harold Wilson never did, that the Treasury was the real enemy, and that until the Treasury was stood up to and defeated no real progress could be made in anything.

September 20th

From today's *Scotsman*: James Burke (18), a deaf-mute who appeared at Glasgow Sheriff Court charged with committing a breach of the peace by 'shouting, bawling and swearing' appeared again yesterday and was found guilty of an amended charge, that he committed a breach of the peace by waving his arms about.

September 25th

To Parliament House for the start of the Session. The usual service in St Giles', but a number of changes which brought it more in contact with realities. They included a five-minutes sermon from the new minister, Rev. Gilleasbuig Macmillan, whom we had thought highly of when we heard him in Braid Church before he was named for St Giles'. It was sensible and to the point. I was pleased to find that despite Dr Whitley's departure the one echo that remained of the old order was the singing of Chesterton's hymn about how our earthly rulers were faltering.

October 1st

The Labour Party conference, on television: Denis Healey winding up a debate on prices and taxation. I never feel that he really knows what he is talking about, and this morning he was worse than usual: a disastrous speech emphasising how his tax policy when he got into office would bear hard on everybody, without at all explaining what it was intended to achieve. As a potential Chancellor of the Exchequer, he is a serious liability.

October 2nd

Began hearing evidence in *Duncan's Hotel (Glasgow) v. J. & A. Ferguson*. There was some slight difficulty when counsel were arguing about the admission of productions to the accompaniment of a persistent hammering noise from somewhere outside. I summoned Almond and told him to find out what it was and get it stopped; and he came back shortly afterwards and said it would stop in about ten minutes. Nobody told me what had been the cause of it.

October 3rd

The notes of today's evidence include Fiddes' examination of the hotel's managing director about a diary he had for 1968:

Q.—I think at the beginning there is a summary of damage observed during 1967? A.—Yes. Q.—Was that written at the time of the damage it records? A.—No, it was written later. Q.—Do you now have the notes from which that summary was compiled? A.—No, I don't. Q.—What happened to them? A.—They were in the 1967 diary and were so badly damaged that I took these notes. Q.—The 1967 damage, you mean the damage in the fire? A.—Yes, it was lost. *By the Court:* Q.—I don't quite see how if the diary was lost in the fire it could contain notes of the damage that arose after the fire. A.—I am sorry, they were taken after the fire occurred and the diary was so badly damaged it was not available. Q.—Well, it is rather mysterious but there may be some explanation. *(No answer.) Examination continued:* Q.—I think the diary must have been available after the fire? A.—Yes. Q.—Because it can only have been in the latter part of the year you recorded any notes of the damage? A.—I am sorry, there is a misunderstanding. The diary was there after the fire. *By the Court:* Q.—What damaged the diary? A.—I haven't got the diary. Q.—What was the damage that you spoke about, to the diary? A.—The damage really is that the diary just isn't there. Q.—When you spoke about the damage to the diary what you mean is you have lost it? A.—Yes. Q.—Well, that may be a possible meaning of the word? *(No answer.)*

October 6th

In the evening on the television we had the Trinidad Philharmonia Steel Orchestra, a collection of black men in sober black jerseys playing a variety of music by striking steel buckets with little steel rods: a virtuoso performance of astonishing skill and dexterity. I cannot imagine how they do it.

October 9th

From today's *Scotsman*: 'An 18-year-old Glasgow youth was ordered yesterday at the High Court in Glasgow to be detained during the Queen's pleasure. Richard Money had pleaded guilty to having assaulted Alexander Munro (63), struck him on the head with a trouser press and a mirror, struck him on the face, head and body with an electric fire, a table and a cake stand and murdered him'.

October 12th
We set off with the dog for Bamburgh.

October 13th
Warkworth. We paid our 7p each to the Department of the Environment and went in to see the castle, on a knoll above the town. It had a big grass courtyard, but the buildings themselves, which are extensive, were dark and cold. Even with the roof on, it must have been an uncomfortable place for the Earl of Northumberland to live in. A pleasant country road back to Bamburgh. Nancy remarked on the great variety of scenery that Northumberland has to offer: undulating country with sea and woods, which at almost every turn has something different for one to see.

October 14th
To the parish church for the morning service. An elderly man with a grizzled beard preached to a tiny congregation: fewer than thirty people. He was rather gloomy, but it was a perfectly adequate, well-composed twelve-minutes sermon. I was sure that he was the vicar, and was surprised to learn at the end that he was a lay preacher. It is a lovely old church; and despite the small numbers it was a pleasant service: everything well done, with a dignity and beauty seldom to be found in church services north of the Border.

October 15th
Home about two. The cat met us halfway down Midmar Gardens and trotted up to the gate after us; but Elizabeth, who had been keeping house over the week-end, said that although the cat had seemed hungry it had been able to eat hardly anything. We motored in with it forthwith to the vet's. Mr Baird agreed that there was something seriously wrong, beneath its tongue.

October 19th
The proof proceeded, with the evidence of a lively little Glaswegian who answered questions at length, addressing counsel by name and using a vocabulary all his own. Speaking of a period when piling had

been stopped for the situation to be considered, he spoke of what was happening 'during the standstill reconstructionwise'.

The news of the cat was not good; the vet thought it might require a major operation. We agreed that if that was found to be necessary the cat should rather be put down.

October 20th

Eleven divorces. Two of the actions were between the same parties: the wife's action of divorce for adultery against her husband, and the husband's action on similar grounds. Counsel explained that each party was particularly anxious to get a decree against the other, but I pointed out that that was impossible—after I had granted a divorce in the one action there would be no marriage left to dissolve. In the end it was the husband's case that went on. I granted decree of divorce and dismissed the wife's action. In one of the other cases the adultery on which it was founded had been committed on 21st September 1973: justice in that case must have been expeditious.

October 21st

A tame grey squirrel in the garden this morning. It ran up the clothes pole to the line on which Nancy had hung a net-bag for the birds, turned the bag upside down, scattering the nuts on the ground, then came down the pole and had a busy time carrying nuts to various caches it had dug in the garden. Not wanting the birds to be deprived of all their nuts, Nancy removed the pole; but that was no deterrent to the squirrel, which climbed up the drain pipe on the side of the house and along the clothes line to the bag of nuts, balancing itself delicately on the line as it manoeuvred the bag until it was empty.

South Morningside Church: Mr Cumming of Palmerston Place preached a fine sermon on Acts 20:13.

October 22nd

The vet told me that the cat had made no progress, and with his full agreement I gave instructions to him to dispose of it. We shall all miss Henry, a cat of considerable character. Like all cats, he went his own way, but though never departing from his air of conscious superiority he was an exceptionally friendly cat and had no enemies. He was friendly to everyone, even strangers in the street. The word 'fish' was of special significance to him in any context. If he was lying apparently asleep on a chair when fish were mentioned on the television, he would start up at once. He got on well with all the dogs, particularly the present one, which would nudge its head in to the cat, wanting the cat to wash it—which the cat would sometimes do, if so inclined. He was as lively as ever right up to the last night at home, obviously enjoying our company. So it has not been a bad way to lose him, when he was still the same fluffy black cat, always interesting, always curious in every sense of the word, and in full possession of his faculties to the end.

Finished reading *Inside Number 10*, by Marcia Williams, an interesting account by a shrewd, level-headed observer of what went wrong with Harold Wilson's Prime Ministership. It really takes the lid off, and demonstrates beyond question how a Labour Government can be frustrated by a predominantly Tory civil service establishment. The portrait it paints of Wilson is much to his credit, and I am sure completely true; but reading between the lines one can see that he was far too kindly and friendly in his treatment of the people he had to deal with, and if one compares his own book with Marcia's it looks very much as if he has not yet realised what kind of people they are. I had supposed when in the Government that Marcia Williams must be a useful person, but until reading this remarkable book I had not realised the extent of her perspicacity and the soundness of her judgment. Without the slightest discourtesy or overt hostility to anyone, she shows that she has them all summed up exactly.

October 25th

The proof continued, with evidence from Mr Nolan, a retired engineer who before working with Wimpeys had been a bridge designer for the Southern Railway and the LCC and naval base engineer at Scapa Flow, and had been brought back into service by Baptie Shaw & Morton specially to supervise the work of pre-loading steel beams in Fergusons' reconstruction. He was a delightful little man, who gave a definite, precise answer to every question, and on being asked what work was done in Fergusons' basement reeled off a complete list of all the operations, in perfect order and without the slightest hesitation. Asked by Davidson whether the job was like any he had done before, he replied that out in Borneo he had a whole tunnel to underpin which was nearly 500 yards long. I met Davidson in the corridor, and he was expressing regret that he had been unable to pursue this with the witness. It occurred to me that Fiddes would be pretty certain to do so, and sure enough Fiddes proceeded to ask him about Borneo. A tunnel, Mr Nolan explained, had been bombed by the Americans at one end and the Australians at the other, and the Japs were all in a train inside. The tunnel started collapsing and had to be supported. The traffic had to be kept going because that was the livelihood of the natives. 'Yes', said Fiddes, 'and what is the point of resemblance between this tunnel which had been bombed by the Australians and the Japanese –' 'No, no', I said, interrupting him, 'not the Japanese—the Americans'. 'The Americans', said Fiddes, correcting himself, 'the point of resemblance between this tunnel and Fergusons' basement?' The witness explained the similarities, and Fiddes proceeded: 'I take it this was some time between 1941 and 1945?' 'No', said the witness, '1951 I went to Borneo'. 'But the Japs weren't in the tunnel six years after the war ended?' 'Yes', said Mr Nolan, without offering any explanation. 'Would you agree,' asked Fiddes, 'that technology had advanced a bit between 1951 and 1967?' 'Frankly, I wouldn't', said Mr Nolan.

October 26th

With Nancy to Parliament House for the Faculty reception. We had a talk with Moira Anderson, who was looking very attractive and was interested in recalling our night with Mr Kosygin. It was obvious that she, like us, had enjoyed the evening with the Russians and had a very clear recollection of it.

October 30th

When the proof was resumed, Davidson got leave to lodge some records of tell-tales that had been fixed on the hotel walls during later stages of the operation. They disclosed that there had indeed been some subsidence, and Fiddes produced a Minute of Amendment alleging fault on the part of the consulting engineers in failing to keep a watch on the tell-tales and take appropriate action. This is the first time that Fiddes has sought to make a case against anyone but the occupiers of the shop, and he included in his Minute a 'small amendment' by which he deleted the words 'not known and not admitted' in relation to the other parties' case against the consulting engineers and substituted the word 'adopted'. This covers the whole case on pile-driving, and means that on the seventeenth day of the proof, Fiddes has realised that he ought to have Baptie Shaw & Morton as defenders—something that I have vainly urged on him ever since the case was in Procedure Roll a year ago. I suppose it is true to say that the pursuers are now on the right lines, but the result of today's proceedings is that the case is now in complete confusion, the bulk of the evidence having been taken while it was pleaded on quite a different basis. It was an ingenious idea of Fiddes' to take advantage of the late lodging of documents which Davidson should have produced earlier, but they have nothing to do with the piling case.

November 6th
Fiddes produced some adjustments to his Minute, and we had a brief argument about whether amendment should be allowed at all at this stage. I castigated Fiddes for not bringing the consulting engineers in as defenders at the start, but balancing any prejudice to them against the manifest disadvantage to all the parties in the horrifying prospect of having all the evidence led again in a new action by the hotel against the engineers I allowed the amendment.

November 13th
We are having a fortnight's holiday from Duncan's Hotel, counsel and shorthand writers having gone off to Kyle of Lochalsh for a public inquiry.

Lyceum: *Much Ado about Nothing*. This I think is far and away the best of Shakespeare's comedies, sparkling with wit and character, a feast of fun. The Lyceum Company carried it off superbly. The theatre was crowded with teenage school parties, who sat stolidly through the first half sucking sweets and rustling sweetie papers. But they succumbed to the production after the interval, and were carried on willy-nilly to an enthusiastic finale.

November 23rd
The Pollock case is at present before the High Court on appeal.

November 27th
Spoke to Wheatley about the Pollock case. He told me they were going to refuse the appeal. Davidson told me that Dr Silver had had a coronary thrombosis and was supposed to be dying. I motored to the Church of Scotland eventide home where Dr Silver has been staying. A very nice matron told me that while Dr Silver had not been at all anxious to live on she had rallied a lot since last week. She took me to Dr Silver's room, where the patient after she discovered her visitor's identity was quite extravagantly delighted to see me. She

recalled how I had come when the Australian grandchildren were there and had spoken to the children, and when I heard there was a younger child who had gone to bed had taken the trouble to go and speak to her. It was quite a joy to have given her such apparent pleasure simply by paying her a visit. On the way out I encountered the matron and said I thought that under her care Dr Silver was not going to get her own way just yet so far as dying was concerned. Dr Silver herself had been almost apologetic about it: her daughter had been summoned, and they all thought it was a matter of saying goodbye, and now here she was seemingly getting better. I assured her that it would never have done for her to die last week before I got a chance to see her.

November 28th
About 2.30 the evidence in *Duncan's Hotel v. Ferguson* at last came to an end. I called on Fiddes to begin his speech, but he asked to be given till Friday morning 'to collect his thoughts'.

November 30th
Fiddes began his speech, and continued throughout the day. Today he was dealing mostly with law. He had obviously done a lot of work on it, and spoke well. I found what he said very interesting.

December 3rd
Finished reading *Hammarskjöld*, by Brian Urquhart, an exceptionally fine biography—depressing in so far as it is dealing with national stupidity and jealousy, whether outright obstruction by the Russians, or the mindless anticommunism of the Americans, or the even more sinister undercover work of the British and French, but encouraging too as showing how much can be achieved in spite of all that by one man of integrity and determination who is prepared to disregard misrepresentation and to work away quietly and impartially for the right solution. Influenced no doubt by the calumnies of the time, I had had a vague idea of Hammarskjöld as an unpractical person, out of touch with realities. This judicious, well-documented, exciting book dispels any such notions.

December 4th
Hunter regaled us with an account of the cottage set apart in Barlinnie Prison for the accommodation of Boyle and two or three other noto-

rious criminals who were segregated from everyone else and passed their time working on sculpture or fashioning ladies' handbags. Boyle, he said, had sculpted Father Ross, the vice-chairman of the Parole Board, and although it was not in the least like Father Ross he had been pleased with it and set it up on his mantelpiece, so that it gazed down on students who came to see him in his capacity of chaplain at the University. Hunter referred to the chairman of the Parole Board as 'that lunatic who used to climb up ropes when he was Moderator'.

December 6th
Fiddes concluded his speech, and asked if he might withdraw, as work on this case had meant that his other work had got very much behind.

December 8th
Nine divorce proofs. One had to be continued because it turned out that counsel was conducting the wrong case. A cruelty action must have been thrown overboard and a new action raised when evidence of adultery came to light; but Drummond & Co. had fixed a proof in the old action while supplying counsel with the papers in the adultery case. So the proof came to an abrupt stop. The pursuer, a cheerful Glasgow woman, did not seem to be unduly put out. 'Sorry about that', I said, 'but you had better get on to your lawyers and tell them where they get off'. 'I will', she said. 'You wait until I get hold of them on Monday morning, and see what they're like after that'.

In the afternoon we motored to Longniddry. There was a dead creature on the beach which looked like some kind of porpoise or shark. A young couple whom we met seemed to think it was a seal, but we were pretty sure it was a fish.

December 12th
In the course of today's hearing I was referred to a case in which a man had sued Cecil Rhodes and Dr Jamieson for injuries he had sustained when taking part in the Jamieson Raid. I was amused at the particulars of the damage: 'Loss of kit £25; loss of pony £120; loss of earnings £433; loss of leg'.

December 13th
Installation of R. H. McDonald as the new judge in place of Milligan, the first judge to retire under the 75-years age rule, introduced just before he came on the bench.

On television tonight we had Mr Heath giving an address to the nation on the Government's fantastic decision to introduce a three-day working week in industry and shops in order to conserve fuel, a decision said to be necessitated by the effects of the miners' ban on overtime working. This pigheaded diktat seems to give some support to Mr Powell's contention that the Prime Minister has gone out of his mind and is prepared to allow the whole of British industry to go to ruin rather than concede anything to the miners. He ended up by saying that it would now be necessary for everyone to work harder than ever in order to increase our exports sufficiently to meet the vastly increased cost of our imports of oil: an exhortation that was difficult to reconcile with a compulsory three-day working week. A discussion programme which followed in ITV's 'This Week' was grossly unfair—the representatives on the workers' side were Joe Gormley and the TUC secretary Len Murray, both competent debaters, while the employers' side was represented by the assistant secretary of the CBI and by Kearton, who as usual was all the other way, leaving the unfortunate CBI man to put the Government's case against the other three. Needless to say, he did not make much of it, and Kearton was devastating in condemning the Government proposals as 'the economics of the lunatic asylum'.

December 14th

Mr Wilson had his turn on television tonight. Instead of saying, as I think he should, that the Prime Minister had taken leave of his senses, he chose to adopt an attitude of sweet reasonableness: that if only Mr Heath would be nice to old age pensioners, and put a tax on property speculators, we would all be able to work together for the saving of Britain. It was good in its own way, but feeble and namby-pamby in the face of what the Government is doing. Enoch Powell or Lord Kearton would have dealt with the situation much more effectively. Manifestly it was time for someone to speak out plainly about what was happening, and Harold Wilson, it seemed, was not the man to do it.

December 15th

Nine divorce proofs. In one, a pursuer from Dumbarton did not turn up. His brother, who had come as a witness, said he had called in for the pursuer with his car, but was told that the pursuer had already left, with the intention of coming by train. I pointed out that on a previous occasion the diet of proof in this action had had to be discharged because the pursuer did not appear. The brother explained that that was his fault—they had both come in his car, but it had broken down halfway. That being so, it was perhaps not surprising that the pursuer had decided to come by train; but train services being somewhat disorganised these days he has not yet succeeded in getting himself divorced.

December 16th

Finished reading *William's Mary*, by Elizabeth Hamilton, an interesting biography of a deservedly popular Queen whose death at the age of thirty-two must have been a serious blow to the people of England. William and Mary's tolerance and good judgment is well illustrated in their choice of Archbishop of Canterbury: John Tillotson, who read over to himself every morning a resolution 'not to be angry with anybody upon any occasion, because all anger is foolish, and a short fit of madness; betrays us into great indecencies; and whereas it is intended to best others, the edge of it turns upon ourselves'.

From today's *Sunday Express*: 'At present we have a first-class Government led by an intelligent hard-working and talented Prime Minister'.

December 18th

James Leechman having moved up to the Inner House to replace Milligan, I put in a claim to take over his court. Having discovered in the course of the Duncan's Hotel case how much better I could hear witnesses from a witness-box on the left I decided to move to a court which had the witness-box in that position. It used to be called the 'forum non conveniens', away at the end of the main corridor, and is quiet and comfortable, with the further advantage of having a retiring room of its own where the judge can work.

December 19th

A pursuer seriously injured when he fell from a rock face at Furnace Quarry blames his employers for failure to provide a safe system of work. The defenders say they had safety harness available, and aver that if the pursuer had used it he would not have sustained fatal injuries. This averment the pursuer admits, subject to the explanation that he did not sustain fatal injuries. At home I had to look up an authority in a volume of the *Scots Law Times*, and was pleased to find a dividend warrant of Nancy's that had been lost for some months. I knew it was missing, but had not realised I had the book out at the time and put the warrant into it to keep my place. It was lucky I had to consult the same volume today.

December 20th

Fifteen undefended divorces. The pursuer in one of them, speaking about the break-up of her marriage, said it was quite true she found two fleas on the cat—that was right enough, and she admitted it. But her husband had said that the cat or he himself would have to go. 'I kept the cat', she said.

December 21st

Motion Roll. In *Thomson v. Cluny's Executors* the motion did not get very far owing to a misunderstanding between the two counsel, each of whom thought the other was there to oppose him until they found out that they had both been instructed on the same side. I was amused to observe that in an adultery divorce the defender's maiden name was Barbara Innocent. The pursuer was resident at the Central Volcanological Observatory, and the adultery was alleged to have taken place in New Guinea.

December 22nd

Completed the term's work by granting decree in nine undefended divorces. Miss Aronson, Almond told me, as she was going out of court and passed Horsburgh on his way in, said to him 'You'll be all right—he's in a good mood today'. The pursuer in one of this morning's cases was founding on a conviction for rape. Her husband had written a letter from prison to the court, agreeing to his wife's having custody of the child. 'My wife has been a loyal, faithful and devoted young woman, unsurpassed in all aspects of marriage, she has been a wonderful mother to our child and it is only fit and proper she should continue to be in her mother's care. I have already signed into my Wife's name, our house, furnishings and bank account. It is with deep regret that I must admit this conviction and having wrecked a very happy home and marriage'.

December 28th

Finished reading *CB*, a biography of Sir Henry Campbell-Bannerman by John Wilson: a good biography, detailed, well informed, judicious and extremely readable—a most encouraging book, for it discloses that however badly Harold Wilson may think he is treated by the newspapers it is nothing to what they did to Campbell-Bannerman. He is maligned, abused, belittled, not only by the press and the Tories but by supercilious people on his own side. With imperturbable good humour, he simply ignores it, and emerges without any effort on his part as a Prime Minister in complete control of his party and the House of Commons, and leads the Liberals to their greatest electoral triumph by carrying on in the way he believes to be right. 'If people should say of me that I tried always to go straight there is perhaps no credit to me in that. It may have been mere indolence. The straight road always seemed to me to be the easiest'. It is obvious too that though no great orator he was a witty, cultivated man, who spoke fluent French, a shrewd judge of character who nevertheless gave most people the benefit of the doubt and never harboured a grudge, and a man of much personal charm, whose sense of humour never failed him. His life makes an interesting, rewarding story, with plenty of lessons for present-day politicians.

December 31st
We watched a Hogmanay programme on television until Big Ben struck midnight.

Index

Where appropriate, entries give the position of a person at the
time of writing of the diary. In some cases what the person
later became is given in parentheses